1

Preserve the Value:
... A Novel/Guide to Successfully Integrate an Acquisition

By: Michael P. Gendron

FOREWARD

The past 5 months have been the most challenging since I started the business. Fortunately, Joseph alerted me to the many challenges that we would encounter. His advice in four areas was instrumental to our successful sale:

- During the sale process we must continue to manage the business consistent with our principles, and also serve new masters – potential buyers who were investing millions of dollars after investigating the business for a short time.
- Know the reputation of the potential buyer, and understand if their operating

style and culture are consistent with our business model.
- Prepare for an intense period of Due Diligence review that examines every facet of the business in a way that we've never done before.
- In addition to running the business, integration is a full-time job causing inefficiencies for the buyer and the target.

Of course, we initially thought Joseph was exaggerating to prepare us for the worst, but his advice was perfect. The number of questions and detail that the *potential* buyers required was mind numbing. And I said *potential buyers*, since several suitors engaged in the process. Yes, Joseph prequalified each of them before we formally launched the process, but if you want to sell, you entertain suitors. In addition to all the extra work, we still needed to manage the business, which has always been more than a full-time job.

The executive team performed extremely well during the past years, and was the key to sale and integration.

Jackson Manufacturing

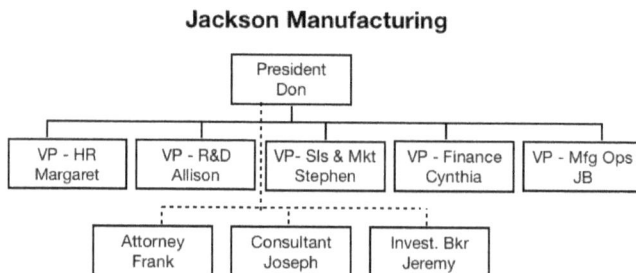

President Don

| VP - HR Margaret | VP - R&D Allison | VP- Sls & Mkt Stephen | VP - Finance Cynthia | VP - Mfg Ops JB |

| Attorney Frank | Consultant Joseph | Invest. Bkr Jeremy |

Joseph frequently reminded us that suitor companies were putting millions of dollars at risk, based on a few hundred hours of investigation. Of course, it made sense that buyers would be thorough in their Due Diligence review.

We disqualified one buyer purely for cultural reasons. I didn't want the Company to be acquired by a ruthless investor. Several others were disqualified because they didn't operate in a manner that we liked. Fortunately with Joseph's counsel, we selected a perfect match that respected our hard work, the employees and our customers, and they paid a fair price. They were not the highest price if everything went perfectly, but Joseph pointed out that seldom do things work perfectly. He suggested that if we didn't get the money at the closing, we might never see it. I guess that *earn outs* may be disputed by the parties, since there are many elements to the contract.

The integration was very thorough – a lot of extra work – and unfortunately some of the folks weren't able to continue with the new Company. Although the pre-planning was extensive and the buyer managed that process well, we – the buyer and us – had some major challenges. The Company provided outplacement counseling and generous exit packages for displaced employees. I did not agree with some changes, but it was no longer my Company.

The integration activities included three major segments:

- Day One activities
- First 100 days
- Second 100 days

Initially, I thought that it was overkill, but breaking the integration into three segments worked well. We focused on near-term goals so that we could measure accomplishments. The initial focus was, "How do we keep the customers and employees fully engaged the day of closing?" The 1st hundred days focused on preserving the value of the acquisition. The 2nd hundred days focused on the long-term strategy. This was interesting since their goals differed from our strategic goals. But again, it was their Company.

The staff again had to change the way they managed. As a global Company we now had an entirely different scale, and the Newco strategy was more visionary than we've ever experienced.

So now, I spend a few hours each month *consulting* with the new owners. Occasionally I meet with the Company executives, and I have improved my golf handicap to a 9.

This has been a perfect ending to a lifetime investment in Jackson Manufacturing.

The Journey

First Management Meeting - Introductions

The Hagstrom Company team arrived at the Hyatt conference room adjacent to our meeting room about 30 minutes before the scheduled meeting. We selected the Hyatt to avoid revealing confidential information not requested in their checklists, to minimize interruptions to our executive team, and avoid disrupting Company employees.

The broad conference table was organized with a dozen chairs, neatly squared with the table – each place with a note pad and a Hyatt branded pen. Refreshments - coffee, hot water, a carafe of orange juice and a selection of pastries from the Shadeau bakery - were arranged on the buffet table as if prepared for Bon Appetit Magazine.

Don, Joseph the consultant, Frank the Company outside attorney, and the Jackson (JAX) executive team milled about waiting for Hagstrom's CEO to arrive.

The hotel, anticipating a room full of uncomfortable executives, chilled the room to 68 degrees.

In quiet conversation Frank cautioned the team. "We haven't completed the deal yet. My concern is that we may disclose information today that could influence the deal – pricing, or worse, even kill the deal. It is important that we are completely truthful, and if the questions are appropriate, we can respond to them. My role at this meeting is to listen and, working with Joseph, advise you when it seems that we will be giving them too much information. It is not a problem to deny them information initially, if we are not sure about the business impact. If they think that we are being unreasonable about the information available, we can discuss their concerns at a later time. Any questions?"

Cynthia, the CFO, tapped the conference table with her pen, "Glad you prepped us on the ground-rules. I'm always concerned about telling them 'No' and killing the deal."

Stephen further challenged, "How will we know when they've asked for too much."

"I won't leave anything to mystery. You'll hear me redirect the question so that we can give them an answer without disclosing too much."

Don, fully confident with his experts' advice, summarized, "Let's make a deal… and thanks for your support, Frank."

A double knock on the door immediately preceded two Brits' entry into the room.

With outstretched hand, a distinguished gentleman with a welcoming smile and a British accent said, "Don it's great to see you again and finally to personally meet your executive team."

Hearty handshakes and brief introductions around the room settled everyone's nerves. "Starbucks Americano for all. And a selection of teas for our international guests." Don gestured all to the buffet. For the next 10 minutes, folks made small talk at the buffet as they selected pastries and drinks.

Elton, the CEO of Hagstrom's, was an accomplished, 30-year veteran of their global medical device business. A marketer by training, during the past 13 years he has served as the CEO of Hagstrom. During his tenure, Hagstrom acquired several businesses in the EEC – each one a success ranging from modest to an once-in-a-lifetime success. His reputation for acquisitions was one of being a tough-but-fair negotiator, and once a deal was complete, a master at interpersonal skill and executive management. His actions were always based on 'doing the right thing… the right way, every time – no matter what the cost.'

His associate, thoroughly British Jaclyn, bobbed hair, dressed in fine wool navy colored jacket and matching skirt, remained seated.

Jaclyn's background, not as deep in mergers and acquisitions as Elton's, was based on a PhD in Marketing granted by Oxford University, after completing an MBA in Supply Chain Management. Her 20 years of experience included industries such as Pharmaceuticals and Medical Devices at Bayer Gmbh, Roche, and several smaller startups.

As folks settled into their seats, Jaclyn launched into the integration topic. "Thanks for joining us today, folks. We know that you've got a full schedule managing the day-to-day operations, and it is very difficult to carve time out for the integration planning. However, based on our experience, it's critical to plan before the deal is done. We also know that, since the deal is not yet executed, you may have some reservations about sharing information with us. When you consider the information to be confidential, tell us, and we'll review our minimum requirements and if possible, wait until after the closing.

We are extremely pleased to merge with Jackson Manufacturing Company. We envision this to be a partnership that will aggressively launch Hagstrom's into the US market, and will also give us expertise in the niche implantable device market.

M&A integration is an extremely challenging task, since each of you has a *day-job* that consumes a normal workweek, and each day of integration will also be a major responsibility. Each day of preplanning and successful integration activity represents a big investment. But that investment is really just protecting the $60 million that we'll pay for Jackson Manufacturing.

We like to aggressively plan the integration. Think about it for a moment. If the integration requires 6 months to be substantially complete, the Company employees may be doing two jobs every day – normal operations and the integration. Would we really want to do two jobs for more than 6 months? And during the integration, competitors will be trying to take our customers. Do we really want to extend that vulnerability?

When we plan the integration, we identify three major segments to the integration process:
- Day One activities;
- The first 100 day's activities, and
- The second 100 day's activities.

Generally, we like to be substantially complete with the integration process within about 6 months.

Anybody nervous yet?"

Cynthia waved a hand, "Yes, you can be sure that I'm nervous… I think this is the first corporate integration for all of us. Anyone else agree?"

Silent nods followed among the executive team.

"Nervousness is actually a good sign. I'd be concerned if you were first-timers and you weren't apprehensive. See that tall gentleman seated to my right? Well, as you know, Elton is the CEO of Hagstrom. He's been through M&A integration many times, as have I. It's also significant that he is sitting here at our first organization meeting. Anything that you want to say, Elton?"

"Just that we are extremely pleased that you will become a part of Hagstrom. I'm here because this investment is critical to Hagstrom's global strategy, and I want to be sure that you get what you need to be successful in the integration. Thanks Jaclyn."

Jaclyn continued, "The integration requires thorough *initial* planning and dynamic planning throughout the process. Dynamic planning – how's that for an original term? That means that we know that our best-designed initial plan never comes true as we planned it. Things change. Perhaps we get a major new customer … or perhaps lose a major customer… the competition gets more aggressive…. Things happen.

Communication is key. We need a continuous flow of information to the integration leaders throughout the integration process. Although we do prepare a master plan – hopefully before we close the deal - there are obstacles. Confidential information that may affect planning may not be readily available before the closing.

We take that into consideration during the planning. But the integration plan is *our* plan including you folks – not just Hagstrom's. We need your insight.

We don't want you to feel stranded with that responsibility. Our role is to be sure that you get what you need to be successful.

We'll prepare a master integration plan, based on our expectations of the transaction. We'll look out 3 years and describe what we think we'd like the combined Company to look like.

Knowing where we want to go, we'll ask you how we're going to get there. And we truly want your input, since you know how this business is managed.

In addition to planning, we'd ask that until the deal is closed, you freeze all organization changes (…hiring, promotions, special incentives etc.), and all major purchases, until the transaction is completed.

We do this to avoid any whipsaw activity affecting the employees during the next few months. Think about it. Would you consider it fair to give a promotion to an individual today, and in three months, the Company reorganizes and no longer needs the position? We're not aware of any such pending actions, but if we can avoid the turmoil associated with such moves, we'd like to do so. This is your business until the closing, so this is just a request for the benefit of all.

Also, we'd like to avoid the reconciliation work that would be required, as we look at existing payables and commitments disclosed in the closing documents. If you can avoid major commitments during the next few days, that would be great. Of course, commitments not in the ordinary course of business should be avoided, according to the contracts now being finalized.

We'll set up some Day One deliverables, and also have a series of deliverables for each functional area to be implemented during the first and subsequent 100 days. Ideally, we will schedule the activities so that the integration flows well and is coordinated among all the functional areas in all the Companies involved.

We'll develop a communication's process that will allow anyone in the organization to raise an issue if something goes awry.

Communications – both outbound to all our constituents, and inbound, *listening to feedback* – are critical. We want to hear what's happening. We'll set up a hotline that can be used to inform management of integration concerns, and a separate secure website to share our accomplishments compared to the integration plan. We'll have weekly progress meetings with the executive team, and formal monthly reports will be sent to the Board of Directors.

Yes, this transaction is that important to the Company.

Our goal is to make this the most successful acquisition in the Company's history. We cannot complete the transaction without your support, and Hagstrom's personal commitment to the transaction success.

Questions?"

JB whispered to Cynthia. "Nice soliloquy. …Think she really wants our input?

"Guess we'll find out."

Stephen broke the ice. "What about our routine commitments – travel, meetings with customers and vendors. How will that fit into the integration activity?"

"Good question, Stephen. We still need to manage the business, so let's do so. However, you've hit on the reason that we want to move quickly. Studies have shown that during integration, Company efficiency drops by as much as 50%. How much inefficiency can we tolerate? And how long do we want to be inefficient? Six months? Nine months? … A year?

And when we discuss Company inefficiency, we mean the entire Company… including Hagstrom and Berkshire.

Basically, I can't answer your question right now – and that's why your input is critical to the process. You'll have to make those decisions as we proceed through the integration.

And did you notice that I included Hagstrom and Berkshire?"

"What's a Berkshire?" JB never missed an opportunity to challenge the unknown.

"Berkshire is our other US investment - a Company that we acquired several years ago. I included Berkshire since Jackson will be the Hagstrom US headquarters, although for tax reasons, Berkshire is buying the Jackson assets. Congratulations to all on your promotions to leaders in the US headquarters." Jaclyn's smile and outstretched arms welcomed the team to their new role.

"Here's what the legal organization looks like."

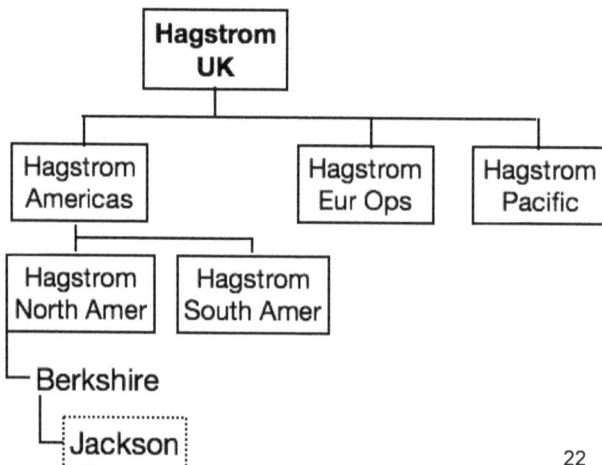

"Yes, this is news for you, and only the beginning of the transition. You each have a packet of information that we'd like you to review. It includes background information about Hagstrom's and Berkshire. We've tried to include many of our planning assumptions and how Jackson will fit into the global organization. It's our best guess – based on analysis and the Due Diligence work we completed thus far.

We know it may not be accurate since we don't have your input. We'd like your insight – as much as possible before the deal is executed – about the realism of our plans.

You are the experts. Help us better define the future. As you review the information you may see errors in our assumptions. For example, it is not unusual for us to assume away a *simple* systems conversion to the Hagstrom manufacturing software. Well, if you don't see enough time or investment in our general plans, shout it out. We want to have the best information possible as we finalize the integration plans. And if we've missed some major investments required, our model will be off."

Cynthia leaned toward Don and whispered, "And if they've missed too much and we alert them, it might kill the deal."

Don winced.

Although Jaclyn spotted the whisper, she did not react.

"Questions?"

"So let me understand this. We thought that Hagstrom was buying us, and it's really the US subsidiary that is buying us, and you're only buying the assets?" Stephen shared his concern, perhaps considering this somewhat of a demotion – not reporting directly to the Worldwide Headquarters.

"We'll get back to the overall structure, Stephen. For now, based on the information that we have, we'll structure the deal that way for legal and tax reasons, but we expect that you will report directly to the UK and directly to Elton. Other questions?"

After a brief pause, Jaclyn continued. "OK. Please review the packet. We'd like to begin the planning tomorrow morning. We'll start with Day One planning, since we want to immediately launch the plan. How does 10 AM tomorrow look for you?"

The rustle of pages signaled the end of the meeting. Tense smiles and nods given from all attendees… Jackson executives remained in the conference room in silence.

As the Hagstrom executives left the conference room, Elton observed the silence and motioned for Jaclyn. "Any surprises in their reaction?"

"No surprise. This is a major event for them. We'll see how well they adapt to the planning. Our first meeting is complete. Now for the real work. See you later, Elton."

After Elton and Jaclyn left the room, JB was first to speak. "Don, what the hell are they talking about on this integration planning stuff, and the fact that they want us to talk in detail about our business before we cash any checks. I'm nervous like crazy thinking that I'll say something that will kill the deal. Right now, my position is that, 'I ain't talking." While speaking, JB rustled the papers Jaclyn referred to, and then, unread, pushed the stack to the center of the conference table. "I'm not playing the game, Don. I'm very concerned about what could happen, and I don't want to mess things up for you – and if things go south, well, I'm out a big check as well."

Steve's ability to manage these emotional outbursts was proven. "JB-great observation. For sure we don't want to let them peek under the kimono too soon, since that may risk completing the transaction. Let's all take some time to look at their requests, and see what they are trying to do. Elton doesn't want to lose the deal either. Based on his experience,

I'm sure he's seen this kind of reluctance before. Let's try to work with them and get the deal done. The way we treat these unusual requests will be a window into our professionalism and competence – and for now, we're representing Don, not Hagstrom's."

JB scowled and was silent. After a brief pause, he agreed to work through the planning. His final plea was, "I hope I don't mess this up."

DAY ONE PLANNING

The scent of fresh brewed coffee invited the executive team into the Hyatt conference room. The broad array of fruit-filled Danish pastries, bagels and a mound of fresh fruit decorated the end of the conference table. The tense executives milled about the steaming carafes while waiting for the *potential new owner* to arrive. Each executive carefully avoided selecting a seat.

Muted conversations centered on politics, sports and family vacations.

Finally, Cynthia broke ranks, poured a coffee and paired the java with a buttery Danish, topped with a dollop of blueberry preserves and a generous swirl of sugary glaze.

"Guys, these won't last forever and the Shadeau bakery makes the finest pastries in the city. Have a calorie willya?"

"Hey, I'm trying to keep my trim figure," as Stephen took a matador's pose. "But I guess only 1 pastry won't hurt t-o-o much."

"Just add another 3 miles on the tread mill, Big Guy." JB couldn't resist the comment as he reached around Stephen to snatch a bagel. "No cream cheese for me... dieting," as he pinched a chunk of bagel.

Don *sold* the Company and the deal was expected to close within about 10 days. We all knew he would sell, but reality finally set in. In about a week, the British Hagstrom Instruments will own the Company.

Throughout the sale process we met with many acquiring executives – specialists in finance, marketing, FDA regulation, sales, manufacturing, IT, human resources – from several different companies. Initially, it was exciting to boast about our recent accomplishments, but after the third repetition, it was a nuisance. And during this time, it was critical that we met our weekly sales and profit goals.

Some of the visiting executives were true professionals, while others were under-qualified reviewers trying to score points with their bosses, by asking pointless questions seeking useless information.

Some companies sent two or three executives to investigate, while others shuttled planeloads of experts to scrutinize the operation. Thank goodness Jeremy, our investment banker identified the tire-kickers early and suggested that there was no fit with our organization. He sent them home before we wasted too much effort.

And then there was Hagstrom. Two senior executives – the CEO and the Senior VP Marketing – met Don and Jeremy for dinner, just to talk about the business.

Jeremy, our investment banker, coached Don to, "Just be yourself. Sometimes this is more of a personal chemistry check than anything else."

Apparently the chemistry was good, since Hagstrom - in their thoroughly British manner - asked for permission to spend more time in a Due Diligence review.

Throughout the ensuing weeks of review, Hagstrom's team was highly professional, courteous, and focused on critical issues. They were considerate of our time commitment to their review, while always allowing us to focus on the day's responsibilities.

A few weeks ago, the deal was basically sealed, awaiting the final closing. And here we are today – planning the Day One post closing activities.

As the clock chimed 10:00 AM, Don, and the Hagstrom executives strolled into the conference room.

Don's broad smile reflected that the deal was virtually complete – within the next nine days, the cash would be in his accounts.

"Welcome folks. Thanks for joining us today. You all know Elton and Jaclyn from Hagstrom's. Well, the deal is virtually complete and they will be your new bosses within the next week or so. They wanted to get together with you informally to talk about the integration process and answer any questions that you might have."

Don waved his hands motioning all to be seated, "Let's all grab a coffee and get into the planning."

"I don't want to step on Elton's meeting, so, welcome Elton." Don smiled, nodded to Elton, selected a gooey Danish pastry & coffee, and quietly moved to the end of the conference table.

"Welcome Jackson manufacturing. Thank you for joining us today. We've enjoyed working with you for the past few weeks and are extremely pleased that we will conclude the transaction shortly." Elton scanned the uneasy executives carefully making eye contact with each one. His unpretentious manner and welcoming smile put all at ease.

"I hope that you have had a chance to review the information packet distributed yesterday. This Company represents our largest investment in the US. We are proud to have worked through the details with Don, and candidly could not have reached this successful conclusion without your help and dedication to the Due Diligence process.

Acquisitions are disruptive – yes, they're a pain in the butt. Your engagement with several Due Diligence teams during the past few months stressed each of you. Some of the teams perhaps were discourteous and demanding. Hopefully, our reviewers were professional and well behaved. We have thoroughly trained our teams to be respectful of your time and all your efforts throughout the process. Although the deal won't be concluded for a few days, we request your insight – at a later date – about how we can improve our Due Diligence process.

But today we just want to say that we are pleased that you are on the Hagstrom team and invite your questions about our immediate goals and how we'd like to proceed. We have a brief agenda to cover, but first, what questions do you have?"

Elton smiled; raised eyebrows, hands extended as if welcoming an old friend, and scanned the audience.

As VP Sales and Marketing, and effectively the COO of Jackson, Stephen cleared his throat and said, "I can honestly say that I was surprised that we would be part of Berkshire. Can you elaborate a bit?" It was clear that he wanted to have a direct reporting relationship to Elton. Stephen knew that the best way to get the resources essential for growth and meet their projections would be through unrestricted access to the Hagstrom CEO.

Elton moved to the whiteboard and started sketching. A solid line split the board into two major sections. One labeled "Tax/Legal" and the other labeled "Management". An array of boxes and arrows on each side of the board resembled a European football play.

"I'm not an expert at this, Stephen, but our advisors have given me the 50,000 foot version. From a legal/tax point of view, Jackson will become a wholly owned sub of Berkshire. For some reason the tax laws have allowed us to grandfather certain tax benefits using this legal structure. The structure also provides some legal protection for Hagstrom global. Operationally, we fully expect that Jackson will report directly to me."

Stephen challenged, "You did say *expect*, correct?"

"Yes, and until we have fully completed the Due Diligence process, and get alignment within Hagstrom – understanding how we expect everything to flow operationally – that's the best I can commit to at this point."

Stephen nodded in half-hearted agreement, and made a note.

JB – never the shy executive – cleared his throat. "I probably have the most staff members – many blue collar workers with unique skills. They've heard the acquisition rumors and they're all concerned about their jobs... their health insurance benefits ... their vacations and all the other benefits that Don has provided. Any comments?"

"Excellent question, JB. As you know, we've spent a lot of time understanding your Company. We've had our best executives investigating Jackson, and also trying to understand how our companies may fit together – organization structure, comp and benefits, policies, product lines, culture etc. Without getting into too much detail, we created a matrix that identified gaps and opportunities, and determined – from our side – how we'd like to run this operation."

When JB heard, "… run the operation …" he winced at the thought of being directed from the UK.

Elton recognized the discomfort. "And remember, I said from our side. But folks, you run a good operation. I will state emphatically that it would be foolish for us to take a myopic, one-sided view. We need your input.

So to answer your specific question, our goal is to keep a well-run organization intact and moving forward in a responsible manner. That does not mean we won't make changes. It does mean that we want your input to make the right decisions.

Throughout the Due Diligence process we've had strategic goals in mind that we've modified to reflect information discovered during Due Diligence. As issues arose, we've documented them and tried to understand how they affect our strategy, and what costs and benefits will result from alternatives that we've considered. Thus far, you'll note that I've said *we*. Well, now that *'we'* includes you as team members.

For those who have checked our reputation, you'll know that we like to have a fully engaged organization, and we are not afraid to compensate our associates very well as goals are achieved. Let me emphasize that during the next few weeks, as we work through detailed matters with you and your associates, we will keep the employment status quo. That is to say, everyone should report to work as usual... fulfill their daily responsibilities ... benefits and compensation will continue exactly as is for now. We – that is the JAX Manufacturing executives and Hagstrom's - will analyze the organizations, and will announce changes as quickly as they are known.

We've examined your compensation and benefits, organization structure, Company policies etc. and we can say comfortably that both Companies are consistently managed.

You now know this is our second medical investment in the US, and there may be synergies. We do not have sufficient insight into the core of Jackson Manufacturing to *finalize* transition plans, but we do have draft plans that we'd like to review with you."

At the word 'synergies,' Cynthia immediately sat upright, steely-eyed, gazed toward Elton and said, "Synergy means layoffs! Comment?"

"Cynthia, we understand that associates immediately jump to the conclusion that synergies means layoffs. I won't deny that there may be some dislocation, but at a high level, this investment combined with our other medical investment gives us a critical mass in one of the largest, wealthiest medical markets in the world. Jackson has demonstrated a unique ability to design and properly launch innovative, ultra-high-quality devices that have historically been well accepted in the US.

We expect that with Hagstrom's depth of resources and Jackson's extraordinary talents, we can grow this business to unexpected levels. We need your support to think through the details.

We will pay a premium for this business because we want this team of associates to continue with us, and profitably grow the business. Do you remember the latest strategic plan that you developed? I want you to think about that plan, considering our depth of resources, and let your imagination run. Hagstrom's has resources previously not available to Jackson.

In the packet distributed yesterday, you'll note our strategic goals are to:
1. Launch US products in Europe and Asia.
2. Launch UK products in the US.

3. Invest in targeted R&D projects such as nanotech and, using resources in the UK and the US, rapidly launch new innovative products worldwide.

When we say synergy in this transaction, we are referring to leveraging current resources to achieve more than we could as two independent Companies. I'm sure as we get into the planning you'll readily see this goal.

Other questions?"

Don remained silent at the end of the conference table, pleased that he selected Hagstrom. Their reputation was a good proxy of what to expect.

Elton paused, sipped his coffee as if to allow for more questions. As he scanned the room, he focused on each executive as if to say, "Questions?" In a moment, he introduced Jaclyn.

"Thanks for joining us. I've enjoyed working with you immensely, and asked Elton if I could liaise with your team."

Margaret immediately challenged. "Does that mean that we report to you?"

"Good question, Margaret …the quick answer is no. At this point we expect Jackson Manufacturing will report to directly Elton. As liaison, my role will be to ensure that the transition from private US Company to a part of a publicly traded British Company goes smoothly. Said another way, *any questions that you have about anything* related to Hagstrom's, our other US investment, or the steps that we will complete to effectively integrate the companies – let's talk.

And, if you don't get the answers that you're looking for from me, call Elton directly. I'm not meant to be a gatekeeper to the boss, but rather a facilitator to the process.

I'll lead this integration team to help us identify all the issues and solutions – for all sides of the businesses - the UK headquarters, European business units, and our other US Company. Whatever you need, let's talk.

Let me frame how we look at any company. We like to think of a company as a living being – one that must adapt to a dynamic competitive global environment. We believe that a company is composed of 5 essential elements – People, Processes, Plant/Assets, Product and Market. Think about your operation – what are the key elements of your business.

People – for example – includes what?"

Margaret volunteered, "Employees of course."

"Certainly, Margaret – any others?"

Stephen rapped his knuckles on the table as if to punctuate, "Customers!"

Absolutely, Stephen. Any others?" After a moment's pause, Jaclyn volunteered. "Let's cast the net wide. We consider every person or organization that the Company interacts with, as *People*. It doesn't matter if we control the contact, whether they are an outside organization, government agency – whatever. If we interact with them, we call them part of the *People* segment."

"Interesting that you think that way, since we've defined *People* in the same way. We sort of sandbagged you, Jaclyn."

Jaclyn smiled and almost imperceptibly nodded to Don who was seated quietly in the back. Don warned Elton that the team would test them early to discover the depth of their experience and commitment to a quality Company.

Jaclyn continued, "Folks, we have a lot to do today. I don't want to cut the dialogue short, because we want you to have 100% confidence in our commitment to doing the right thing for the business. Here's a roster of everyone that may be involved in the integration process. You'll note that we've included email addresses, mobile phone numbers for the Hagstrom's senior leadership team, and also the contact information for our other US investment.

Key Personnel - Hagstrom HQ			
Elton Robb	Pres & CEO	011-44-355-0811	Erobb@Hagstrom.com
Jaclyn Finch	Sr VP Marketing	011-44-355-0807	Jfinch@Hagstrom.com
Geoffrey Simblast	VP Consumer Affairs	011-44-355-0899	Gsimblast@Hagstrom.com
Elizabeth Stumpfel	VP Customer Service	011-44-355-0810	Estumpfel@Hagstrom.com
Jennifer Spritely	VP General Counsel	011-44-355-0813	Jspritely@Hagstrom.com
Vito Santucci	VP Operations	011-44-355-0825	Vsantucci@Hagstrom.com
Antonio DeSteffano	VP Regulatory Affairs	011-44-355-0855	ADeSteffano@Hagstrom.com
Jeremy Fitzworthy	VF Finance & CFO	011-44-355-1000	Jfitzworthy@Hagstrom.com
Reginald Worthy	UK- Chief Scientist	011-44-355-1537	Rwrothy@Hagstrom.com
Jason O'connel	GM-Berkshire	617-449-8844	Joconnel@hagstrom.com

We're committed to doing this right. While we don't expect that you to need to talk with all these execs, we want you to be v-e-r-y comfortable with our transparency, Company goals and willingness to share whatever you need to be successful. If you aren't successful, WE are not successful.

As part of the overall integration process we want you to think of this as a $60 million investment that _we need to protect_, and ultimately grow to be the single most important part of our global Company. I say this because often there is a tendency to manage as you have in the past - thinking of each decision as a component of your typical spending. When you act, considering those constraints, you may make bad decisions – so think about our planning as _preserving our investment of $60 million._

As an example, we bought a private Chinese Company a few years ago for $100 million. When we met with the target Company executives, we asked, 'What do you need to be successful?' Before the acquisition, a very frugal private equity firm tightly managed the Company. The Company couldn't spend a dollar without extensive justification. As we pressed for creative solutions, the CFO finally – and with great trepidation – asked for a PC. Yes, *one* additional Personal Computer. Their office was in Hong Kong – and yes, the price of a personal computer would be perhaps $300. After further discussion, we determined that the ideal solution would be 10 additional computers… a total investment of $3,000 to protect – and grow – a $100 million investment. We bought 10 PC's immediately.

So what's our message to you? We want you to carefully manage your business, but we want you to think of our goal – grow and successfully integrate your operations into a vital component of a $500 million global Company."

"So we've got an open spending ticket to rock 'n roll," JB volunteered. "I could use several additional CNC machines… a total of about $1.2 million. You ready to invest?"

"Thanks JB – and we'll definitely consider such an investment – if it helps us achieve our mutual goals of profitable growth and the successful integration of operations into a vital component of a $500 million global Company.

JB, I like your challenge – make us work! Be tough on us!

OK – let's focus on Day One issues.

Several items on the docket - concentrating on People. In a role-play, now that you've been acquired, with whom should we be talking on Day One? Any thoughts."

The team, in rapid fire, volunteered, "Employees …Vendors …Customers… The FDA…Community leaders…"

"Hey, don't forget the bank. They could get really nervous if they don't know what's happening."

"… critical that we talk with benefit's providers…"

Jaclyn interrupted. "Do we want to talk with everyone personally on day-one?"

Stephen volunteered. "Impossible to talk with them directly. Maybe some emails, a press release. Hey, how about a Skype video conference?"

"One-to-one - can't be done… we need to prioritize and use the right medium for the right group."

Jaclyn pressed, "Help me out."

"So I think Don should be on the phone with the top 2-3 customers and vendors. JB - can you talk with the top vendors? Stephen, how about the rest of our customers? Maybe have Allison talk with the FDA contact."

"I like it. And what's our message?"

"Yeah, what is our message?"

With that, Jaclyn opened her portfolio with a draft press release, a series of anticipated questions and answers, and core talking points about some of the basics of the transition.

Hagstrom Corporation
Press Release – 6/15/17 *draft* (4:15 EDT)
For Immediate Release

Hagstrom Corporation, a global British Company, is pleased to announce the recent acquisition of Jackson Manufacturing. The acquisition represents a significant investment in the Americas, and will serve as the headquarters of all North American representation.

The Jackson senior management team will continue to lead the Company, as they have historically done an excellent job managing the successful growth of the Company. Jackson will continue to be a leader in medical device innovations in the US, and will serve as a foundation for Hagstrom's global efforts in new medical device product development.

This investment will demonstrate Hagstrom's commitment to enhanced patient comfort through innovation and a quality manufacturing process.

The Jackson operation will continue to be based in its current Cincinnati location.

Contact:

Stephen
Jaclyn Finch   JFinch@Hagstrom.com

"OK – this is definitely not final. Note the draft stamp. This transaction has moved very quickly, so we haven't had a chance to thoroughly review this document with everyone. We appreciate that Don and Stephen have provided insight into these points. Let's look at the points and let's add to the FAQ. We don't need to know the answers to all questions, but before the closing, we'll review all the questions, prioritize those we believe should be broadcast, and have a script ready for us to respond to those questions not answered in the published FAQ.

The key in these early communications will be to focus on facts whenever possible, and if we don't have an answer – well, '… we don't know…' - is a factual answer – we default to the Company's operating principles. It's OK to say that we don't have an answer, but let's document the question and resolve the open item ASAP. Our goal is to ensure that employees, customers and vendors are our priorities as we transition the Company into the Hagstrom's organization.

Next point. What about Processes? Anything important on?"

Cynthia stood as if stung by a bee. "Cash… cash… and did I mention cash? We better understand our cash processing, or we can be in big trouble."

"Shipping and billing. We want the customers well cared for."

"And we damn well better have employee payroll and insurance in place, or we won't recover from that."

Jaclyn smiled, "You've got it now. Think through the processes that we perform every day, and then ask yourself, 'How will we do this on Day One?'

We've established a new legal entity, and also have established bank relationships to be prepared for Day One. Since this is a new legal entity, we have acquired liability/property and casualty insurance. We're not overly concerned about leases since provisions for assignment are already in process.

I can tell you that we want to change as little as possible on Day One. A thing like Cash activity always has a trail. We can make accounting adjustments in the weeks following Day One.

Most times we can also just extend the coverage on existing benefits, and Hagstrom will cover every dollar of cost, effective with the transaction date.

I'm not trying to wish away the complexity. Let's list all the issues that you think will be important on Day One, and we will ensure that they are properly resolved before a major problem arises.

We're counting on your insight… but sometimes things are missed. What then?"

Don cleared his throat, "We default to the guiding principles? Do the right thing every time – no matter what the cost?"

"You bet, Don. In an earlier acquisition, we missed a remote payroll. So do you think we just told the employees, 'we'll take care of you next month?"

"Not if you wanted them to show up the next day!"

"Right. I called the GM at the 75 employee unit, discussed options, and that afternoon, manually issued 75 checks for the Net Payroll from the prior week. I overnighted the checks to the GM – each with an apology and an explanation of what went wrong. I also included a $25 coupon for Domino's Pizza with each check. What do you think was the response?"

"I'm guessing some happy folks."

"Yes, and several requests for more missed payrolls – from those who enjoyed the Domino's Pizza." Jaclyn enjoyed telling the story, but the chaos behind the scenes that week was horrific.

Jaclyn was ready to wrap up the first serious meeting. "Let's take the rest of the day and think about *Day One* activities. What actions do we need to take? With whom do we need to talk? How should we communicate? Webcast…press release … personal meetings… phone calls … email? They're all available to us. So, think about your constituents, and the processes that we complete every day. Let's get together later today to build a matrix of actions to be completed on Day One.

We've developed some preliminary worksheets to help us think through the day-one activities, and also the first 100-days. These are thought provokers for your reference.

Let's spend a minute to look at the template.

Integration Planning Template							
	Day One	First 100 Days			Second 100 Days		
		30	30	30	30	30	30
People							
Inside							
Employees							
Outside							
Customers							
Current							
Potential							
Vendors							
Contractors							
Agencies							
Retirees							
Community							
Process							
Primary							
Logistics							
Operations							
Sales							
Marketing							
Service							
Support							
Human Res							
R&D							
IT							
Finance							
Legal							
Other							
Plant/Assets							
Primary							
Logistics							
Operations							
Sales							
Marketing							
Service							
Support							
Human Res							
R&D							
IT							
Finance							
Legal							
Other							
Product							
Current							
Pipeline							
Market							
Customers							
Competitors							

Initially, this looks like a frightening matrix. Our rationale behind the template is simple. We've outlined what we believe every business includes. That is People, Processes, Plant/Assets, Product and Market. Within each of those elements, the business can be further segmented. People certainly includes employees, but as we think of a fully functioning business, we know that we must interact with customers, vendors etc. The many squares on the matrix include all the various elements of any business.

And each square can represent many people and activities. So, for example, employees, Day One can include employees on disability, local, and/or remote and full time and part time. Each element may require special attention.

When we examine the components, we then bring time into the integration analysis. Some things need immediate attention – employee payroll and benefits – while others such as retirees may be addressed at a later time.

	Mergers & Acquisitions Planning			
Task	Description	Resp	Due Date/ Time	
3.0	Day One			
3.1	People			
3.1.1	Employee compensation & benefits			
3.1.2	Employment offers/promotions			
3.1.3	Freeze other personnel decisions until organization review completed			
3.1.4	Establish lines of communications & business processes for action - e.g. approvals levels			
3.1.5	Meet/communicate with key customers & vendors discussing the acquisition - use prepared script			
3.1.6	Establish communications with other key constituents - e.g. regulatory agencies etc.			
3.2	Processes			
3.2.1	Cash management process established & fully implemented			
3.2.2	Ensure that all payroll process & benefits procedures are in place			
3.2.3	Establish updated security measures (access to websites, email, cash etc.)			
3.2.4	Establish rules of governance - e.g. approvals le~ ~nnel actions reporting relationships etc.			
3.2.5	Establish/confirm business proces: vendors.			

NOTE: A MASTER LIST OF STEPS TO BE CONSIDERED FOR INTEGRATION IS IN APPENDIX 1.

This is a simple example of a plan for Day One. We list the description of the task, responsibility and due date/timing.

The integration analysis requires that each of you consider your responsibilities and activities, and determine the best action to make this integration a success. Thoughts?"

Jaclyn continued. "Here's where we need your help. Looking beyond Day One, we've included the Deal Summary. This describes our financial goals related to the acquisition,

HAGSTROM ACQUISITION JACKSON MANUFACTURING
MERGERS & ACQUISITION SUMMARY

TRANSACTION SUMARY	NOTES:	SUMMARY CASH FLOW:		YEAR		

Purchase Price: (Millions US $)

Description	Resp	1	2	3
			(Millions US $)	
Baseline		12.0	14.0	15.0
Reduce DSO	Cynthia	2.0		
Inventory Turns	JB	0.5	1.0	
Sales Synergy	Stephen	6.0	7.0	7.0
COGS Reduction	JB	1.0	2.0	2.0
R&D Rationalization	Allison	1.0	1.5	1.5
Total		**22.5**	**25.5**	**25.5**

Purchase Price: Millions US $

Cash	45.0
Stock Val	
Debt Assumed	5.0
Subtotal	**50.0**
Earnout	10.0
Total Cost	**60.0**

This Acquisition Will:

1. Increase Jackson Sales through expanded US Dist of Jax products. (A)

2. Focus JAX R&D on critical products; rationalize company prod line; expand Titanium products. (B)

3. Sales synergies-broaden global distribution. (C)

4. Establish Hagstrom US base. (D)

5. Reduce Mfg costs. (E)

6. Improve inventory turns by 2.

7. Reduce DSO by 2 days.

Year One Objectives:

1. JAX sales force to include all Hagstrom products.

2. Eliminate distributors in Central America.

3. Rationalize Corp. product portfolio.

4. Accelerate R&D Titanium & launch new products

5. Add 3rd shift to JAX manufacturing

6. Add JAX products to global distribution.

Hagstrom US Operations (Year 1)

	Baseline	Baseline	Synergy	Total
Sales	45.0	6.0	7.0	58.0
Gross Profit	30.0	4.0	5.0	39.0
SG&A				
Marketing			2.0	2.0
R&D				
Duplicate			1.0	1.0
Incremental			1.5	1.5
IT Reduction			0.5	0.5
Total SG&A			5.0	5.0
Pretax Profit	30.0	4.0	10.0	44.0

NOTES:

A= Sales will increase due to broader distribution nationwide rather than regional.

B= Rationalizing R&D will eliminate Corp duplicate projects and focus on critical new products.

C = Sales synergies due to selling US products in EU, and EU products in US.

D = Hagstrom will now have a major presence in the US.

E = Upgrading manufacturing equipment and introducing new metals technology will reduce manufacturing costs.

We've developed these drafts by blending the Due Diligence information that we've obtained during the past few weeks and our investment goals. That includes a multi-year strategy based on your strategic plan, modified to reflect our goals and resources. This is a one-sided summary that does not reflect your insight with respect to our investment objectives.

We will meet with you individually and as a group during the next few days. We want your insight. Please keep the information confidential.

Questions?"

At this point, Jaclyn leaned back in the chair suggesting that the most challenging part of the discussion was complete. "...Any tea with these refreshments?"

The most challenging topics complete, the formal meeting concluded. As the Jackson executives were leaving, Cynthia and Stephen motioned to Jaclyn. "Can we spend a few minutes?"

"Of course. What's on your mind?"

Cynthia leaned forward in her quiet voice, "So, you know that we haven't been through this kind of thing before. What can we expect? What kind of time is required for a successful merger?"

Stephen added, "This is a challenging time for us, and we really don't have a lot of excess time to work on the integration. Your thoughts?"

"Well, that's a good question. The answer is yours to determine. Let's frame the question in a different manner. Hagstrom has placed a significant value on this Company – specifically $60 million. When you look at your daily schedules, what actions would you take to preserve the $60 million and potentially accelerate the Company's growth?"

"C'mon, Jaclyn. Not a fair question – we should do whatever is necessary to preserve the $60 million… but that means for the next few months, we're going to be busting our butts doing two jobs."

"Only if you want to preserve and grow the business. And we both know that you will do that, because that is who you are. Stephen, it won't be easy, but as we develop the integration plans, I'm guessing that you're sense of adventure and – let's say thrill seeking, Mr. Ironman – you'll really enjoy the challenge."

"Yeah – you're right, although I was secretly hoping the amount of work was less than I thought."

"And Cynthia, are you in the game on this?"

"Heck yes – I've got 5+ years in the business – can't let it fall down now."

"Stephen, I'm glad you cornered me on this. My challenge to you and the entire team –

push me to my limits. Don't be shy about questions. The sooner we identify issues, the sooner we'll resolve them. While you folks will be working double time on this, I'll be doing the same. You've got my mobile number. If I expect you folks to deliver, then I've got to deliver as well. Call me anytime. And yes, I recognize that European time is ahead of US time by 6+- hours. If you've got a question at 6 PM, call me – I may be groggy at midnight, but we're protecting $60 million."

Jackson Company: Initial Concerns

The Jackson team assembled at 9:00 AM in the conference room to debrief after yesterday's meeting, and to discuss Jaclyn's worksheets. Frank and Joseph joined the meeting about 9:10 to observe the team's process.

Stephen walked to the whiteboard. "OK folks... what do you think? Have you had a chance to review the worksheets Jaclyn distributed yesterday?"

In a rotation around the table, "They must be joking. It'll take a year to get this stuff done."

"Yes, and worse yet, our business will crash and burn if we concentrate on all these steps."

"You'd almost guess that they want us to put in a new ledger and reporting system. You've gotta be kidding me!"

"The factory folks will be very nervous about the potential changes. We all know that they hate change – especially when things are framed as '... we expect...'"

Don leaned forward, "Margaret, we haven't heard from you yet. Any comments."

"Well, yes. We've got folks heavily committed to our benefits – 401-k; pension; tuition reimbursement program. Let's face it, Don has been very generous to all the employees – and that includes us. If folks get uncomfortable, our best people – you know those that are openly recruited by the competition – may bolt with the increased tension. I'm not saying I know of any particulars, but folks have seen far too many times that the 'buyers' tell one story and deliver another. The joke on the floor refers to *'Murders and Executions* not to *Mergers and Acquisitions.*"

"Let's break this problem into a few large chunks." As Stephen talked, he uncapped a marker and scratched out some points on the whiteboard. "We're concerned about the workload, right?" …Nods of unanimous agreement. "Resources?" Again unanimity… "Anything else?"

Margaret volunteered, "We have a general negative feeling in the factory. Change scares these folks – especially since Don has a great track record of generosity, fairness and concern for the wellbeing of the employees. He knows without good employees, there is no Company."

"So, give me a phrase, Margaret."

"I'll give you two – morale, and I'll call it financial security."

JB leaned back in his chair. "Guys, if the folks are unhappy, productivity will drop. We all know what that means right? We don't make our numbers."

"So now we have 6 problems. Any others?" After a pause, he continued, "Let's figure out some solutions. And remember, Elton said that we have unlimited resources – so let's make a list of needs – let's do our job."

For the next hour the team focused on solutions, rather than just complain about the tough challenges ahead.

"OK folks, it looks like we've developed the perfect solutions to these challenges."

Cynthia stood. "Just like always guys. Find a problem… find a solution. Now we get to test Elton's resolve. These *solutions* could cost him a few dollars…er, Euro's. Must start thinking like a Brit. Hey what do you think will happen when the UK returns to the British Pound rather than dealing with Euro's?"

Allison responded, "Leave it to the CFO to bring up the money topic."

Stephen took a picture of the whiteboard. "I'll send each of you a copy of the board. Feel free to add to the topics, but this is a great start identifying problems and developing solutions.

I'll also pretty up a document so that we can discuss with Elton and Jaclyn. Thanks for all the help."

Acquisition Challenges

1. Workload
2. Resources
3. Change is scary
4. Morale low
5. Financial security
6. Productivity

Workload
- Prioritize Activities
- Challenge requirements
  - Eliminate/postpone activities
  - Shift workload to Hagstrom

Resources
- Inside Jackson
- External
  - Hagstrom
  - Consultants

Change is scary
- LEADERSHIP!!!

That's US!!

solutions

Morale
- Information
- Communication
- Focus on issues

Financial Security
- Commitments by Hagstrom
- Honest discussion

Productivity
- Personal pride
- Published goals/reporting
- Management

Smiles prevailed as the group departed. They had again met the challenge with a plan to succeed. Now it was up to Hagstrom to meet their commitments.

Hagstrom-Jackson Integration Framework

The Jackson team, except JB, assembled in the conference room. An array of travel mugs and insulated disposable coffee cups dotted the conference table. Starbucks predominated – some with sugary foam toppings dusted with cinnamon – others filled with intense black liquid the apparent consistency of motor oil.

Stephen was seated at the center of the conference table, allowing Elton and Jaclyn to enjoy the honored #1 and #2 positions.

Awaiting Elton and Jaclyn, some of the executives were answering emails on their smartphones, while others made notes in their journals.

Elton and Jaclyn joined the session – each carrying a journal and a *Jackson Manufacturing* coffee cup. Stephen opened the conversation with, "Welcome Elton and Jaclyn. Yesterday we had a good meeting after your session, and we wanted to share our thoughts with you. I can tell you that initially we were very concerned about the length of your integration checklist. Said another way – incredible detail. You folks have been through this before.

We at Jackson have been through big challenges before, as you know, but this M&A integration is new turf for us. And truthfully, we consider the task to be nearly impossible. But we've done impossible before. Success comes down to time and resources invested. So today, we'd like to share our thoughts with you and would like to understand your approach to our challenge."

Elton sipped his coffee. "We're impressed that you huddled to think through the first level of the challenge, and enthusiastically look forward to this discussion. Since Jaclyn is driving the project, let's turn the meeting over to her. Jaclyn."

Jaclyn's hands were neatly folded in front of her – pen and journal neatly aligned on the table to her right; coffee cup anchoring the left side. "Thanks Elton. Drive on, Stephen. We'd like to hear your observations."

Stephen distributed the summary of their previous meeting and displayed the pages on the screen. Although Stephen introduced the topics, each member of the Jackson team contributed background discussion to further explain the concerns.

Jaclyn winced when the 'resources' discussion arose. She observed, "This could get expensive." The Jackson executives visibly tensed. Margaret immediately scratched a note in her journal, while Cynthia stared motionless at the summary document. JB leaned forward in his seat and cleared his throat as if to speak, all the while doodling many "$" signs on the page. He remained silent.

Elton quickly added, "Expensive, but we've built contingencies into our valuation. I am really excited that you folks have prepared such a thorough summary of the issues. There will be many individual items that we haven't specifically considered in the valuation, but that's the beauty of the contingency fund. Bravo. Let's keep rolling."

The tension continued as Jaclyn nervously repeated, "Yes, you've done a terrific job so far. Let's keep going."

For the next hour, Stephen and the Jackson team discussed the issues as Jaclyn took notes.

As the brainstorming tempo slowed, Jaclyn summarized, "We are very pleased that you've accepted the baton on this marathon. Yes, there is certainly a lot of work to complete, but the only way to get the job done is to break it down into manageable steps… small steps. During the next few days, we'll be meeting with each of you to dig a little deeper to get the specifics of the integration schedule. When we look at the issues raised today, many of these are 'soft' concerns. I don't see millions of dollars of new equipment, scrapped inventory and hard dollar costs. Transition inefficiency and support costs are customary in any merger. The good news: We've identified things right up front. Well done. Thanks for your insight and continued support. Questions?"

Jaclyn advanced to another Due Diligence assessment topic.

"Folks, the matrix that you see on the screen is an overall assessment of your Company through our eyes. Let's take a minute to review what we've done. You've heard us talk about People, Process, Plant, Product and Market. As we completed our Due Diligence review, we assessed how your organization would benefit Hagstrom's.

When you look at the assessment, don't jump any bridges when you see a 'B' or 'C' rating. That only means that when compared to our standards of performance, we see opportunity whenever the function is rated a "B" or "C". So, if you had the resources of a half-billion dollar global Company, we'd rank your performance as substandard. We recognize that you haven't had those extensive resources historically, and we are prepared to provide the resources to raise performance. And, we believe that you are the executive team that can be ranked "A" throughout the organization once resources are available.

But, please take note – you provide us with a beachhead in the largest single medical device market in the world… hence

A's in the Plant location segments.

But you've also got a top-notch Tech/R&D function."

With that, Allison primped, sat more erect and nodded toward Elton.

Hagstrom
Planning Matrix: Jackson Manufacturing

	People		Process		Plant		Product		Market	
	Inside	Outside	Content	Application	Location (US)	Quality	Current	Pipeline	Share (US)	Growth
Primary										
Company	B	?	B	B	A	B	B	C	C	A
Logistics	B	?	B	B	B	B	n/a	n/a	n/a	n/a
Operations	A	?	A	B	B	B	n/a	n/a	n/a	n/a
Sales	B	?	A	B	C	B	n/a	n/a	n/a	n/a
Marketing	A	?	A	A	B	B	B	C	B	A
Service	B	?	A	B	B	B	B	C	B	B
Support										
HR	B	?	B	B	n/a	n/a	n/a	n/a	n/a	n/a
Technology/IT	A	?	A	A	A	A	A	C	B	A
Finance	B	B	B	B	B	B	n/a		n/a	n/a
Legal	B	B	B	B	B	B	B	B	n/a	n/a
Other	n/a	n/a	n/a	n/a	n/a	n/a	n/a	n/a	n/a	n/a

"So let's spend a minute and look at the matrix. You'll notice that Jackson's plant location is rated an 'A'. That would be the established 'beachhead'. The B's play well – you run a pretty good show here in the US. Check out the 'C' rating for Sales. Any thoughts?"

"Nothing from me," Stephen scowled as his temple pulsated, hands clasped tightly and knuckles whitened.

"Don't jump, big guy." JB could never resist the opportunity to provide a good-hearted jab at Stephen.

Stephen tossed a paper clip at JB. "Careful dude, or I'll double my sales and put you in a real production bind."

"Ah yes, the natives are a bit restless," as Jaclyn continued. "Let's not take this too personally. I'd like you to step back a bit and think about what you could do with an extra $2-3 million to invest annually. Now, any thoughts?"

Stephen immediately volunteered, "I've got a home for three additional sales reps to blanket the Northeast. Sign me up for a half-million spending."

"OK, Stephen, if you can use a half-million dollars to expand sales, why haven't you done so thus far?"

"We don't have that kind of money laying around. We do OK, but not that OK. And as long as you're offering, toss in another half-million for 3 additional trade shows – that'll improve our marketing to more of an acceptable standard."

"OK – now you're starting to get where we are going. Jackson is a beachhead, and we have resources that Jackson would eventually have, but we can do this now – immediately."

Allison, always the techie, pulled a laser pointer from her portfolio and circled the Product Pipeline rating of "C". What's this all about? I thought that we were doing pretty well"

"Again, are you considering the available resources? Let me ask you a question, Allison. Do you have any pipeline of Nanotech based products? … And another question, is there a market for such products?"

"No, we don't have the R&D experts in house, but we've been trying to JV with local universities to capitalize on their research."

"Any thoughts about all those '?' in the People – Outside column?"

Cynthia felt a little left out. "Guessing … you're not really sure what our capabilities are in that area."

"Exactly. While we tried to be thorough in our Due Diligence, time constraints cut us a bit short in some analyses. Our valuations and deal structuring have some gaps in the planning. During this early planning period, we'd like to improve our planning with your insight. So while some of our assessments may look harsh and overly critical, they may just reflect a lack of insight. But, to be candid, some of those grades are justified, since Jackson sometimes doesn't meet our performance standards. Once again, not bad, but different. Our job throughout the planning is to identify the items of variance and determine if-and-how we'd like to resolve the differences.

All the "A's and B's" in the People (Inside) and Processes (Content and Application)… well, we think you do a pretty darn good job at those items.

During the next few weeks, we'll go through each of these items with you. Our goal? First thing we need to do is to validate our assessments. Think about this. What if on JB's strategic plan Cinderella wish list – a list that never made it to the strategic plan - he identified a $500,000 CNC machine?"

JB quickly responded, "Boy could I make this place hum with such a machine!"

"But, we didn't see that in your strategic plan."

"You're right – we didn't develop a wish list of things that would be helpful but not essential."

A moment's pause, and as if a revelation, Stephen shouted, "Ahah. That is without Hagstrom's resources."

"Right. So let's say we didn't expose that opportunity during our Due Diligence, while expecting that we could expand internationally without incremental cost. If we completed the deal, told you that we were expanding internationally and didn't consider the capital, our model would be $.5 million short."

"Gotcha. So it's important for us to understand where you're taking the Company to be sure that the proper resources have been identified and the plan is viable."

"Correct. So as we discuss People, Process, Plant, Product and Market, shout out any concerns. And this isn't just about your area of expertise. Cynthia, if you have any major concerns about a new product launch plan, let's hear them. Without the entire team agreeing to mutual goals, we'll have a difficult time delivering the results that we need to justify the deal.

Our planning is broken into three time segments: Day One, First 100 Days, and Second 100 Days. The implication is that all major transition items will be fully completed within the first 6 months."

Don, silent up until now, suggested, "That's a very aggressive plan, isn't it?"

"Not as fast as others, but certainly not a simple task. That is why we need everyone to be on the same page. So at this point, if no other questions, we'll adjourn and begin individual meetings with each of you. These initial meetings will help us develop a coordinated plan that achieves our goals."

A brief silence, and Jaclyn adjourned the meeting with a final remark, "We'll start our individual meetings later today. Thanks all."

Jaclyn organized individual planning meetings with each executive.

Throughout the discussion, she focused on the 5 priority areas – People, Process, Plant, Product and Market. Exploring each area sequentially, she reinforced the rules guiding the analysis.

Whenever possible, she organized the meetings to be in a conference room which provided ample space to walk around, scratch things on the whiteboard, and also provided an LCD projector.

The Jackson executives remained in the conference room after the meeting.

Elton and Jaclyn relocated to the temporary office.

"Jaclyn, I liked the way you picked up on my interruption. You looked a bit nervous about those costs, but hey, we both know that we have the contingency fund, so let's not get too upset."

"OK, boss. But this could get very expensive, and I'm not sure that I want to risk my reputation on a high-risk operation."

Somewhat perturbed, Elton quickly responded, "This isn't your reputation, Jaclyn, it's mine. We've worked together long enough that you know I'll give you all the support you need to make this successful. Our job these first few weeks is to *manage* the process. So let's focus on the issue – identify all the obstacles and possible solutions to a successful merger. Our job is to make sure that we work with these execs to get the job done. If they see us become overly concerned about a few hundred thousand euro – well, we'll lose them. This is a big acquisition for Hagstrom and we need creativity and problem solving, not angst. You ok with that?"

"You're right, Elton. I slipped... just messed up. I just wasn't prepared for those questions so early in the process. I'm where I need to be – we're aligned - and I'll be more careful in the future. Damn, I can't believe I did that...."

Jackson Debrief

Once the Hagstrom execs left the conference room, JB stood, looked at the other execs and said, "Well, what did you think of the Hagstrom leadership. Looks like we could have some trouble with Jaclyn."

"You might be right, JB, but Elton didn't let her comment live for long. He stepped on it and immediately crushed the doubt."

"Yes, but the comment happened. How committed do you think she is?"

Stephen let the comments among the team continue for a few minutes, anxious not to discourage the discussion. "Yes, it was bothersome, but Elton – remember that CEO guy in the front of the room – he set things straight immediately. And, as we know from our own experience, it is actions that count. Let's give them some space to see where this thing goes.

Also, as we continue the detailed meetings with Jaclyn and Elton, let's remember that the deal isn't done yet. Frank has prepped us about what we can or cannot disclose. If you have any concerns, don't disclose and let's put the item on a checklist. Whatever they ask for may be required immediately, and we can huddle to determine how we want to respond. Questions?"

"So it's as if we're being audited? Answer their questions truthfully and directly when we can. No sideline discussions... no rambling answers," Allison summarized.

"That's right. And Joseph and Jeremy can be the main clearinghouse for any concerns about confidential information. We OK with that direction?"

Several of the team nodded agreement. JB unenthusiastically agreed.

Attendees organized their papers, pens and journals and left the room.

Jaclyn's first one-to-one meeting was with JB. Her goal was to schedule the most difficult meeting early in the process to understand the biggest challenge.

JB was particularly tough on 'Miss Brit' as he sometimes referred to Jaclyn.

"Hey Miss Brit – how long have you worked in manufacturing ops? I'm trusting my career to you, and just want to be sure that I should be following you as the master of my universe."

Jaclyn, never one to be a shy executive responded, "Good question, yank. I haven't worked directly in any manufacturing operation. But I've done a lot of reading – just like your president, Abraham Lincoln. JB, I'm not an expert at manufacturing. But let's get to my added value. I know the – let's call it – the facilitation business. I know our investment goals, the Hagstrom resources, and I'm familiar with Jackson Manufacturing at a high level. One of my strengths? I tend to be able to spot an empty suit when they're in my face."

She paused momentarily as if to let JB self-examine and speculate about her assessment.

JB's face reddened.

Jaclyn continued, "I've reviewed your past performance – remember all those Due Diligence questions that you answered? I've looked at the financials for the past 3-4 years and know that you sharpened your game about two years ago. Not sure what did it, but Inventory Turns improved by about 40%, scrap and rework virtually disappeared, and new product launches accelerated. Not just for a quarter or two – no window dressing here - but sustained performance over a two year period.

I know that you graduated from Purdue, spent some time at Caterpillar, and decided to move to an entrepreneurial company that offered you challenge and responsibility. And you made good. Figures don't lie, JB. Now, based on the numbers, we've got to understand if that was *your* performance or some young hotshot that you hired.

Remember your two hours of personal interviews during the Due Diligence? Vito, our VP Manufacturing, grilled you to discover how good you were. You're here, JB – you passed. You're not an empty suit."

JB's intense stare softened – and with a hint of a smile, nodded. "And you left out that I'm a good judge of character," JB responded. "Not many folks challenge me like that, but you're not just a pretty face – you know your numbers and you've done your homework."

"Now JB, you've just violated the Jackson harassment regulations. That's a free card this time, but I don't expect that silly sexist behavior in the future. Shall we just dial back the BS and get to work?"

Without displaying excessive concern, she noted JB's cavalier attitude toward *sexist* behavior. It may have been JB's testing her mettle, and not characteristic of his work attitude, but she would carefully observe his future methods.

Jaclyn continued, "My role in this whole process is to help you folks align with the Hagstrom's investment strategy and objectives. So when you – the manufacturing expert – identify issues and opportunities, we find solutions for those items. It might be introducing you to the Director of Metallurgy ops in the UK – or perhaps the VP Manufacturing at the other US location. It may be tapping our global resources in universities, or some of our other unique resources, such as engineering firms or governmental agencies.

And yes, we'll spend the money necessary to get the job done right.

My goal – get you to identify issues early, and help you coordinate solutions considering *all available resources*. That doesn't mean that you have an open ticket to spend on anything you want, but if _we_ – that would be you and I – decide that you need something, you'll get it."

"Gotcha – so here's one for you. We're having a tough time milling the newest Titanium alloy. What can you do for me?"

In the following rapid-fire exchange JB divulged far too much information. A new product in development may require new computer-based milling equipment that costs about a half million dollars. Up until now, there had been no mention of the capex requirement, and he may have just added an unknown half-million dollars to the investment. Said another way, he may have just reduced the purchase price. The R&D project team expected the new product to be launched in a year. The team identified the possible need for the advanced equipment a few days ago. Only Allison and JB knew of the potential requirement. The R&D folks were still analyzing a potential solution using existing equipment, so no formal Due Diligence disclosure would be required. The technical challenge was to produce at market volumes, since pilot batches worked very well.

"Is it a today problem – something that needs resolution within the next few weeks, or a strategic challenge that we need to resolve within the next 6-12 months?"

"Six to twelve months."

"Then put it on the issues worksheet – we'll log it into the system and within a few days, we should have a scheduled response. As you might guess, we've got to resolve today's issues first. Make sure that people get paid… have health insurance … make sure the customers know we care about them."

"What is this issues worksheet? Nobody's talked about that yet."

"I've gotten a bit ahead of myself, JB. Your right – we haven't talked about that yet. Since you're the first, let's spend a minute. Our goal is to be sure that any issues that require resolution are listed on an issues worksheet. We want to be sure that we don't lose track of anything that is important to the transaction. We'll log the item on the sheet; prioritize the issue, value the issue, and potential solution. Working with a sponsor – the person who owns the issue – we'll be sure that everything is properly resolved."

As she was talking, she selected a worksheet from her portfolio. "This worksheet is on the website – it will take 2 minutes to complete, and then we've got it in the system for resolution. We've set up a system to log everything that affects the success of the acquisition. Include the timing in the Description section. We review this daily to be sure that we don't miss anything. And if the timing changes, we'll update the form.

Due Diligence Issue Summary												
Ref	Res	Validate	Upside	Downside	Integration	Description	Date		Financial Impact *(000's US $)*			
							Open	Resolve	Sales	Gross Margin	Expense	Capital
						Enter a brief description of the issue, and if multiple years, describe.				If multiple year impact, explain in description		

JB eased back from his desk and leaned into the deep seat cushion satisfied that Jaclyn wasn't all fluff – a prim and proper inexperienced PhD wonk. She had some guts – some substance - pushing back on the manufacturing expert.

"So, Jaclyn, tell me about these headings: Validate; Upside; Downside; Integrate."

"Let's think about our investment process, JB. We have a brief opportunity to investigate potential investments – the Due Diligence process. Throughout the process we're trying to understand the strategic fit for any investment. That fit comes down to economics. Each of our reviewers is responsible to understand our strategic goals for the investment. As such, we've developed a business case with assumptions.

We charge each reviewer with a responsibility to help us make a good investment, and they all have an equal voice. We group the responsibilities by:

- Validate our investment assumptions.
  Each of the reviewers knows the
  strategic investment goal, and the
  assumptions used in the model. Their
  job is to validate those assumptions
  whenever possible, and/or provide a
  judgment about the assumptions. Are
  they reasonable and achievable?
- During the due diligence process we
  want to continuously search for
  - Upsides to the transaction. Think
    about it. We have very little time
    to investigate one of the largest
    single investments made by the
    Company. The reviewers are
    experts in their function. We
    want them to analyze what they
    see, and using their judgment,
    identify things that we haven't
    considered in our model.
  - Downsides to the transaction. It's
    the same logic. Reviewers
    observe and identify things that
    we haven't considered in our
    model.
- Integration issues. In our very limited
  time at the target, we *must* consider
  integration issues. Think about the
  process. We have a few hours to
  observe and think about our *tomorrows*.
  What will the investment look like in 6
  months... or maybe a year? We send
  experienced execs on the Due Diligence
  review, and their job is to simulate the
  integration during their review. Some
  integration issues may be critical – so

let's say a *key* employee may appear to be nervous about the acquisition. Well, the reviewer needs to highlight that, and we may do something special – like have the target company offer some golden handcuffs. We might also focus on key customers that may be a bit nervous about the transaction and spend additional time with them, assuring them about how the integration will proceed.

As best we can, we quantify the value of any of these items and build the impact into the model. We only send our best people on Due Diligence reviews – and we don't mean just those with technical skills, but true executives that can assess the overall business environment. That helps us protect our investment.

A few minutes ago, you mentioned the computer-milling machine for the Titanium alloy. Now that's a downside that we included in our initial assessment a few weeks ago. Our estimate is about a half-million dollars. Does that sound about right to you JB?"

"That's about right."

JB attempted to disguise his surprise at her knowledge. He was very thankful that he hadn't cost Jackson a half-million dollars.

JB and Jaclyn continued to discuss the manufacturing operation. It was as much sharing information about the global Hagstrom operations as it was probing for additional information about Jackson. Jaclyn wanted to demonstrate her openness about the Company, while acquainting JB with the capabilities of Hagstrom. She continued to probe for synergies and issues that may affect the success of the merger.

The meeting concluded on professionally friendly terms after about an hour. Jaclyn mentioned that she would meet with Margaret at 1 PM to brief her about the transaction.

Shortly after the meeting, JB was brewing a Sumatra Dark on the Keurig, sharing the story with Allison, Cynthia and Stephen.

Surprised at Jaclyn's response, Stephen challenged, "You mean that young marketing brit pushed back on you?"

"You betcha – surprised me as well. I think that they have a qualified no-nonsense exec driving this integration bus. This might be a lot of fun – lots of work as well – but I don't mind working with demanding folks if they know what they are doing.

And she knows how to play a target for information. She pushed me enough that I got a bit emotional and talked about the Titanium milling machine."

Allison's eyes opened wide. "JB, you and I are the only ones that know about that."

Stephen stared at each of them, his eyes drilling them… digging for information. "Anyone want to tell me about the Titanium milling machine? I don't recall ever discussing it."

Allison inhaled deeply. "Stephen, you know that we have that new product scheduled for introduction in about a year."

"Yes, the breakthrough product…"

"Well, last week the project team discovered that the Titanium alloy density, and the tolerances required may require some additional equipment. We're not sure yet if our existing equipment can produce at the required market volumes. We have a tiger team working on potential solutions, but – well, we may need an additional half-million investment to properly launch the product with our planned margins."

The vein on Stephen's temple throbbed and he lowered his voice to almost a whisper. "So what you're telling me is that Jaclyn knows more about our business than I do?" His jaw tightened and his eyes narrowed.

Defensively, JB offered, "Stephen, I messed up. I know that you and Joseph have warned us about disclosing too much information. The conversation got away from me. Now if there is any good news about this mess, it is that Jaclyn already knew about the new mill requirement."

"And would you care to tell me how she knew?"

"She mentioned that her Due Diligence team already identified the need, and I don't have any idea how they discovered the requirement."

As if a gun turret, Stephen turned to Allison and repeated, "If you and JB were the only ones that knew about the requirement, would you care to explain how *they* knew before I heard about it."

"I can tell you that I've had no discussions one-on-one with them since we discovered the need. I don't have any idea about how they knew. We should check with them."

JB interrupted. "Jaclyn gave me a quick tutorial on their Due Diligence process. Basically they send in their best talent to look at a potential target. They're looking at the business in a completely different way than we do, day-to-day. I'm guessing, but given their metallurgical experience in Europe, and their existing businesses, they've probably already identified the high-speed milling requirement in their new product development."

"OK, JB. I'll buy that for now. Let's call this a teachable moment, guys. We need to be exceptionally careful about disclosures. We MUST be truthful in any responses, but let's not volunteer information if it's not specifically requested."

JB and Allison both agreed.

As the effective COO, Stephen continuously observed and evaluated the team. Yes, this was a good outcome to a burly manufacturing VP's challenge. It was also evident that the Hagstrom Due Diligence team was very thorough in their investment evaluation.

Human Resources: Jaclyn and Margaret

Jaclyn had an interesting rapport with Margaret, and she wasn't sure why. She knocked on Margaret's open door more to announce her arrival than request permission to enter. "Good morning, Margaret. Is this still a good time to meet?"

"Sure thing. Come on in." She carefully stacked the papers on her desk, clipped them with an alligator clip and slipped them into her top drawer. She slid her journal to the center of the desk and folded her hands, smiling, and asked, "What shall we talk about?"

Jaclyn responded, "I just want to talk about the transaction and integration. Nothing hard and fast, but more a 'get acquainted' meeting. Have you given much thought to the integration?"

"Yes. I've thought about how simple this could be, but I'm also a bit concerned about foreign ownership. The simple side – I'm guessing that we will be a freestanding operation with minimal interference from UK-HQ."

Jaclyn keyed on the word 'interference' as something that she would have to overcome through diplomacy. As an owner, Hagstrom had a responsibility to its stockholders to oversee their investments. 'Interference' is an uncomfortable term with negative connotations. She reasoned that direct confrontation about *interference* would not go well.

Jaclyn smiled. "Well, for sure let's talk about the Jackson op as the US HQ. You're right about what should be simple from the administrative side. But when you consider our global presence and the Berkshire operation, it may be a bit more twisty. Let's spend a minute and think about the transaction strategy. We're a somewhat vertically integrated global operation. When we looked at our expertise with exotic metals, our ability to manufacture complex medical devices and our minimal presence in the US, we knew that we needed a foothold in the US. Our initial investment in Berkshire allowed us to familiarize ourselves with US customs. That's worked out well for us.

We're now looking at Jackson as a way to rapidly leverage our European technical expertise in the sciences and manufacturing, expand our global reach with our European approved products, and launch the Jackson FDA approved products into the European markets. We'd also like to market these products to the Asia market.

When you think about all the interaction that will be required to be successful in this venture, well, we quickly move from simple to somewhat complex. "

Margaret listened attentively, nodding occasionally while taking brief notes in her journal. "So my assumption that we would just operate as the US branch is oversimplified. We're not just sending you profit checks in the UK?"

"Right. But while this sounds somewhat complex, it really is just the result of small, individual decisions made in a chain to accomplish our objective.

One of the first things we want to ensure is that the employees are fully engaged. We're early in the integration planning, but what's your read on the temperament."

Knowing that the deal is still not complete, Margaret carefully crafted her answer. "Jaclyn, we're very excited about the opportunity to work with Hagstrom. Throughout the due diligence you've demonstrated a thoroughness and professionalism that fits our culture. I won't lie to you – we are apprehensive about foreign ownership, but thus far your actions have been sensitive to the Yankee culture."

"Yes ma'am. We cannot be successful as dictators from the other side of the pond. Let's spend a minute on some of the mechanics. We mentioned that Jackson would be combined with Berkshire. We don't expect much disruption in that combination, since we'll fold them into your responsibility. Your benefits are superior to Berkshire, so they will have no issues aligning with your benefits. The management team will be folded into Jackson's, and the Berkshire CEO is comfortable – maybe even thankful – to be reporting into Stephen in his prospective role as COO, Global Medical Devices and US operations.

That said, we're buying the assets, folding all the assets into Berkshire for liability and tax reasons.

But the heart of our strategy is the intimacy required among all the operating functions. Think about the linkage required for new product development, blending the science and manufacturing operations to quickly launch existing products across the borders. Better yet, how about developing new products?

Let's spend a minute discussing JB and Allison. How will they play with the Europeans?"

Margaret wasn't expecting such a direct question about the two executives, but she knew the script.

"JB is a real character... gruff and sometimes blustery, but he is great at his job. He can easily relate to the folks on the floor, and he can get the teams to go far beyond their imagination when they understand the challenge and his commitment to support.

And Allison? Well, she is definitely a team player. Technology is her specialty, but she is one of the few scientists that I know who can easily understand the business goals when we're talking about new product development, cash flows and profitability."

Just as expected, each executive team member is presenting a favorable summary of every element of the business, always trying to get the deal done.

"So Margaret, talk to me about the Company culture. I'm trying to scope out how the integration will progress, and where some of the personnel issues might arise."

For the next few minutes, Margaret continued to 'sell' the Company, never varying from the *internal marketing* script.

"And Margaret, what's the biggest challenge that you folks have conquered during the past year."

Joseph had prepared the team with similar questions, and the team, while not fully scripted, had already identified some of the keys to their success.

"Just about 6 months ago, we had a real problem with some of the materials delivered by the supplier. Something about the titanium alloy and concentration of carbon. Whatever the issue, JB and Allison put a cross-functional team together to identify and solve the problem. Engineering, R&D, Purchasing, Regulatory Affairs and Sales met to brainstorm the scope of the problem and possible solutions. As a fix, we bought some stock from a previously validated backup source. "

When Jaclyn heard 'regulatory affairs' she listened attentively to be sure that she understood the situation, since no one had mentioned this problem before. She thought, '...could this be a major problem for us?'

"So why was sales involved if it was a manufacturing problem?"

"Customers are number one in this business. We wanted Jeffrey – the Director of Sales - to hear what was going on so that if there were any rumors in the field, he could thoroughly explain the issue and our solution."

"And what was the solution?"

Margaret continued, "Once we identified the alloy issue in our routine testing, we retested the shipment, confirming the results. Then we rechecked existing stocks to be sure nothing got through in an earlier batch. Our entire existing inventory was within spec. From there we notified the vendor of our test results.

They immediately froze all shipments from that lot number.

"So it sounds like you cast a net around any possible technical problem that could have resulted from the bad materials. What was the timing of all this activity?"

"All completed within 72 hours. And when I say 72 hours, I mean around the clock. Labs were running ..."

Margaret continued to discuss the issue for the next 15 minutes.

Jaclyn's take-away... the Company was fanatical about quality, and was critically aware of the need to have flawless product related to implanted devices. The team was unafraid to shut the business down when a serious problem arose. This attitude was consistent with Hagstrom's culture and operating philosophy.

"OK, Margaret. This has been helpful. Now let's spend a few minutes on the integration. I mentioned that, while this is a fairly simple transaction – buying the Company assets – the integration includes a function-by-function integration. Jackson will be the US headquarters, but we want the global organization to function as one. You'll lose a bit of autonomy. Any comments?"

"For sure, it will be different. Today we just stroll down the hall and meet with Don and Stephen. Now, I guess that we'll do a video conference."

"But that's not all, Margaret. The executives will now be one operational family. So Jackson will now sell Hagstrom products suitable for the US. Hagstrom R&D will now be a part of a fully integrated development team. You will have access to all our research… our scientific resources in the European universities etc.

JB will now be required to work with our European manufacturing operations when new products are developed. And JB will have to comply with European regulations for products destined for Europe.

How will Allison and JB react to that?"

"Both Allison and JB are team members. Once the guidelines are established, we execute against a plan. It will be a bit more difficult since historically, they are at the top of the food chain, but they can get the job done."

"And when we have global Company reporting requirements?"

"As I said, once the rules are defined, they'll get the job done."

Jaclyn continued to discuss some expected integration factors, but no major issues were identified.

R&D: Jaclyn and Allison

Jaclyn's schedule was overpowering today. In sequence she would be meeting with each of the Jackson senior executives. She anxiously anticipated meeting with Allison since they were both women executives in challenging and very technical roles.

At the appointed time, she knocked on Allison's door respecting Allison's professionalism and awareness of business etiquette.

"C'mon on in, Jaclyn. I've been anxious to meet with you. Shall we meet here, or would you like to meet in the conference room?"

Jaclyn entered, extended her hand guiding both to the casual setting – deep cushioned chairs in the corner of Allison's office near the windows. The feng sui of a casual setting seemed to break down the perceived barriers of an acquirer and target company.

"Would you like a coffee or tea, Jaclyn?"

"You know that would be good. Shall we walk to the kitchen?" Jaclyn was well aware of the need to break any tension with casual discussion and a stroll to a new venue.

"You know, when I looked around your office I noticed several photos of broad landscapes with – I think it was you in those sunglasses and backpack. Interesting pics…"

"Yes, one of my bucket-list challenges… I backpacked the Camino de Santiago a few years ago. … No revelations, but getting unplugged was pure magic. Kind of helped me realign some of my priorities."

"So was there any one thing that startled you on the trail? I mean, did you solve the world's hunger crisis or, were you ever afraid or did you feel threatened while hiking?"

"I can only say I was surprised at the outcome. When I planned the trip, I believed that it would be a life-changing event… not sure what to expect, but thinking that when in the middle of nowhere, I would have a startling revelation about life and the world order. My hiking days would be filled with inspiration… Instead, the days were filled with absolutely nothing. I spent 22 days walking about 6-8 hours a day, thinking about nothing. When I finished the trek, I celebrated, and came back to work. I won't say completely energized, but realigned. Not that my day-to-day routine changed, but it just felt different."

"So did you decide to hang up your spurs when you returned… you're happy that the Company would be sold so that you could dial back an intense work schedule?"

Jaclyn probed the soft side of business during planning and Due Diligence. During these *informal* discussions, her goal was to peel back the executive's *sales orientation* to better understand his/her personal goals.

Joseph explained that during Due Diligence and any discussion with potential buyers, buyers continually evaluated key executives for their leadership and technical skills, and their personal goals and motivation.

"You know, before the trek, I thought that I would develop a plan to unwind my career in those long hiking days. In fact, since I didn't think about much – other than the next food stop, or the beautiful scenery – I absorbed the cultural journey.

When I returned, for some reason I found that I had more commitment than ever to grow this business. I was surprised – let's say pleasantly surprised - at the excitement and level of commitment to the business. But I broadened my approach to better consider business alternatives as the executive team evaluated strategies. It's hard to explain, but my commitment was deeper or more substantive than my earlier superficial commitment, by comparison."

While in the kitchen, they brewed the coffee casually discussing Cincinnati sports teams. They returned to Allison's office with steaming cups of brew.

"So, Allison, what are your expectations of this merger? Any concerns – questions?"

"I'll let you explain a bit more about the Hagstrom approach and your business goals. It would be foolish of me to talk about my expectations, since you folks know your strategic objectives and will be leading this merger."

Jaclyn described the merger goals and a broad outline of the near term objectives, including creating a global R&D strategy with focus on specific technologies including Nanotech.

"So, what is your initial reaction, Allison?"

"It seems that you have thoroughly considered our strategic fit and have some interesting goals. I'm a bit concerned about globalizing R&D, but we scientists tend to get ultra focused on goals, and as long as the goal is commercialization of technical products that best serve the patients, let's do it."

"Yes, the patients are a critical part of our strategy, but we also serve our stockholders, so we need to balance the tech focus with the P&L. You know, I like the way that you focused on the non-technical integration element. Culture is a key… working together in a global organization gives us leverage, breadth of vision to a broader patient base. So how do you think we should handle the culture challenge?"

"This is moving very quickly and I haven't given much thought to the merger. Just thinking out loud… I think the teams should develop common goals so that all their energy is focused on mutually agreed deliverables. Of course we know that scientists can go down a rat-hole for the sake of science, so we'd have to coach them to focus on goals that would be acceptable to Hagstrom."

Allison paused with furrowed brow, and focused on her coffee.

After a few moments she offered, "I think some kind of team meeting – you know, some of the European folks and some of the US folks. But, Jaclyn, that could get expensive, and I'm not sure we could afford it."

"Glad that you are cost conscious, but remember, we're guarding a $60 million investment, and launching a renewed global Company. We might surprise you about what we're willing to invest to achieve our goals."

"OK – got it. You mentioned that earlier, and I'm just going to have to think differently – and maybe a bit bigger – as I consider the integration. So let's see, we'd need a meeting – maybe 15-20 key folks depending on the R&D strategy… we'd want to have the meeting somewhere away from the day-to-day so that we could focus, and we may want to have it close to a Company facility so that we could expose 'the other team' – whoever that may be - to the other Company.

You've seen our operations. Any insight?"

"You're right on the track that we've developed in our preliminary planning. We like to describe a strategic framework and let the team of professionals – the folks that will have to execute the plan - develop the details. Allison, I really like the way you think about assembling the participants from both sides develop the plan. Talk to me…"

"Jaclyn, I've been through development projects where two groups work in isolation – for example, manufacturing operations and R&D. Heck, the R&D folks developed the most incredible products you can ever imagine. Trouble was, manufacturing couldn't manufacture the 6-headed hydra the R&D gurus developed for less than 3 times the estimated selling price. What a mess. After the management stumbled a half-dozen times… incredible infighting and loss of key people … the execs finally figured it out. Get the damn teams together to design the product.

I can assure you that there will be planning challenges to overcome, but I'd rather be resolving the differences on a whiteboard than thrashing through tens-of-thousands of dollars spending trying to fix something later.

If the meetings are properly facilitated, good things happen."

"OK, Allison, brainstorming for a minute, do you see any scary issues?"

"Well, one thing that jumps at me is the prioritization of the projects. We've got a certain process that works here. We developed the process through trial and error, and it yields good results. If we are to be the global HQ, how will we prioritize the global projects?"

"We'll just step back and look at all projects on a global scale, and based on required investment, expected timeline to product launch, and probabilities of success, we'll select the projects to be developed. We have some notions about future value of some of your projects, but we're empowering you folks to do the global analysis and recommendations for continuing projects. Of course the overall evaluation needs to be approved by Corporate, but I can assure you that since our goals are aligned, things will work just right."

Jaclyn was pleased with the discussion. For the next hour, they covered the highlights of Hagstrom culture and broad strategic goals.

Sales/Marketing: Jaclyn and Stephen

At this point, Jaclyn was exhausted, but knew that she had to meet with Stephen before the end of the day. Her steps a bit slower and the sparkle in her eyes somewhat dimmed, she knocked on Stephen's door.

"Who goes?"

"It's Jaclyn, Stephen. Still time to meet with me?"

Almost before she finished her sentence, Stephen opened the door. The crisp white shirt and $200 necktie broadcast professionalism. His broad smile welcomed her into his lair.

"Jaclyn – great that you could fit me in today. I wasn't sure if we'd make it. I understand your schedule has been very hectic today. C'mon in… would you like a mineral water?"

It was clear that Stephen was in sales & marketing, having a ready supply of Perrier, often the desired beverage of European visitors. His firm handshake and broad smile left Jaclyn wondering if he had just returned from a workout.

Knowing the challenge that such a professional presented, she dug deep into her energy reserves.

"I apologize for the late meeting, Stephen. I just got a bit behind at every stop. Is this a good time to talk?"

"Sure – let's have at it. What shall we talk about?"

His triathlon training prepared him for such challenging times. Now he would reap the benefits of his offsite hobby.

As Jaclyn settled into the comfort of his deep cushioned chair, she said, "Stephen, we'd just like to get your initial insight into the transaction and integration. But before we do that, what are those pictures on the wall. It looks like you in some kind of presentation." She knew there was no better way to break down barriers than scan the office and select a memento or personal picture to relieve some the *interrogation type* pressure.

Stephen's wall had several photos – some with professional golfers, and some just ribbon ceremonies for his completion of triathlons. Since she didn't specify, he opted to boast about a triathlon.

 "Not a big deal – just some mementos of a few competitions?"

"So it's true – you are the IRONMAN."

"Yes, I've done a few of them, but those were the old days. I can't do a full Ironman anymore – ' I'm into the *half* competitions. They're still plenty tough – but I just don't have the time to train for the Full Monty anymore."

"What got you into such a challenge to begin with?"

"Simply put, if I don't have a challenge, I'm miserable. I was feeling a bit underwhelmed–maybe it was a mid-life crisis, I don't know. But one day I awoke and said, 'I'm doing it!" From there, months of training, and a few near-last positions in competition, and I decided to get serious. My best finish was in the top 25% - but you've gotta see some of the guys in the competition."

"So, you like to have challenge. Perfect fit for a merger environment. These tend to be very challenging."

After a few minutes of storytelling, Jaclyn refocused the discussion to the acquisition and integration. "So, you've heard us describe the overall strategy. What kind of snakes do you envision – with the strategy and with the integration?"

"How long do you think the integration will take?"

"Good question. The complete integration could take up to a year, while the critical elements will be done within 6 months. Our goal is to avoid confusion for too long within our ranks, with customers, vendors, and governmental agencies such as the FDA. When we think of the transaction, we break it down to People, Process, Plant/Assets, Product and Market.

You'll be responsible for the US market and Hagstrom's Global Device segment. That includes all your existing products, new product development – both here and Europe – and existing products from Europe on which we expect imminent FDA approval. We also want you to launch US products in Europe, once they are approved by the EC.

It's going to be a major task for you, but we believe that once you folks are focused on the integration objective, we can make it happen."

"It sounds like a huge task – aligning organizations, new product launches etc. My initial reaction is that it's a gut buster."

"Spoken like a triathlon master. So how do we train and plan the events? What is your initial reaction?"

"Well, for sure, I'll need to know what and when you expect the European products to be approved here in the US. And then, when you expect to get the US products approved in the EEC.

Getting ready for a launch here in the US doesn't scare me since we launched several new products during the past few years. We have a good process for product launch and I'll guess that we should put the marker at 4-6 months if everything is in order. We can bridge off the marketing that you've done successfully in Europe.

As far as launching our products in Europe – well, I don't have any idea about marketing in Europe."

"We understand that you haven't launched any products in Europe, and that you will rely heavily on our experienced teams in Europe for a successful launch. When I said that you would be responsible, I meant that we would collaborate with you to be sure that we accomplish all the critical steps and milestones.

Any other concerns?"

"Sure. We now sell through distributors in Latin America and the Far East. Do we have any overlap with Hagstrom's existing distribution channels? We've been very protective of our distributor relationships and want to treat them fairly. Not only that, we have some contracts with some of them, and now that we are no longer a small US manufacturer but rather a *deep pockets* global company – well things could get expensive."

"We're aware of the distributor contracts, which, based on our Due Diligence, seemed to be boilerplate. Do you have any particular concerns?"

His carefully worded response was, "You know these distributors. No major conflict – just the usual sabre rattling and trying to push us to the limits. Nothing extraordinary."

Shifting quickly to another topic, "It seems that the integration of product launches will disrupt our normal sales process – learning about the European products, and training the European sales team about US products that could be sold in Europe. I'm concerned that our compensation plan and sales commission for the sales force will be disrupted. It's conceivable that the diverted resource to these unplanned product launches could result in our missing sales targets. Our guys work hard and they deserve the real chance to achieve their commitments."

"Agreed, Stephen. We've seen similar concerns in some of our other integrations. Once we understand the efforts required, we make adjustments to the compensation goals so that we continue to have happy, well-compensated reps. Anything else?"

"Sure. Just how do you think I'll fit into this new global organization?"

"We'll need to work that out. Just remember that our policy is to treat people fairly, and we want your insight. We've known that you are a team player from the get-go, and we hope that cooperation will continue. What do you see as day-one issues, now that we've discussed the overall integration strategy?"

"We've absolutely got to assure the troops that they are valued components in the new venture. If I have to ensure a successful launch of the US products in Europe, I won't provide the same support to my team as in the past. That's a gap we have to consider."

"I understand Stephen. We've already discussed that the integration means nearly double-time for anyone directly involved in the integration. I think that you're really starting to appreciate that commitment.

The integration team is not just the senior executives, but everyone is part of the integration process. We know that this requires extra effort by all, and we – and that includes the executive team – need to define what are essential activities during this period, and what activities can be postponed. In past integration efforts, we have intentionally eliminated low value activities - sometimes indefinitely.

An effective integration requires that we examine the entire value chain and determine what is the best use of our limited resources.

Remember how Elton said, 'We need your help.' Well, now you can understand how foolish it would be for us to simply dictate activities in a merger. Our lives will change – on both sides of the transaction. So let's not just think of *adding* responsibilities to your team, but when we consider the universe of activities, some of our current activities will be low priority, and some activities will be eliminated.

Stephen, I think you get it... and in particular, I like the way you press on the important issues. So yes, we know that there will be pressure on both teams, and we'll have to figure out how to focus on critical activities, eliminate non-value added activities, and create proper rewards for the extra effort involved."

Jaclyn paused as she shifted topics. "So back to Day One priorities... people, processes, plant, product and market.

Let's take a minute to brainstorm. People – you've hit on employees – great. How about outside the Company?"

"Customers. And we should probably think about potential customers. Our sales cycle time for major accounts sometimes goes for months – perhaps years before we close the account. We need to keep them on the radar."

"And knowing your organized approach, you've got a history on all those potential major accounts?"

"Yes, for sure. And when I think of your template approach to integration, I think of Process. We have a well-defined approach to selling. How do you think that will match with the European team?"

"You've developed a well-regimented approach to selling. Although I'm not thoroughly familiar with the European sales force, my sense is that you have a more sophisticated sales method. I think that the Europeans would benefit from your tactics."

"So does that add yet another 'demand' on my time? How do you think that we should prioritize the sales training in European ops?"

"It's definitely something that we should put on the list… perhaps as something in the 2nd hundred days. What do you see as Day One requirements for sales/marketing?"

"OK – just brainstorming, but I think that we need to develop some marketing material that anticipates questions from customers. We'll need to discuss the 'new' organization and the fact that we'll have some new products to sell in the near term. And what do you think of including some information about the global R&D effort and concentration on Nano technology? Gosh, it seems that there are many potential positives from this.

I think we should also be ready to implement some tactical SPIFS for the sales force – you know, something that gets them focused on performance rather than the transition.

You know, Jaclyn, I think I need to do some serious brainstorming about Day One, and all the positive things that could result from this merger."

"Great, Stephen. I'll let you develop some thoughts and I'll get out of your way. I think you're exactly on track when you think about all the benefits of the merger. When you get your list together, don't forget to prioritize the activities, and don't be shy about asking for Corporate resources."

"Got it."

With that, Jaclyn returned to her temporary office to summarize her day.

Jaclyn summarized her notes from the morning's meetings to discuss with Elton.

"Elton, in my meeting with Margaret, she mentioned an alloy assay failure that we hadn't picked up before. It sounds like the problem was properly handled, but I'm putting this on the Due Diligence hit list.

There a few other items that need attention:
- Retention contracts for the senior execs, and a few critical employees in R&D.
- Performance bonuses for certain employees with high priority tasks (e.g. IT integration).
- New product launch could be a real challenge, especially since we have the synergy value in the justification.
- Stock options to director level.

Pre-Closing: T-6 Days

Transaction Summary to Jackson Executives

At 2 PM, each executive received a 'High Priority' confidential email jointly signed by Elton and Jaclyn ominously labeled, "Deal Summary".

JB, Diet Dr. Pepper in hand, strolled to Allison's office. Unannounced, uninvited, and without hesitation he disregarded her closed door. "Allison, have you had a chance to look at the Deal Summary yet?" as he waved the email in the air.

"Yes, I've been reviewing it. It's an interesting transaction summary. Better yet, it pretty well lays out the transaction goal. While I haven't thoroughly understood the strategy, since I don't have the Hagstrom background, it looks like this could be quite favorable to the Jackson team – that is, if we can pull this off."

Yes – I was surprised that they expect to spend an additional $2.5 million in capital to get the expected results. Honestly, I never considered a complete overhaul of the shop floor and inventory control system. It's a bit shocking to think that they believe they can get us to 6 inventory turns a year, while they grow the business by 20% per year during the next few years. We've done a credible job during the past two years, but I couldn't even dream of that kind of progress."

"Feeling the heat, eh? You didn't even mention the additional new products that they expect to launch during the next 18 months. That average cycle time will beat our historical performance by about 7 months. And yes, I thought we were doing a darn good job all along - at least compared to where we were three years ago. Damn! Can't believe their expectations. Wonder what's up their sleeve."

"Allison, have you talked with anyone else about this? It would be great to get insight from the numbers expert, and I'm sure that Stephen will have a reaction to the hyper-growth expected."

As they continued their discussion, the computer alert signaled another email arrived at Allison's computer.

"Well, how about this? A meeting invitation to meet with Elton and Jaclyn to discuss the 'Deal Summary' with the team. Things could get interesting tomorrow morning.

JB launched a quick salute and left the office as quickly as he arrived. Making the rounds of the other executives, he tested their acceptance of the "Deal Summary". Each exec was somewhat surprised – perhaps skeptical - at the aggressive growth goals, and the creative thinking that reflected a fully integrated organization. The big question – could we execute in the manner described?

After meeting with each VP, JB stopped in the kitchen and fed $2 into the vending machine for 2 bags of peanuts, walked to Don's office, knocked and announced his arrival.

"Here ya go boss … a bag of heart-healthy nuts to munch on."

Don smiled, head slightly bobbing in amusement. "Thanks JB. You concerned about my heart-health these days?"

"No… just kind of strolling around checking things out. Wanted to chat a bit about the 4 PM meeting. What did you think?"

"Interesting for sure. Have you had a chance to talk to the others?"

"Yes – they're all a bit… well, I'm not sure if it's apprehensive, overly concerned, or just a bit skeptical. We've made a lot of changes during the past few years, and I'm not sure that the energy needed to pull this off is in the reserves."

"Personally, JB, I was impressed with Hagstrom's vision. Think about this. They're a bunch of Brits taking over one of the colonies. They only know our business through the trade and a few weeks of Due Diligence, yet they're willing to put $60 mil on the table. They're going to trust you folks to make something happen that seems – well, it just seems a bit overly aggressive."

"So you're skeptical too, boss?"

"I think a better term is intrigued. If they weren't paying virtually all cash, I'd be concerned, but they're – a poker term – 'all in' and I can't accuse them of being timid. You folks have been through major change during the past few years. You've earned some wonderful bonuses, and you'll enjoy the buy-out for cash – remember all your options will be vested when the transaction is complete.

Elton and Jaclyn have been through this before. Let's give them some space. While I want you folks to give them honest feedback on their plans, the check isn't in the bank yet, so we may want to be careful – truthful, but careful. They have a good reputation; they seem to be very competent. Let's see what happens. My suggestion? You and the entire team, in a professional way, should challenge those items that you think are – maybe not unachievable, but very aggressive.

My guess is that they truly want your input. I would also assume that whatever the team signs up for would be goals in any upcoming performance evaluations … that will drive bonus and stock option awards. It's a multi headed hydra. Slay that serpent, JB

And thanks for the health food, Mr. Peanut."

JB returned to his office to continue his review of the "Deal Summary". Although not a financial exec, he understood the financial summary. As he settled deep into the leather cushion of his office chair, he stared at the "Deal Summary," tearing the corner off the peanuts package while saying to himself, 'Heart healthy – but 200 calories.'

He liked to sip a Diet Dr. Pepper and munch on healthy snacks when he reviewed complex concepts. This summary was compact, focused and not overly complicated. How were these results possible?

HAGSTROM ACQUISITION JACKSON MANUFACTURING
MERGERS & ACQUISITION SUMMARY

TRANSACTION SUMARY

Purchase Price:	Millions US $
Cash	45.0
Stock Val	
Debt Assumed	5.0
Subtotal	50.0
Earnout	10.0
Total Cost	60.0

This Acquisition Will: (Notes: A, B, C, D, E)

1. Increase Jackson Sales through expanded US Dist of
2. Focus JAX R&D on critical products; rationalize company prod line; expand Titanium
3. Sales synergies-broaden global distribution.
4. Establish Hagstrom US base.
5. Reduce Mfg costs.
6. Improve inventory turns by 2.
7. Reduce DSO by 2 days.

Year One Objectives:
1. JAX sales force to include all Hagstrom products.
2. Eliminate distributors in Central America.
3. Rationalize Corp. product portfolio.
4. Accelerate R&D Titanium & launch new products
5. Add 3rd shift to JAX manufacturing
6. Add JAX products to global distribution.

SUMMARY CASH FLOW: YEAR

Description	Resp	1	2	3
		(Millions US $)		
Baseline		12.0	14.0	15.0
Reduce DSO	Cynthia	2.0		
Inventory Turns	JB	0.5	1.0	
Sales Synergy	Stephen	6.0	7.0	7.0
COGS Reduction	JB	1.0	2.0	2.0
R&D Rationalization	Allison	1.0	1.5	1.5
Total		22.5	25.5	25.5

Hagstrom US Operations *(Year 1)*

	Baseline	Baseline	Synergy	Total
Sales	45.0	6.0	7.0	58.0
Gross Profit	30.0	4.0	5.0	39.0
SG&A				
Marketing			2.0	2.0
R&D				
Duplicate			1.0	1.0
Incremental			1.5	1.5
IT Reduction			0.5	0.5
Total SG&A			5.0	5.0
Pretax Profit	30.0	4.0	10.0	44.0

NOTES:
A= Sales will increase due to broader distribution nationwide rather than regional.
B= Rationalizing R&D will eliminate Corp duplicate projects and focus on critical new products.
C = Sales synergies due to selling US products in EU, and EU products in US.
D = Hagstrom will now have a major presence in the US.
E = Upgrading manufacturing equipment and introducing new metals technology will reduce manufacturing costs.

While overall Company results were important, he concentrated on the Manufacturing Deliverables.

Cost of goods sold reduction of $1-2 million per year, and improved inventory turns give a cash flow of up to $2 million annually. These metrics are worrisome – likely that we can't do those. Since we're meeting at 4 PM today, I need historical metrics to demonstrate that the goals might be difficult to achieve. I don't want to scare them off, but if I sign up for that performance, I want to be sure that I can deliver.

How could I possibly improve inventory turns by 1 turn per year? Two years ago we scrubbed the place clean. Eliminated bins of questionable material... reduced the WIP by changing process flows... got rid of the "Just-in-Case" inventory. Heck, 4 years ago we didn't use the FIFO – First in First Out - method of inventory management, we used the FISH method – First In Still Here.

What a pain in the butt the F-I-S-H method was. Pushing stock all over the warehouse and shop floor holding it to be conservative.

And if I have to sign up for this performance – well, I'm just not sure I can hang my reputation on this. But I sure don't want to mess up the deal. Don's earned an early out. And the immediate vesting of options and quick sale ...

that money will look good in my personal account.

As he sipped the Diet Dr. Pepper, he leaned back in his chair, entertained by the squawk from the tilt mechanism in the chair. Thankfully he had lost 40 pounds or the chair might be a broken relic in the trash bin. Thinking out loud, 'I wonder what Stephen thinks of the $13 million sales increase he will be signing up for. And Doc Allison might lose a few pet projects with this acquisition. Could be a very interesting meeting today.'

That afternoon, Stephen's office buzzed with activity. He and Cynthia were scanning the prior year's sales results attempting to rationalize the $13 million sales growth expected on the Deal Summary.

"Cynthia, I think these folks have been smoking some of that legal marijuana sold in Colorado. They must not realize that marijuana isn't legal here in Ohio. These numbers are scary. An additional $13 million – and add the evil serpent 'synergy' to the deal. Damn, I can't believe that these people can put this kind of junk together. When I met them and their team during Due Diligence, I thought that they had some common sense, but this seems to be just plain stupid."

"Off the ledge, Bubba. We know they're not stupid, because they've done this before. There must be something that we're missing."

She had a gallows laugh and added, "Yes, we're missing sales."

"Stephen, let's wrestle with some assumptions. Let's scratch some things out on the whiteboard. What possibilities... what ways to make this work? I don't know about you, but the payday from a successful deal closing ... well, I'd like the challenge of finding a home for the half-million+- dollars that I'll get from exercising the options. And it seems that they are keeping the exec team together. C'mon, Stephen, let's do some brainstorming."

Stephen stretched to reach the markers.

He started to write 'Baseline' and the marker was dry. "Damn thing – I'm going for the green one. ... Maybe green's prophetic," as he tossed the marker into the nearby wastebasket.

"OK Cynthia, let's think."

During the next 50 minutes, they scratched words, circles, asterisks and dollar signs across the white board. After several false starts – and complete erasure of concepts – they resolved that, 'yes, it's possible – but who would believe it?'

* New prods from sister US sub @ $1-2 mil

* New prods from accelerated R&D = $1.5 mil

* Expanded global JAX Diet.. $3 mil

* Price increase... none in 3 years - $1M

Acquire orphan prods from Mom & Pops - $.5 mil

* New prods from UK $1.5M

* Expanded supply $$-outsourced & JV @ $1.5 mil

* Organic growth= $1.5 mil

"OK Bean counter, we've done our duty. I can't believe it, but I suppose their goals are not stupid. Not sure how *accurate* these guestimates can be, but heck, if we're 80% right, we have a chance. And they did say that they are ready to invest. I guess I'm anxious to hear their story.

Cynthia, I like the way you've built some probability into this brainstorming. Squares more likely than circles. Really appreciate your pushing on this – I was feeling fairly negative an hour ago, but now there's hope. And yes, I'd like to stuff a half-million-or-so into my bank account as well."

Cynthia's phone always came in handy, and rather than let this *creative brilliance* disappear under a cleaning cloth, she snapped a picture and sent a copy to Stephen. "Let's sandbag them a bit and see where they want to take us. We've got some thinking behind the numbers… wonder how this compares to their detail plans. Yeah, we've figured out how it's conceivable, but can you imagine how much work it will be to make this happen?"

That afternoon, the rest of the executive team analyzed the deal summary without consultation.

Pre-Closing: T–5 Days

Margaret and Allison were early risers and often arrived at the office by 7:00 AM. Tradition required that they share observations about the day's early news. Margaret's source was the New York Times, while Allison read the Wall Street Journal and Washington Post.

As they queued for the coffee, Margaret snickered about the government's *plan* to provide free college tuition to all who attended. "Great idea, but who's going to pay for it? I mean, yeah, it would be wonderful for all the millennials to graduate debt free, but even I can't understand how it's possible. Heck, when I graduated with the Bachelor's degree, I owed about $4k – about 40% of my first year's pay – and I survived. Typically, I'm for benefits to the common man – or to be politically correct, person – but jeesh."

"Don't get in a dither, Margaret. Everyone knows it's a political football tossed to ensure that someone with common sense opposes it. Just a political chip for some senator in the next election. Can you see the headline? 'Senator Sampson opposed free tuition for blah-blah-blah…' Sometimes I wonder about the political process and where these crazy ideas come from."

Allison – a coffee aficionado – informally managed the coffee specialties. This month, her favorite was the Gloria Jean's Butter Toffee selection.

"How can you drink that syrupy sweet coffee so early in the morning, Allison? For me, the more pure the coffee, the better the taste, first thing in the morning."

"Sure, simple can be a good choice, but I've been exploring various flavors so that I don't get stuck in a coffee rut... same-old-same-old. I'll probably shift back to the real stuff – maybe the Green Mountain Dark Extra Bold next month. Hey, what did you think of the 'Deal Summary page?"

"C'mon over to my office." Margaret touched Allison's elbow, guiding her to the office. "Probably shouldn't be discussing the 'Deal Summary' in the kitchen area. I'm puzzled how they can summarize such a complex deal in one page. I mean, there are a lot of moving parts, and everything is on one page."

Continuing on, Margaret offered, "I'm sure there is a lot more to the deal than is on that page, but these points are the priorities... the absolute essential parts for the next few years."

"I'm anxious to hear the team's response to the expected sales growth and manufacturing cost reduction. Should be interesting. Anything in the 'doc' that scares you?"

"I think it's what's not in the summary that worries me. In yesterday's meeting they mentioned synergies. That pretty much means *layoffs* in most deals, doesn't it? Sure, they said no layoffs, but…"

"Yes – I've seen lay-offs in many deals. Hopefully they have a few tricks up their sleeves. I'd hate to cut staff just so they could make more money. … Profits from a stream of corpses resulting from the deal."

"On the other hand, if we can make that summary come true – well, this will be a vibrant Company. … Wonder how Stephen, Cynthia and JB feel about the summary. … Guess we'll find out in a few hours. Have you talked with anyone about the summary?"

"… Spent a few minutes with JB yesterday. He's definitely anxious… maybe I should say nervous. …Likely that they will tie performance bonuses to those numbers, and if they're unachievable, we just took a pay cut."

"…What's Don's take? Did you see that line called earn out? Can it be that they will hang some of the purchase price on performance?"

"It's not unusual to do so. We'll have to ask that question at 10 AM. Gotta run… "

Hagstrom and Jackson – First Issues

The conference room was chilled today – thermostat and heat balancing still a bit off, but

119

it will keep the team alert. Don's assistant prepared the room for the 10 o-clock meeting. Two carafe's of coffee, a carafe of steaming hot water, a selection of teas – from English breakfast to Chamomile – and a mound of warm bagels accompanied by a variety of herbal light cream cheese. Drapes were open to the brilliant morning sun that glistened off the pond.

The polished wood conference table, arranged for today's meeting, had manila envelope packets aligned with each chair.

Executives drifted in 10-15 minutes before the scheduled start, uncertain of the seating arrangements. Historically the team always selected the same seats, as if assigned like in grammar school. Now that Hagstrom's executives were informally driving a transition team, the established order was disrupted.

Jaclyn's quick steps echoed in the hall, announcing her arrival. As she appeared in the doorway, her smile and glacier blue eyes invigorated the team.

"Mornin' Jaclyn – check out this morning sunshine. We arranged it just for you."

She squinted from the reflected sunlight, and walked to the window. "Brilliant – absolutely brilliant. Thanks for the welcome sunshine. Everybody have a good night? I'm still struggling with the jet lag – been up since about 4:30 and my body is screaming for lunch. Fresh bagels?"

"Yes, and some *light* cream cheese – if there could be such a thing."

"Thanks for the Deal Summary yesterday." JB was first to raise the topic. "Interesting reading. Should be a v-e-r-y informative meeting this morning."

"Glad that you had a chance to read it JB. Everyone else get a chance to open the email?" Nods of agreement followed. Jaclyn assessed the team's response – nothing yet observed about their reaction.

Don arrived and immediately suggested that the team pour a coffee, *schmeer* some cream cheese on a bagel and let's get started.

The bumbling seat selection was silly to watch as these accomplished executives attempted to be courteous – stumbling over etiquette - allowing the guests to select preferred seats. Unfortunately Elton selected the only squeaky seat in the conference room. The team knew that with every move, the chair squawked like a wounded pig.

Allison arose, and suggested that Elton take her seat not wanting to prolong an embarrassing situation.

Elton dressed down to business casual today to blend in with the more mid-west Jackson

Manufacturing environment. "Thanks for joining us, folks. I hope that you all had a chance to read the Deal Summary last night. Not formally study the doc, but just get familiar with the highlights. It is a v-e-r-y compressed document. When we do a deal, we like to focus on the critical items – key deliverables – so that it is easy to understand why we did the deal. There are many more objectives, but if – I should say when – we accomplish these goals, we've completed a good deal. For both the seller – that would be you folks and Don – and our shareholders."

"Compact is right. Do you always summarize a $60 million transaction in 6-8 points? Man, that is tight."

"Yes JB. It provides focus, but there is a lot behind those few numbers. And that's why we wanted to familiarize you with the Summary before we get too far along. Today's meeting – well, we wanted to share our expectations. We also want your insight about how these goals can be accomplished. Initially, they may seem aggressive, but the goals have been developed based on observations made during the Due Diligence, and our assessment of your Team's capabilities.

Today's meeting is meant to fill in some of the blanks. Our assumptions include considerable information about Hagstrom's team, our financial resources and organization. Without that background information – well, you just might think that these goals are unachievable."

"Is there any contingency built into the Deal Summary?   Sometimes things just don't go according to plan, Elton."

"Excellent question Cynthia, and yes, in the presentation to our Board of Directors, we've built in a contingency to this plan. As we review the elements of the Deal Summary, you'll also identify some very conservative assumptions that create some slack – just in case. So Jaclyn, I think it's your turn to explain how this Deal Summary works."

JB decided to stir things up. "Say Elton, when I look at that 'deal summary' and see three year sales growth of 50%, I don't think that you've paid enough for the Company."

Total silence – not even a paper shuffle. Most of the team merely looked silently down at the package. Don, somewhat startled, picked up his head, but didn't say a word.

Jaclyn smiled during that prolonged silence. "We can understand why you might say that, JB. But let's look at this from a long-term strategic point of view. We're putting $60 million at risk as an entry fee. Part of that sales increase is due to your introduction of the European products already approved. Do you agree?"

Somewhat humbled, JB quietly responded, "Yes, I saw that."

Jaclyn continued, "So we're just asking this team of experts to do what they do best – launch new products – and you've demonstrated that during the past few years. Have you lost that skill?"

Stephen leaned in, "No, Jaclyn, we haven't lost that skill, and in fact, we've now got a repeatable process."

"Right... and we're paying a premium for that skill. And another element of the growth will be new product development – that is a joint effort of both the European and the US R&D teams. Allison, would you rate your nanotech expertise at an A+?"

"Our folks are working incredibly well, but we really haven't been able to afford an A+ team."

"And based on our discussion, would you believe that we have an A+ European Nanotech team of experts?"

"Yes, it seems so."

JB was now mindlessly shuffling papers, feeling somewhat self-conscious about his remark.

"JB, yes, it will be quite an accomplishment to increase our US and incremental European revenue as a result of this transaction by 50% during the next three years. It won't be easy, but let's canvas the team. Has the last three years been easy? And three years ago, would you have believed you could have accomplished your three-year growth and profitability?

And JB, we hope that you can improve inventory turns and reduce cost of goods sold. Comfortable?"

"Heck no. We've squeezed the cost and improved inventory turns dramatically during the past three years. There's not much left."

"And do you have the latest ERP software in place and fully functioning? And how about that $500,000 CNC machine that will reduce production costs? And did I mention the advanced R&D technology that we have available for you to improve your manufacturing process?

JB, I'm not here to corner you, but I want you to think of virtually unlimited resources, if the need can be justified, that can be applied to your production processes. Any thoughts?"

"OK, so you're going to give me resources to make things happen?"

"Yes sir. And if given the resources, we – you heard me say WE, right – can't make it happen, we'll accept that outcome."

After a few moments of silence, Jaclyn smiled broadly and said, "Hey folks, we've made a $60 million bet on your past performance. We've interviewed each of you and have full confidence in your ability to accomplish our goals. But, when we peel the layers of this strategy, we're bringing major elements of this future success, but we can't do this without you. You've done this before – you know that aggressive growth thing – and we believe that you can do it again. So rather than just beat up the concept, let's slice this into meaningful components, and see if we believe that each step has a high probability of success. We're not afraid of a major challenge, so shall we get at this?"

All nodded agreement.

"OK team, I'd like to get your initial impression of the plan. So, raise your hand - 'who thinks that there is a 90% probability of success?"

… And no movement.

"Anyone believe this is 75% achievable?"

Don raised his hand. "I'll go for 75% - just trusting your judgment and experience at the M&A business."

"Anyone else?" Stephen reluctantly raised his hand. "If Don has a 75% confidence level, I'll go with him." Margaret, and Allison squirmed a bit in their seat, and then raised a hand.

"OK then, I've got my work cut out for me. I'm 95% confident that this plan can be achieved. And when I look at the talent around this table, if we're committed to the goals, well, I'm 100%

confident that we can deliver this plan." Her bright blue eyes and enthusiastic commitment were inspiring.

"So let's talk about the plan and your concerns. We've got the white board, so let's use it. I'd like to get all your concerns out – no matter how small. And challenging our plan won't be a one-time activity. Whenever you identify a problem or concern, let's share it with the team. I've found that while there may be a specific problem, there may be many answers that resolve the issue. So, let's have at it."

JB leaned forward, "Your improved inventory turns don't make any sense… far too aggressive. We've been concentrating on inventory reduction for the past two years, and I think that we are where we need to be."

Jaclyn quickly noted on the whiteboard, with the initials JB.

"Others?"

Stephen was laid back – somewhat reclined in the chair, legs extended and crossed at the ankles. "You know, I've been thinking about the sales synergies. Thirteen million +- in the next year is worrisome – not that it can't be done, but … well, let's break the point into two points. Year one sales synergy increase of $7 million on top of the $6 million baseline. And then additional synergy on top of that. Yes, I'm a bit concerned."

Jaclyn continued to press for the issues –
scrawling words as quickly as she could. As a
marker dried up, she stood the marker on end
as if a soldier at attention. Fortunately this
conference room had 24 feet of white board
and a half-dozen colored markers. Throughout
the session, Jaclyn commented about the timid
execs – always with a big smile, challenging
them to raise questions. She paced around
the room, making eye contact with each exec,
encouraging them to be tough on her… make
her work.

Jaclyn highlighted important issues with a red
asterisk – sometimes two or three for additional
emphasis.

The brainstorming session continued for about
45 minutes and covered the financial metrics,
and at Jaclyn's encouragement, went well
beyond the financials. Other areas of concern
- organization, personnel development
philosophy, promotional opportunities for all the
staff, cross-development with other Hagstrom
divisions… no topics to be avoided.

True to her PhD background, the list was
neatly prepared, color-coded with appropriate
notations as if the basis for a thesis

-Synergy sales too high***
- Baseline sales too aggressive
- Cutting R&D limits N+D
- Invent turns- too many
- DSO now well managed...improvement
 can't be done ***
-Personnel development programs
-Mfg cost decrease? How?
-Little In'tl Experience
-Comm with other Hag divisions
- Capex needs $2.5 mil ***
- COGS reduction-too much
- Who's in charge?
- What happens in 1st few weeks?
- Personnel cuts?
- What is that earnest $$$?
- Comp & bonus plan
- Stock options
- Exec roles & staff cuts
- Plant relocation***
- Shifting production to US sister co.
- Tuition reimbursement prog.
- Maternity benefits
- Compliance with US regs?
- FCPA***

This has been superb. As I said this isn't an all
or nothing exercise. You can't scare me, so
keep up the brainstorming.

Jaclyn paused to allow participants to ponder
the many issues. Cynthia jotted some notes

on the deal summary as others just sipped their coffee.

"So let me give you an initial response – let's call it a preliminary policy response as a bit of framework for this business combination.

First, let me say that we always comply with the law - no matter what country we operate in. Our goal is to comply with the strictest requirements of any country in which we operate. So for example, the Foreign Corrupt Practices Act popped up as an item. Hagstrom and all its subsidiaries ALWAYS comply with that regulation, regardless of the cost to the Company. We can discuss some specific examples, but be assured that we are among the most conservative organizations on the planet.

There were also questions about personnel cuts. Our initial response is that you have a well-managed Company that is properly staffed. We do not intend to have any major staff reductions related to the combination. The dreaded term synergies relates primarily to sales growth and product synergies. We're going to merge your operations with Hagstrom's – a Company with another US business, and several global operations outside the US. Our goal is to have a well-managed, appropriately staffed *global organization*. Our priority is to ensure that we treat all employees in a professional manner. As we review the requirements of the global organizations, and Company strengths and weaknesses, there will likely be some employment disruptions."

Allison and Cynthia shifted nervously in their seats.

"Areas of potential risk include R&D, Finance and IT. During the first 30 days, we'll review each functional area, understand today's demands and the impact of future plans, define the appropriate organization and skills required for success, and make fact-based decisions. We'll avoid emotional decisions. Our history in M&A is our best advertisement of how we deal with transitions and we invite you to examine our approach.

Allison, in R&D you have an exceptionally talented research organization. However, we've noticed potential organizational gaps in Nano-technology – a specialty segment in our UK operation. We'd like to expand your knowledge base using our expertise. A question for you to think about Allison. How do you feel about the future of Nano-tech versus general research? No need to answer now – we'll discuss the topic later. But if we focus on Nano-tech, we may discontinue some of your current, potentially less profitable projects.

Finance and IT are unique. In today's world, these administrative tasks are based on information and transaction processing. While many acquiring Companies simply 'centralize these functions, we'd like to better understand the functions performed. In some business units, finance and IT are critical on-site functions, since they are integral in planning. In each of these areas, we have some initial thoughts based on our Due Diligence and your input. We'll need your insight to ensure that we make the best decisions."

Jaclyn leaned forward, hands resting on the conference table, scanned the team and said, "How am I doing, folks?"

This break in the discussion was well timed. Unconsciously, the steely-eyed US team had leaned into the conversation – some hands tightly folded and resting on the table, while others propped on their forearms. Jaclyn's question had a calming affect and all relaxed in their seats. Some sipped the steaming coffee, while others just stretched in place.

To further break the tension, Don's voice from the back of the room, "Sounds like you've done this before, Jaclyn. Although I'm a bit uncomfortable with the possibility of layoffs, you've got a process that leads to sound decision-making. Let's keep this thing moving."

"The other major areas that I'd like to touch on are sales growth, manufacturing cost reduction, and new product development. We have numerous products developed and approved in Europe that historically we haven't had a means to sell in the US. You have a competent, well-trained sales force in the US. When we say sales synergy, we expect to launch several new products here in the US through this Company – hence, sales synergy.

I think that you can see there are many moving parts in the integration planning. Elton and I have a responsibility to share our expectations with you. There are many facets to the transaction that you have not seen until now. Sales synergies – new, previously approved products to be introduced here in the US; specially trained UK personnel who can accelerate your New Product Development projects; and yes potentially some layoffs.

We need your insight into how these and many other factors will affect the future deliverables. We appreciate your help and your commitment to whatever the final integration plan. That plan will be one that WE – that is all of you, Elton and I – assemble during the next few days."

As Jaclyn rested the marker on the tray, she scanned the room and said, "Thank you for your input. Remember, every question is a good question."

Elton, until now a quiet observer, walked to the front of the room. "Thanks Jaclyn. Don, Stephen, Allison, Margaret, Cynthia, JB. This was an excellent session. We've talked a lot. During the next few days, Jaclyn and I will work with each of you – individually – to develop Day One and the first 6 month's plans. I encourage you – don't be shy. We are not afraid to resolve the difficult questions. We are an honorable Company that respects employees, customers, and vendors – our constituents.

Let me talk about one other matter circled on the board - compensation & bonuses. We have aggressive – but in our opinion realistic – plans. We will review the details, but I can assure you that we can - and will - be generous with our compensation, bonuses, and stock options.

This was a superb meeting. Thank you for your input." Don nodded agreement.

"Jaclyn or I will meet with each of you to discuss detailed integration plans. Questions?"

After a brief pause, "Thanks…meeting adjourned."

Jaclyn took a picture of the whiteboard.

Let's get together tomorrow at 10:00 AM to discuss your initial plans."

Stephen mildly objected. "Jaclyn, I've got a business to run. Getting any planning done between now and tomorrow at 9 is a bit of a crunch. … Not sure if I've got the time to do it."

Margaret added, "I'm with you Stephen. I've got some reports to file with the Workers Comp Bureau – due at noon tomorrow. Can we push this a bit?"

"And now the crunch time. Remember a few days ago, I mentioned that for a few months we'd be doing several jobs at once. Well, we have arrived. Our goal is not to be foolish with overtime, but the closing is next week, and – well, let me ask you a question.

If we don't develop the integration plan – and Day One in particular - between now and then, and if we don't develop a consistent message, and if we don't identify the critical processes and plant items... what happens on Day One?'

"Yeah, I got it, Jaclyn, but this is turning out to be a real crunch... damn, this is a lot of work."

"OK – so do we push the closing so that we have more time? Don, you OK with that?"

"Hey troops. It's a lot of work, but let's think about the last two years. We've remade the Company – not an easy task – and here we are at success' doorstep. I know it's a lot of work. Here's a suggestion. What resources do you need to get this done? I'll give you an open ticket to spending during the next few days – just let me know what you need. Whataya think?"

Allison was doodling on the file cover. Never looking up, she said thoughtfully, "... home stretch...not easy, but we can spend the next hour debating, or we can actually get something done. Hey, remember when we started this journey two years ago? Joseph told us it would be a lot of work, but we might enjoy some of it. He was right, and now we're at a point where we can realize the benefits of our efforts. Let's dig in... quit whining about the work and let's get it done – grab this beast by the horns and wrestle it to the ground... just like the last two years."

Margaret rose and approached the window overlooking the pond. "I remember the days before we started to plan our business – the stress was incredible because we never knew what was going to blow up. We've now got a chance to control the pace of change. I'll be done with the HR function tomorrow at 10 AM."

Now, as the team realizes the amount of work to be completed, Elton broke into the conversation, "Folks, I've been through this before. In several other earlier deals, we accepted that the work was excessive, and postponed the detail work until – well, until it was too late. The deal closed, and there was chaos – we were 100% in a react mode and we never caught up.

I committed to our Board that I would never close a transaction until the planning was substantially complete. We will postpone the closing until you folks are comfortable with the preplanning. So, if doing the planning in the next 5 days is too heavy a load, we'll push the closing for a month to give you some breathing room. I say a month, since a clean monthly cut-off saves a lot of work. Jaclyn and I will leave the room for – shall we say for 30 minutes – to give you the chance to discuss timing. This is your deal."

Jaclyn and Elton moved toward the door to give the executives some privacy.

Don stood, silhouetted against the bright sunshine glaring through the windows. "Hold on Elton. Let's take a quick vote of whether to proceed on the current timetable. I know these folks and they're not afraid of some hard work. I think that this may have caught them by surprise." Turning to the team, "OK, we've all been through challenging times before. This work is a bit of a surprise to me, but I trust Elton's judgment about when the work must be done. Here's my commitment. I'll provide the resources that we need to get through this – so let's get creative and solve this problem. During the next few days, let's start the planning. If it doesn't look like we can develop a reasonable plan, we'll postpone the transaction.

I can't remember a time when we conceded defeat before we at least tried to get the job done.

If you're in favor of spending the next few days – and yes, they'll be long days – to get a draft plan together, raise your hand."

Moments passed in silence. Stephen stood erect as if volunteering for a deadly mission, "I'm in. I've never given up before I even tried a challenge. Heck, my first Iron Man – I didn't have a clue, but I didn't bail out."

Allison and Margaret agreed in unison saying, "I'm in."

JB scowled, staring at the tabletop, mindlessly shuffling pages. "I'm not in favor."

Don looked at Cynthia. "You'll bear a heavy burden in this, Cynthia. Admin in the early times could be a bear."

Cynthia scanned the executive team, hands folded neatly in place, almost imperceptibly nodded agreement. "In."

"OK, JB, will you give it a run? ... Couple of long days to see if we can pull this off?"

"I'll play this out for a few days. I don't think I can be ready, but I'm not dumb enough to wreck the deal without a try. Let's get on with this."

"Before you leave, let me share several checklists with you that we've used in the past. This is absolutely not a complete list of everything that must be considered. We want to be sure that people feel loved. We always want to take care of PEOPLE... employees, customers, vendors etc. Basically anyone the Company engages anytime during the course of business. You folks are the key to doing the right thing, every time, every day – but especially on Day One. Take these templates and use them as a brainstorming *jogger.* And if you have any questions, contact Elton or me. Thank you for your time today – we all know that even without an acquisition, you have plenty of things to do."

The meeting dispersed as each executive returned to his or her offices to begin the planning.

Manufacturing Operations: Jaclyn and JB

Jaclyn followed JB to his office. "That wasn't a whole lot of fun JB. I know exactly how you feel about this. My question – what do you need to make this work? Shall we spend a few minutes sorting out an approach?"

"You guys boxed me in and I'm not real happy about it. In fact I'm furious." Seated at his desk, he opened drawers, shuffled some papers and slammed the drawers successively. "The way you handled that meeting - you set me up. I don't like set-ups. Dirty game you play, Jaclyn."

Jaclyn let the fury play out, silent, observing the energy.

After a few minutes of silence, JB looked directly into Jaclyn's eyes. "Aren't you going to say anything? I'm mad as hell about this."

"I can only say, I've been in your seat. Packaged and shipped by a democratic vote.

Yes – it's infuriating. Can't say anything else, except that you folks get to drive the transaction timing. I think part of your concern is that you may have a built-in expectation about how much work this can be. I'm here to tell you that in 4-5 hours, we can complete a first-pass plan."

"BS!"

"JB, is 4-5 hours too much to ask during the next 24 hours to get this transaction ready to go? Knowing that I'll help you through the process." She let that thought linger – let it steep as if a fine tea. "If we can't get it done in 4-5 hours, I'll agree that we shouldn't proceed with the transaction."

"You mean that you'll go into that meeting tomorrow and say we should postpone the closing?"

"Guaranteed!" Jaclyn didn't waver, her intense gaze as if through a rifle sight focused on Big Game.

"Pretty gutsy game you play, Jaclyn. Get your butt back here in an hour. I'll clear the schedule – you've got 4 hours to convince me.

Jaclyn extended her hand to formalize the commitment. "Deal!"

"OK Jaclyn – come back in an hour."

She immediately left JB's office and walked to the conference room. Elton was speaking on his mobile phone and gestured 'one minute…'

His call complete, he looked concerned about the transaction. "And?"

Jaclyn approached the window watching the flock of ducks paddling in formation across the pond. "This could be a tough one. JB's pretty well locked into a failure mode. I've made a promise to him that if we spend 4-5 hours, we can complete his preliminary planning. If we can't get it done, I told him I'd vote against the transaction timing."

"And?"

"I *will* get us there. Not exactly sure how, but we will have enough of a plan that JB will be comfortable, and the transaction will get done."

"Make it happen, Jaclyn. The Board and I are counting on this deal closing on the 30th. It won't be a total disaster if we postpone, but it will be a big mark on our strategy implementation."

"Elton, since I'm booked with JB, can you check in on the other folks. A bit of rah-rah to demonstrate your commitment?"

"Will do."

Jaclyn appeared in JB's doorway one hour after their meeting.

"Good timing, JB?"

"Yeah, let's rock 'n roll. Since you've left, I asked for a few pieces of info – high-low listing of customers, and vendors. I've also asked the engineering department for a listing of all active and inactive contract employees or organizations, and I sent Allison a note requesting her contacts. It seemed only fair to turn the heat up on her.

And I've got a pad of flip-charts to scratch things on."

"Wonderful prep, JB. I notice that you have an LCD projector. Can I suggest that we just hook up the laptop to the screen and use an excel spreadsheet to do the brainstorming? It gives us a lot more flexibility to change things in a simple way, and once we're done, a little finesse & formatting, and we'll have a finished product."

"Whatever you like – we've got 3 hours and 45 minutes left to get this done."

JB was serious about the 4 hours… this could be a real challenge.

"OK, JB, what are the most important components of your responsibility? What do you do every day… week … month?"

During the next 2 hours, JB shared the highlights of his responsibility. Primary responsibilities included manufacturing, quality assurance, government relations, patent and intellectual property. Within these areas, deliverables included:

- Meeting production schedules,
- Managing production costs,
- Managing inventory levels to avoid stock-outs,
- Managing critical sub-contractors,
- Working closely with *critical* material vendors such as the primary Titanium source,
- Coordinating new product development and manufacturing prototypes and bringing pilot projects to manufacturing scale,
- Union relationships,
- Coordinating outsourced labor supply,
- Working with Freight Forwarders,
- Procedural reviews with government agencies such as OSHA, Worker's Compensation, EPA,
- Coordinating inspections with insurance inspectors,
- Managing environmental consultants,
- Coordination of NPD with Allison,
- Etc.

Jaclyn's initial strokes just jammed information onto the spreadsheet, starting with basic responsibilities. As she probed each responsibility, new column headings appeared as if by magic.

"Why did you add a column for Notes and one for Priority?" Jaclyn kept typing without looking up.

"Seemed like a good thing to do. Maybe we'll use the columns… maybe not. But since I can delete them as quickly as I put them in, what the heck!"

She numbered each line (a clear trail to the initial order – she claimed it was good to do so, but it was not essential).

She kept pressing JB for more information – as quickly as he could shout it out. Spelling errors popped up like weeds in a field. "No worries, JB – a quick spell check will fix those. I want to keep the ideas flowing. You know the way this works, perhaps 20% of this brainstorming will be a complete waste of time, but – oh those gems that you're identifying – absolute magic. Keep up the heat, JB."

JB enjoyed the challenge of creating ideas and concepts well before Jaclyn was capable of typing. "Hey, let's add a column for 'timing.'

"Excellent, JB. Keep 'em coming."

The screen quickly filled with columns and concepts.

"Hey, JB, you're slowing down. How about we take those high-low lists that you prepared and add some of that info to the lists?"

"Deal. I'm going to start with vendors. If it's OK, I'd like to start with the big dollar vendors?"

"Rock 'n roll, JB. You're in charge."

Playing to the male ego was a great thing … created a sense of JB's true ownership of the process.

Once JB finished with the largest vendors, he questioned, "What's next, Jaclyn?"

"You're in charge. Whattaya think?"

"I want to focus on some of the crazy PhD's we deal with. They're sometimes a quirky bunch, and I definitely want to keep them happy. You know, Jennifer Delaney is a critical person. She knows more about our designs than anyone on the planet. It would be a catastrophe if she didn't feel like a key part of the process."

"I guess that means we just don't send her an email. What do you think we should be doing?"

"I'm a bit concerned that when Don no longer owns the place, she may feel less allegiance to us. Don helped her out as she was developing her thesis. This may sound a bit of overkill, but she would really appreciate a personal visit from the new owner – you know, Elton. That would be the icing on the cake, but I can't ask him to do that."

"And why not? Remember, he said anything we need to make this go well – no holds barred. Let's put it on the list and see what happens."

"Are you serious? He's the CEO of a half-billion dollar global Company. He'd do that?"

"Make us work JB!"

JB's concerns about getting things done seemed to evaporate. … Such a great commitment by Elton. This may actually work out.

As Jaclyn probed routine activity, it was clear that union representatives and retirees were important constituents. Surprisingly, JB included several local charities and a halfway house for convicts as part of his 'routine contacts'.

"OK, JB – let's understand that we're not exactly a social organization. I'm not opposed to the half-way house contacts, but can you help me understand the context?"

"In today's economy, it's nearly impossible to find highly qualified, motivated people ready to work. Yes, these folks have been in trouble, and yes, we do occasionally have problems with some of them. But more often than not, they are desperate to get back into society. While they're in the halfway house, we provide training and use them in the warehouse."

Two hours after the initial keystroke Jaclyn suggested that JB step out to the kitchen and grab a couple of Pepsi's. "JB – take a walk – grab a drink for me. While you are gone, I'll pretty this up a bit, and let's see what we have."

"Gotta tell ya – this has been a bit simpler than I thought – and you still have about 1 hour left. Be back in a minute."

During JB's stroll, Jaclyn tapped the keys furiously creating a bit more structure – a little bolding here… a little centering there… an occasional note.

She heard JB's footsteps nearing the door. "Hang on JB. Don't come in yet."

"Going to be some kind of unveiling of the stone tablets?"

"Just one more minute. OK – c'mon on in. And take a peek at our accomplishment."

MANUFACTURING

Ref	Key responsibilities	Type	Description	Notes	Priority	P; E;V;PR	1st Day	1st Week	1st Month
1.0	Meeting production schedules,	Vendor	Vendors		3	PR			
2.0	Managing production costs,	Employees	Employees		2	E		✔	
3.0	Managing inventory levels to avoid stock-outs,	Employees	Employees		2	E		✔	
4.0	Managing critical sub-contractors	Vendor	Substore Metals		1	V	✔		
5.0	Working closely with *critical* material vendors such a the Titanium sole source,	Vendor	Jason Trucking		2	E		✔	
6.0	Coordinating new product development and manufacturing prototypes and bringing pilot projects to manufacturing scale,	Consultants	Harold D. Grandin, PhD		2	E		✔	
6.1			Jennifer L. Delaney, PhD		2	E		✔	
7.0	Union relationships,	Employees	Shop foremen		1	V	✔		
8.0		Union	Blue Collar/mechanics		1	V	✔		
8.1		Union	Union - local President	B	1	V	✔		
8.2		Union	Shop steward		1	V	✔		
9.0	Coordinating outsourced labor supply,	Vendor	Development		3	PR		✔	
10.0	Working with Freight Forwarders,	Vendor							
10.1		Vendor	Dragon Welding		2	E		✔	
10.2		Vendor	Turnstile Spinning		3	E		✔	
10.3		Vendor	Syms Packaging		2	E		✔	
10.4		Vendor	Jackson Metals	A	1	V	✔		
10.5		Vendor	A-B-C Temps		2	E		✔	
11.0	Procedural reviews with government agencies such as OSHA, Worker's Compensation, EPA	Agencies	Regional EPA		2	P			
12.0	Negotiating with insurance inspectors,	Agencies	OSHA		3	E		✔	
13.0	Managing environmental consultants,	Consultants			2	E		✔	
13.1		Consultants	Hayward Environmental		1	E	✔		
14.0	Coordination of NPD with Allison.	Consultants	Johnson Design		1	E	✔		
14.1		Consultants	University of Cincinnati		2	E		✔	
15.0	Customers - Product development support	Customers	J&J	A	1	V	✔		
15.1		Customer	Alpha Diagnostics		3	E		✔	
15.2		Customer	Beta Change Mgmt.		3	E		✔	
15.3		Customer	Clinical Dynamics		2	E		✔	
15.4		Customer	Diagnostics Inc.		1	V	✔		
15.5		Customer	Projection Diag GmBH		1	P	✔		
	Employee Duties & responsibilities	Employees	Employees		1	V	✔		
	Employee Benefits	Employees	Employees		1	V	✔		

A = Personal visit from Elton
B = Personal visit from Don

LEGEND:
P - phone call
E - Email
V = Personal visit
PR = Press release

148

"OK JB, this isn't my best work, but I think that we have basically done the job. Let's think about what we've done. We've looked at your routine responsibilities and thought about the impact of a merger. Some of the routine activities are time critical – and let's face it – it would be a disaster if we messed things up.

So we've looked at risk and considered communication's timing. We've considered the type of communication, and thought about each audience individually. In some cases – where we need either Elton or Don, we've put a note in the file.

Now we have a shape of the most important items, how, when and with whom. Our job is done – for a first pass. Thoughts?"

"OK – I'm just blown away at what we've accomplished. I've never done anything like this before, but just simulating routine activity, and knowing the importance of some items – well, the matrix sort of built itself. Amazing. And using a simple excel spreadsheet and the projector, we did the brainstorming and basically developed a finished product."

"JB, of course we're not done with this, but we have plenty to get on the table at tomorrow's meeting. Planning is never complete, so keep an open mind to additional items that we may have to include in the future – and as we get

into more of these transitional tasks –
brainstorming and Excel spreadsheets are your
friends. Using a bit of technology can get us to
a finished product very quickly.

I'll email you the spreadsheet – make changes
if you like - and you can discuss this in
tomorrow's meeting. I'm off to check in with
Elton…"

Update: Jaclyn and Elton

She caught up with Elton in Allison's office.
Allison was joking about the perils of flying
General Aviation, single engine. Allison was
just finishing a story about an engine-out, 8
miles from the airport.

"Yes, Elton, stress like that makes this seem
simple by comparison. It won't be easy – but
landing a plane without an engine isn't so
simple either. I'm glad that you stopped over
to make a *personal* commitment to give us the
resources that we need to get this job done. By
removing resource constraints I'll spend time
on solutions – regardless of resources
required. At first, I panicked, immediately
defaulting to, 'How am I going to get this done,
knowing that I've got to keep the business
running?' I was thinking of how I'd shift
resources around… changing priorities etc. -
rather than trying to identify the items that must
be completed." She arose, and gestured Elton
to the door, "I'm going to throw you out of my

office so I can get some work done. I'll be ready tomorrow at 10."

Elton's years of experience and previous integration efforts – and his personal assurance of *'no resource constraints'* - has the team focused on solutions, and not reasons why the task cannot be done.

"C'mon Jaclyn, let's have an espresso."

The idle coffee machine awaited their selection. Elton shuffled through the disorganized bin of single serve k-cups. "San Francisco Bay Espresso Roast? Shall we sip as they do on the west coast?"

"Sign me up."

"So, Jaclyn, how did it go with our tough customer?"

"Excellent. While he seemed to be a non-conformist with a negative attitude, he did a bit of research before I got there. Within two hours, we talked him off the ledge, and I think he is fully committed to the project. One problem with middle-market companies is that they haven't been through this before - they overestimate the task, and they also underestimate the task."

"OK, Jaclyn, help me understand what you just said."

"Well the first thing the execs do is think about their current routine, know that they are working – oh, let's say 50+- hours a week – and immediately default to, 'can't be done.' So they overestimate the initial task – and it is much easier to say 'can't be done' and try to get off the hook.

The underestimate? Well, once they identify the individual tasks, they underestimate the time it takes to complete certain parts of the work. As long as we continue to reinforce the 'no resource constraints' we'll be ok. That will get them to focus on solutions."

"Sounds like you got a great jump on the issues. I've met with Allison, Cynthia and Don. They're sort of 'on-board'. Or let's just say they haven't gone negative. We've got to continue to reinforce our position and keep the communication lines open. Can you pop over to check on Stephen?"

"On the way."

Stephen was at the easel jotting notes. Several completed pages were hanging on the walls between the photos of his Ironman challenges.

"Hey Stephen, what kind of bike is that you're riding in this picture – Hawaii, right?"

"That is a real beauty. A Cannondale Super Six Evo. Carbon frame… weighs about as much as a laptop."

"So you really enjoy the Ironman competitions. You're a dedicated competitor, Stephen."

"Good choice of terms – enjoyed. I've done 4 so far."

Smiling, Jaclyn shifted to, "What are all these sheets distracting me from the Ironman photos?"

"Been working my butt off, trying to get ready for tomorrow. Lots to do."

"Do you want to spend a few minutes talking about it?"

"Jaclyn, a key to being successful was your definition of people. At first I wouldn't have considered *potential customers* in the first pass for communications. I would have concentrated only on my biggest existing customers. But when you hit me with potential, I immediately thought of a couple of hospital accounts that I've been working for about a year. The acquisition brings an entirely new dimension to the negotiation.

I'm now a part of a global half-billion dollar Company. I've got critical mass… substance."

"Agreed. There may be several helpful elements. Yes, your critical mass is now that of a half-billion dollar company – one with staying power. But we also have other products that could be useful to hospitals –

pharma and other devices. In fact, they may already be customers of Berkshire.

So in this case, we just don't want to think like Jackson Manufacturing, we want to approach them as if we are a half-billion global medical products Company – because we are. That may immediately convert them to current from potential customer. When we get together tomorrow, toss the challenge to Elton. Give him the names of all your potential customers – you know – the bigger ones initially – and add in some of the *desirable but not touched accounts* that have been on your radar for a few years. We may be able to accelerate the sales process for you."

"I get the sense that you folks are serious about 'make you work.' I like your style, Jaclyn. Let's make this happen."

For the remainder of the day, Jaclyn and Elton circulated among the Jackson executives coaching them through the brainstorming process, continually reinforcing the critical nature of the preplanning.

After several hours, Jaclyn and Elton adjourned to the local steak house to summarize issues.

During the next two days, Jaclyn met individually with the executives to discuss the open issues. In addition to scheduled meetings, she strolled into offices unannounced to check on progress and coach the executives when necessary 'Is this a good time?' If not convenient, she scheduled a convenient time.

Throughout the process, she explained the broad integration plans, always probing for faulty assumptions. During these discussions, she identified several additional challenges and possible solutions. If solutions were not identified, she added the items to the master list of unresolved items.

Jaclyn, true to her word, continued to encourage all to raise any issues, and also talk among themselves to discover any new issues.

Human Resources

Jaclyn and Margaret developed the master matrix of all benefits for all employee levels.

Human Resources - Benefits Matrix

	Hagstrom								Jackson							
	Senior Exec		VP's		Directors		All Other		Senior Exec		VP's		Directors		All Other	
	Y(N)	Note	Y(N)	Note	Y(N)	Note	Y(N)	Note	Y(N)	Note	Y(N)	Note	Y(N)	Note	Y(N)	Note
Health Insurance																
Hi-deductible	Y		Y		Y		Y		Y		Y		Y		Y	
Best Coverage	Y		Y		Y		Y		Y		Y		Y		Y	
Health Sav Accts	n/a		(N)		(N)		(N)		n/a		Y		Y		Y	
Worker's Comp	Y		Y		Y		Y		Y		Y		Y		Y	
Disability Insurance																
Basic	Y		Y		Y		Y		Y		Y		Y		Y	
Enhanced	Y	1	n/a		n/a		n/a		(N)	1	n/a		n/a		n/a	
Unemp Insurance	Y		Y		Y		Y		Y		Y		Y		Y	
Grp Life Insurance	Y								Y							
Profit Sharing	N		Y		Y		Y		(N)		(N)		(N)		(N)	
Maternity leave	Y		Y		Y		Y		Y		Y		Y		Y	
Flex Work Hours	n/a		n/a		n/a		Y		n/a		n/a		n/a		Y	
Day Care Comps	N		Y		Y		Y		N		Y		Y		Y	
401-k	Y		Y		Y		Y		Y		Y		Y		Y	
Charity Match Gifts	Y		Y		Y		Y		(N)		(N)		(N)		(N)	
D&O Insurance	Y	1	n/a		n/a		n/a		Y	1	n/a		n/a		n/a	
Co. Automobile	Y	2	n/a		n/a		n/a		Y	2	n/a		n/a		n/a	
Tuition Reimb	N		N		Y		Y		N		N		Y		Y	
Gym Memberships	Y	3	Y		N	3	N		Y	3	Y		N		N	
Key Person Life Ins	Y	4	n/a		n/a		n/a		(N)	4	n/a		n/a		n/a	
Annual Physical	Y		n/a		n/a		n/a		N		n/a		n/a		n/a	
Deferred Comp	Y	5	Y		Y		N		Y	5	Y	5	Y		N	
L T Incentive Plan	Y	6	Y		N		N		Y	6	Y		N		N	
Stock Options	Y	7	Y		Y		N		Y	7	Y		Y		N	

1. D&O limits to be increased to $1.5 million.
2. Automobile allowance provided by Jackson to Senior executives @ $500/month. Hagstrom allowance will total $1,000/month.
3. Gym memberships now to extend to Director level and above
4. Improved Key Person life insurance equal to 3x annual base salary
5. Deferred Compensation to expand to include Director level+
6. Long Term Incentive Plan enriched and will be vested over a 5 year period rather than 3 years.
7. Stock Options to be vested over 5 year period rather than 3 years.

Margaret was concerned with some of the potential benefit changes. Jaclyn understood Margaret's initial concerns, but as they talked through the potential changes, it was clear that although benefits differed, there was a net of *additional* benefits for employees rather than a reduction.

"I'm glad that you didn't just throw this analysis over the wall, Jaclyn. Yes, it took a bit of time to understand the nuances, but I now feel comfortable representing this as a positive change to the employees.

While we are discussing fringe benefits and my concerns, did you intend to keep all the existing staff, or will there be layoffs?"

"Margaret, we mentioned that we want a fully functioning Company going forward, and this Company is already well-managed. We are concerned about potential redundancies in R&D– mainly related to scientific specialties – and in administrative areas, such as IT and Finance. I'm not prepared to discuss them without more input from Cynthia and Allison, but I've scheduled some time with them later today and will circle back with you."

"You can be sure that they share concerns as well. We are family at Jackson. Every employee is personal with us, and we don't want to harm anyone's career.

I'll let you meet with Allison and Cynthia, and I will develop some materials to summarize the benefits."

Margaret accepted the responsibility to develop some collateral materials by the end of tomorrow.

Research & development

Jaclyn approached Allison to discuss the organization.

"Thanks for meeting with me Allison. I'd like to discuss the R&D organization with you."

"So is this the time I run for the exits to avoid bad news?"

"Not at all. No doubt that we have prepared some preliminary plans, but we've got to get your insight. We've reviewed the Jackson and Hagstrom organizations, considered our global strategy and have focused on possible redundancies."

Allison's posture straightened, and she adopted a stern look. "Yes, Jaclyn, I've been waiting for this discussion."

Jaclyn disliked these discussions, but mergers often meant organizational changes.

" OK, Allison, let's follow the guiding principles of the transaction. Our goal is to acquire and integrate a well-managed organization, and return a reasonable profit to our shareholders. Sometimes that leads to redundancy. We've examined both organizations, and we have some preliminary ideas, but without your input, we'd be fools to implement our one-sided analysis.

Here's a summary chart that we developed reviewing the R&D organization. The Jackson organization is expert at developing, and obtaining regulatory approval of implantable devices. You know the FDA regs, and you know how to manage communications with the agency.

To develop these devices, you have certain specialties. As we've examined the organization and identified potential redundancies within the Hagstrom family. Let's look at this chart."

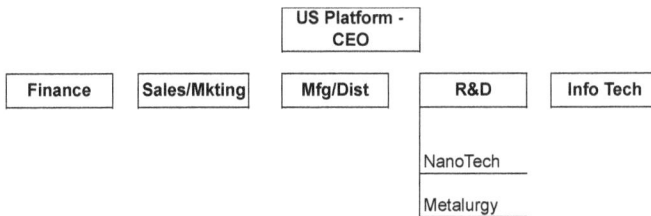

US Platform - CEO				
Finance	Sales/Mkting	Mfg/Dist	R&D	Info Tech
			NanoTech	
			Metalurgy	

As she considered her staff, Allison pressed, "So tell me, what's up with Nanotech and Metallurgy? Why are those functions separated?"

"Let's think about the people involved in Nanotech and Metallurgy. We don't have perfect information, and that's why you and I are talking. You're Nano-Tech staff includes two engineers with Masters Degrees who are doing basic application development. We've taken a preliminary look at their projects and, while they are doing an admirable job, their development work is not as robust as at our UK headquarters. We're counting on you to develop newly approved Nanotech applications within 4 years. The question we're asking you is, "Do you think that it is a smart goal – a reasonable goal - for the US division of a global half-billion dollar Company?"

"Yes, with the right tools, we should be able to do so."

"And what do you *need* to move from '*dabbling in the science*' to a focused project that delivers the results that *we* – that is Jackson and Hagstrom's combined – are looking for?"

"Well, I'd improve the intellectual talent on the project." Defensively, she quickly followed with, "But you know, we haven't been able to do so in the past because we don't have the budget."

"Allison, we know that you've been financially constrained. Not an issue, and I'm not being critical of you or the organization. But what specifically would you like to have?"

"You're catching me a bit by surprise, but I'd like at least two PhD's in the Nanotech discipline."

"And if Hagstrom's had two such experts on staff? Two published, recognized leaders in the field? Would that suffice?"

"Depending on their qualifications, yes."

"Allison, we have two Nanotech PhD's on our headquarters staff. They may be a possible solution for you. I'll get you their CV's this afternoon, and let you take a look at their credentials. Then let's get together tomorrow afternoon to discuss the NPD challenge, and develop the best solution?"

"Deal."

"We'd also like to understand your NPD project portfolio. Do you have anything that might summarize open and pending projects?"

"Sure, I've got some summaries that I can share with you."

At each of these discussions, Jaclyn always refocused the discussion on the agreed-upon goals of the merger. When difficult challenges such as employee redundancy arose, Jaclyn redirected the team to the strategic goals and asked, "How do we achieve this goal?"

Meanwhile, as Jaclyn met with Allison, Elton met off-line with Stephen.

Elton settled into the chair in Stephen's office. "Stephen, we had a great session this morning. Seems like we touched on a hot button with personnel. I'd like to hear your concerns about the proposed HR changes that you have virtually completed. Was it a promotion and additional hires?"

Seated directly across from Elton, a hunter's stare and tightly entwined fingers, Stephen responded, "Elton, I take my goals very seriously, and simply put, I've already agreed to deliver sales results in our strategic plan, and I need those changes to make things happen."

"I understand your professionalism and know your commitment to goals. I want to better understand what's giving you the angst.

But let's start with our mutual goal. We're after a few new product launches and sales growth of 40% during the next three years. Are you comfortable with those goals?"

Glaring at Elton, "Yes, I think I can deliver those goals, but I need the team I've outlined."

"OK, so let's talk about the overall merged Company goals. Now we haven't had much time to discuss this, but the analysis at our end may have a few hidden features. We haven't had a chance to discuss everything with you folks yet – we're still early in the planning.

So here's a bit more information for you to consider. We expect to add three new products to your line from our UK stable. They are EU approved and should be quickly approved in the US – agency reciprocity agreements. Overall, we think that these should bring in an additional $4-5 million annual revenue over the next few years. There will be launch expenses, and some impact on the organization, but we have a very high confidence level for these sales.

We also have excellent distributor relationships with several major hospitals – that are not currently your customers. Have you heard of Austin Children's hospital; San Diego Children's?"

Tensions somewhat eased, and Stephen's glaring stare became more friendly. "Yes, we've been trying to crack each of them for the past three years."

"Well, we sell some products to them now through Berkshire, and we expect that they will expand their purchases to the Jackson line immediately upon closing. Jackson has a high-quality product and it may help to reduce the number of vendors that the hospital works with."

"OK – those factors ease my concern about the sales goal a bit. But I still need the organization changes – a regional manager and an additional sales rep."

"So let's talk about your customer pipeline process, and let me understand how you'll function as a key component of a half-billion dollar global Company."

Whenever possible, Elton reframed the discussion to the "Newco" structure. It was important to get the target Company to start thinking as if they were a part of the global organization. By challenging the executives to change their perspective, and use their analytic skills, they often developed an acceptable business plan.

As Stephen reviewed his strategic sales pipeline, he discovered that thinking as if he were part of the Newco, his plans changed.

They spent the next hour discussing some of the highlights of the proposed merged Company. Elton encouraged Stephen's thinking to develop the strategy and tactics to ensure that he owned the strategy.

Stephen discussed the pipeline of current and prospective customers, his approach to the market and how he allocated his sales and marketing resources. Elton was intrigued with the discussion and asked for more justification for the additional sales force.

Stephen flipped open the leather portfolio on his desk and shared the Company's planned allocation of sales and marketing resources.

Jackson Manufacturing- Sales/Marketing Mix									
	A		B		C		Total		
Millions $	Act	Pot	Act	Pot	Act	Pot	Act	Pot	Total
Resources									
Direct Activity									
Sales Rep	1.1	0.7	0.4	0.1			1.5	0.8	2.3
Manufacturer Rep							-	-	-
Distributor							-	-	-
Catalog/Printer Material	0.1	0.1	0.1		0.1		0.3	0.1	0.4
Direct Mail	0.1		0.1		0.2	0.1	0.4	0.1	0.5
Telemarketing	-				0.2		0.2	-	0.2
Subtotal	1.3	0.8	0.6	0.1	0.5	0.1	2.4	1.0	3.4
Indirect									
Entertainment	0.3	0.2	0.2	0.1			0.5	0.3	0.8
Website	0.1		0.1		0.2		0.4	-	0.4
Advertising - Magazine	0.1		0.3		0.2		0.6	-	0.6
Advertising - On-line			0.2		0.1		0.3	-	0.3
Public Relations	0.3		0.2		0.1		0.6	-	0.6
Trade Association: Orthopedics	0.1		0.2				0.3	-	0.3
Subtotal	0.9	0.2	1.2	0.1	0.6	-	2.7	0.3	3.0
Total	2.2	1.0	1.8	0.2	1.1	0.1	5.1	1.3	6.4
% Total Spending	34%	16%	28%	3%	17%	2%	80%	20%	100%

The matrix showed a concentration of resources allocated to A and B customers, with 20% of the Company's overall sales/marketing resources dedicated to *Potential Customers.* About 40% of the sales force cost was dedicated to *potential* A and B customers.

"OK, Stephen, why so much concentration on the potential customers?"

"We've looked at our market to determine the number of hospitals using our products. We are going up against the big guns like J&J, so it is difficult to match their spending for the major accounts – Cleveland Clinic and Mayo. But we have discovered that the smaller market hospital and surgery clinics represent a huge potential market for us. That's the good news. The bad news is that such smaller health care markets require more personal attention initially. Once we have them as clients, they are "A" all the Way. J&J won't give them the initial personal service they deserve.

We service these smaller markets with the less experienced sales reps that need more sales management. Our goal – spend rep resources and T&E on the A's and B's – both Actual and Potential.

Also, check out our resource allocation between US and offshore."

Jackson Manufacturing - Sales Marketing Mix	United States				International				Total			
Millions $ Resources	Direct	Dist	Rep	Total	Direct	Dist	Rep	Total	Direct	Dist	Rep	Total
Direct Activity												
Sales Rep	2.3			2.3					2.3	-	-	2.3
Manufacturer Rep	-						0.5	0.5	-	-	0.5	0.5
Distributor				-		0.4		0.4	-	0.4	-	0.4
Catalog/Printer Mat'l	0.4			0.4	0.1			0.1	0.5	-	-	0.5
Direct Mail	0.5			0.5					0.5	-	-	0.5
Telemarketing	0.2			0.2					0.2	-	-	0.2
Subtotal	3.4	-	-	3.4	0.1	0.4	0.5	1.0	3.5	0.4	0.5	4.4
Indirect												
Entertainment	0.8			0.8		0.2		0.2	0.8	-	0.2	1.0
Website	0.4			0.4					0.4	-	-	0.4
Advertising - Mag	0.6			0.6		0.2		0.2	0.6	0.2	-	0.8
Advertising - On-line	0.3			0.3					0.3	-	-	0.3
Public Relations	0.6			0.6					0.6	-	-	0.6
Trade Assoc.: Ortho	0.3			0.3		0.2		0.2	0.3	0.2	-	0.5
Subtotal	3.0	-	-	3.0	-	0.4	0.2	0.6	3.0	0.4	0.2	3.6
Total	6.4	-	-	6.4	0.1	0.8	0.7	1.6	6.5	0.8	0.7	8.0

About 80% of our sales marketing resource is invested in the US market.

If you're going to provide us with exposure and sales resource in the International market, and you're going to help us launch some new EU approved products here in the US, I think that we should redo the entire sales/marketing mix… maybe add some additional sales force since we'll have more products to sell. What do you think, Elton?"

"Well, now at least I've confirmed that you are an expert at selling. I was thinking that we were going to reduce some spending when we talked, and now you've got me dipping into my wallet to give you more money. You break me up, Stephen.

So let's think this through. You have a model that allocates the sales/marketing investment to grow this Company by getting new "A" and "B" US customers. You've got a CRM process that helps you identify how the resource is actually used against your plan, and you've identified specific targets to call on. You know your call success rate, and sales cycle time – and you manage the plan.

I agree that there may be a sales upside with the EU approved products being sold here in the US, and the US products being sold in Europe through Hagstrom's company sales organizations.

And you're only asking for an internal promotion and a new rep?"

"Well, that was before we talked about the new products that I'll be getting from the Europe, and the expanded distribution of our products across Europe. Now, I'm thinking of adding at least 2 new reps here in the US, adding a trade show and changing the mix from Distributor to In-house sales reps in Europe. I'd like to add – oh, let's say in round numbers, $1.2 million to the sales & marketing spending, and that's without knowing more about the EU approved products.

Whattayathink?"

Elton immediately clutched his heart with one hand, and grabbed his wallet with the other. With a twinkle in his eye he said, "Call an EMT – I think it's my heart." After a short pause, "Man, I can't believe that you've tapped me for more than a million dollars. I've got to stop talking with you." He extended his hand to seal the deal. "You've got me. Get me an analysis that supports the numbers and – based on what we've just discussed – you've got a deal. I'll get you the product info for the EU products and some information about the European Sales operations. … Prove the numbers to me, and you'll get the resource. You're thinking differently – like you're a part of a half-billion dollar global organization. Excellent."

"Deal, boss."

Elton left the office, pleased that they discussed the 'to-be' state, concentrating on the People, Process and Product, and Market aspect of the integration. Completely satisfied with the outcome of what could have been a very contentious encounter, Elton sought out Jaclyn.

"Jaclyn, sign Stephen up for an additional million dollars of spending."

"Elton, I've got to keep you away from these execs – you're costing me money."

"You'd be amazed at the metrics that Stephen uses to manage this business. We'll do just fine with this organization. He's updating his sales forecast and will get us the details later this week. How'd you do with Allison?"

"I've discovered that these folks are goal driven and manage to their metrics. Tough discussion about potential redundancies. Had to refresh her thoughts about the goals of this acquisition. I think that she'll come along, but it is difficult to require staff reductions. I've left her with a challenge and we'll see how the planning goes?

One-to-One Meeting: Jaclyn and JB

"JB, let's refresh the ground rules. This isn't just about your area, but your observations about the Company. We're definitely interested in your understanding of 'manufacturing fit' with Hagstrom's, but we want your insight about the entire Jackson Manufacturing Company. We'll approach the integration task with each executive the same way.

Talk to me about your staff, management levels and functions served. I'd like to hear how you run the day-to-day business."

During the next few hours they reviewed the organization chart and discovered several critical functions that were not staffed internally. The engineering department was well staffed, but as Jackson ventured into more exotic metals, the Company established critical relationships with alloy engineering specialists.

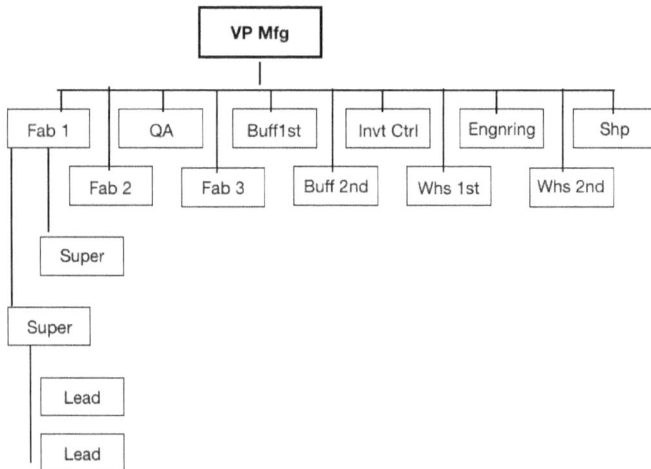

```
                        ┌──────────┐
                        │  VP Mfg  │
                        └──────────┘
                             │
  ┌───────┬───────┬───────┬───────┬─────────┬───────┐
┌─────┐ ┌─────┐ ┌───────┐ ┌─────────┐ ┌─────────┐ ┌─────┐
│Fab 1│ │ QA  │ │Buff1st│ │Invt Ctrl│ │Engnring │ │ Shp │
└─────┘ └─────┘ └───────┘ └─────────┘ └─────────┘ └─────┘
   │   ┌───────┐ ┌───────┐ ┌─────────┐ ┌─────────┐ ┌─────────┐
   │   │ Fab 2 │ │ Fab 3 │ │ Buff 2nd│ │ Whs 1st │ │ Whs 2nd │
   │   └───────┘ └───────┘ └─────────┘ └─────────┘ └─────────┘
   │   ┌───────┐
   │   │ Super │
   │   └───────┘
┌───────┐
│ Super │
└───────┘
   │  ┌──────┐
   │  │ Lead │
   │  └──────┘
   │  ┌──────┐
   │  │ Lead │
   │  └──────┘
```

Jaclyn confirmed that the Company had no long-term contracts or confidentiality agreements with these firms.

"So, JB, are you comfortable with the arrangements with these firms?"

"These folks are honorable folks and we have a handshake agreement that their work is for our exclusive use. It's a Midwest thing. We've never had a problem with them."

"I understand, but with our $60 million wager on this firm, would you still be comfortable with an informal relationship? I guess where I'm coming from is that these folks are critical to the process, and I think we'd like to lock them into some kind of intellectual property agreement – at a minimum. Do you think they'll accept the request?"

"Our relationship is pretty solid – shouldn't be a major problem. I'll put that on my to do list."

Missing these critical resources wasn't necessarily negligence by the Due Diligence team, since when reviews are limited, reviewers primarily concentrate on organizations.

"OK, and as we look at this rough organization chart let me play the devil's advocate. It seems that you have too many Fab Managers – and maybe too many direct reports. How have you challenged the organization to improve?"

"I understand your observation about the Fab managers, Jaclyn. But 11 direct reports is consistent with today's accepted HR philosophy of a flat organization."

Jaclyn was familiar with the goal of flatter organizations, but she was concerned that this organization would not allow JB to grow the Company. With so many direct reports in one plant, JB was more of an operation's manager than a visionary executive responsible for rapid growth in a global Company.

"JB, do you think that we're going to be satisfied with historical growth rates? You've seen our projections... a bit more aggressive than in the past. Your responsibilities will be expanding – not just overseeing existing production, but you'll likely be coordinating among several plants – two here in the US and one in Europe. We have some specialty products, device engineering know-how, and some very progressive research in place at other facilities.

One of our objectives is to leverage your top-notch executive skills and introduce new products through coordinated global efforts.

Said another way, it's not just 11 direct reports, but my concern is that we won't be using your talents for the greatest benefit of the whole Company."

"Jaclyn, you don't understand some of the operating dynamics at Jackson. You know about Chip, Janelle and Robert – Don's family members. Well, we also have a few other family members scattered throughout the organization. In Manufacturing, they do a decent job as Fab Managers, but they can't move up – not the right talent – and I can't get rid of them. So my organization is not optimal.

Sure I see how adding a plant manager would free up some time, but with the organization and financial constraints – well, I'm stuck."

"JB, let's scratch out an ideal organization without any constraints, knowing that you'll have additional responsibilities after the completed merger. We'd like you to spearhead product launch/commercialization activities with the FDA, and also guide other plants and Company specialties to accelerate product launches in the US. You'll also have to work with European manufacturing to help them produce and launch US products.

Your talents are underutilized. When we think of this merger, I want you to think like a senior exec in a half-billion dollar global Company. This will mean a bit more travel for you to properly manage those additional responsibilities, but we are convinced that you can do the job, and new products are a key part to the acquisition."

With that Jaclyn and JB outlined the ideal manufacturing organization, identifying existing non-value added positions.

JB's concern was obvious. "So who gets to break the news to Don about his relatives?"

"Elton and I will do the deed. But don't be too concerned, JB. At Hagstrom's we have a reputation for our generous approach to personnel displacement. It's not unusual for us to have an outstanding severance package, retraining when appropriate, outplacement support and introduction to local organizations that may be in the hiring mode.

As an acquirer, we learned long ago that our integration actions dictate the quality of firms that will entertain our merger advances. We've seen other companies that *slash and burn* organizations in mergers, trying to save every dollar possible. In the long run, that is a very expensive mode of operation... their poor reputation is often a determining factor in future mergers."

JB finalized the draft organization chart. Costs associated with the transitions were estimated and would be added to the Deal Summary financials.

Jaclyn then focused on plant – facilities, equipment, and intellectual property.

"Let's walk through the facility, JB."

They strolled around the generally well-organized facility. As Jaclyn explored production capabilities, she reconfirmed that several machines were at the end of their useful life. While they could do the work required of today's business, the equipment would not reach Hagstrom's production goals.

During the Due Diligence process, the Team discovered that the plant manufacturing software was the same as used at Hagstrom's. Unfortunately, Jackson used an older version that required updating.

"Any thoughts about how much the software upgrade will cost JB?"

"The upgrade itself will be about $200k; installation will take 2 months and take an additional $150k of consulting costs. We've postponed that for a few years – timing of capital spending on a limited budget."

"OK – I'll have to be sure that we've considered these upgrades in the Deal Model.

JB, I'm curious. How do you identify items that can be patented?"

"The engineering folks do a great job – tight ship overall, and they patent everything possible."

"OK – once you get the initial design from the engineers, do you ever make changes to the designs?"

"Sure – occasionally the toolmakers adjust the specs so that the device works better."

"And once those changes are made, do you know if the original drawings are amended so that we have a proper patent application?"

"That's up to the engineers. As far as any changes that we make, we coordinate them with the engineers and leave it up to them to file properly."

"Have you missed any opportunities? And how do you think it should work within the Hagstrom organization?"

Launching new products and the successful commercialization of R&D were key components of the Hagstom business model. Adding another US based manufacturer will complicate the global Company's process, but also rapidly expand the Company's market potential and valuation. Although they were now beyond the 2-hour discussion limit, Jaclyn and JB continued to discuss business processes that could be enhanced as all the Companies were merged.

They explored Company synergies among the various operating companies, while discussing each functional area – strengths and weaknesses – that could add value when adjusted to Newco.

JB enthusiastically challenged concepts, continuously developing ideas that would build value. He clearly understood that synergies weren't limited to cost cutting. Rethinking the new combined Company created value well beyond the basic "2+2=5" universally accepted synergy. After this candid discussion, she knew that JB was a *keeper*.

She gathered her notes, took photos of the whiteboard and, shaking JB's hand, said, "Can you put these notes together for discussion with the executive team? This will be a key component of our 100-day planning. A quick reminder - add, modify, delete anything that you like… this was an outstanding session. …Sorry we went so long."

"This has been great, Jaclyn. I've never experienced *synergy* as anything other than cost cutting. It doesn't have to be a zero-sum game. Profits can increase dramatically without cost cutting."

Jackson Manufacturing
Manufacturing Operations - High Level Transition Plan

<u>**AS IS**</u>

The Company is a non-union shop. The primary functions include FDA validated and approved Manufacturing of precision medical devices (e.g. bones), approved by the FDA; new product prototype development coordinated by Jackson R&D; coordination of production scaling working with outside consultants. The function is also responsible for maintaining proper levels of inventory, in a secure and appropriate warehouse; and product distribution to customers and affiliates.

<u>**TO BE**</u>

The Company is a non-union shop. The primary functions include FDA validated and approved Manufacturing of precision medical devices (e.g. bones), approved by the FDA; new product prototype development coordinated by Jackson R&D; coordination of production scaling working with outside consultants. The function is also responsible for maintaining proper levels of inventory, in a secure and appropriate warehouse; and product distribution to customers and affiliates.

During the transition to the 'to be' state, the function will also ensure the proper and effective knowledge transfer to produce EU approved product for US consumption.

	2017 Current State	Notes	2020 Future State
Revenue *(Millions $)*	35.0		42.0
Headcount			
Individual Contributors	155	A, B. C	175
Supervisors	21	D	15
Managers	15	E	9
Directors	3		3
VP's	1		1
Total	195		203
Contractors	22	F	27
Factory Size	400k Sq. Ft	G	300k Sq. Ft
Inventory Turns	4.5	H	6
New Equipment *(Mil $)*	Amount		
CAD/CAM System, & to UK			
Equip	0.7	I	
Software	0.3	J	
Laser Machining (2 units)	0.8	K	

A = Assess direct mfg. personnel to identify talent capable of: 3/17
   CAD/CAM equip operators
   Laser cell
B = Begin training
   CAD/CAM 6/17
   Laser Cell 9/17
C = Assess remaining direct labor to adjust for new equip. Rationalize organization
D = Reorganize CAD/CAM and Laser cell operations 2/18
E = Reorganize floor management to flatter organization 2/18
F = Engage knowledge contractors, specializing in metallurgy, laser technology (note - these are
   not full-time positions, but rather consultants to fully train workforce. 9/17
G = Inventory reduction to allow for reduced warehouse space; convert to production 3/18
H = Reduce inventory by 30% 12/17
I, J = Install new CAD/CAM equip, train personnel in use of new software 12/17
K = Install laser machining, finalize training 12/17

Stephen requested an early session with Jaclyn – most likely due to his concerns about such aggressive sales goals. Jaclyn understood his concerns and wanted to accomplish two things at today's meeting:
- Listen to any issues
- Identify the first 100-days of deliverables

"C'mon on in Jaclyn."

A warm handshake and a salesman's smile greeted Jaclyn as she arrived at Stephen's lair. Stephen's confident demeanor showed he was in *sales* mode - Jaclyn was on her guard.

"You know, you and Elton seem to have a carefully scripted approach to this merger process. How are we doing? ... Better yet, what should we do differently?"

Jaclyn thought, 'Nice touch Stephen. Get me to do the talking.'

""Things are going well, Stephen. We've completed the preliminary Due Diligence, but we're always looking for additional information. S-o-o-o-o-o tell me about your sales and marketing organization. You know our emphasis – people, process etc."

Stephen motioned Jaclyn to the head of the conference table near the window. At the table, two folders were aligned to seats at the head of the table and immediately to the right.

"I put a few notes together for us to begin. You and Elton mentioned People, Process, Plant, Product and Market. I've got a section for each portion of the discussion. Many of the items were developed in PowerPoint, Word or Excel. I can give you the soft files if you like, but I thought we'd get started with the hard copy. Knowing that you like the whiteboard – well, it's clean & ready for your penmanship."

Jaclyn wasn't sure if there were negative undertones, but her best advantage was to move forward in as positive manner as possible.

"So, let's talk about people."

Stephen continued. "I've had a brief discussion with Elton, and we've concluded that I'll document all the details about the organization chart. But your concept of people includes everybody we come in contact with as we fulfill our responsibilities. So let's talk about our customers?"

With that he opened the file sorted with tabs:
- Key Customers: Actual
- Key Customers: Potential
- Geographic Customers
- "B" Classification Customers
- "C" Classification Customers
- Distributors
- International Operations

"Let's start with the Key Customers. We'll start with our "A" customers. They represent any customer – current or potential – with annual sales of more than $500k. It's a bit arbitrary, but they are the big ones. We have a contact cycle of at least one 'touch' every 30 days for "A" customers. … Could be a lunch, or just a quick call checking in on the quality of our service.

Each call is an opportunity to listen to their needs – whether it's about product, service, pricing or competitors. We also ask about competitors. We've discovered that if we listen, it only creates opportunity for us."

Stephen was in his element. He spoke fluently about his customers – whether current or target customers. The sales team had analyzed the market and competition, and Jackson's strengths and weaknesses. His team prepared and was executing a comprehensive marketing & sales plan within the scope of their product line and geographic territories.

The file included summary progress reports against annual and quarterly objectives. A *crib-sheet* of handwritten adjustments to the expected performance showed that Stephen was current in his sales management.

Distributor and International segments were secured with commitments – such as minimum order levels, sales terms, and renewal options -

and some formal contracts. These external *people* were well managed and current.

"And we meet with the local university med students semi-annually. …Throw them a reception to let them know that we love them. Doesn't cost much, but the goodwill generated from a few bottles of wine, some craft brews and a few trays of hors d'oeuvres. Well, the med students don't make a bunch of money and they'll remember us. And yes, the profs join in as well."

"So what haven't you thought of, Stephen?"

"Well, we're never sure that we have everything, but we ask the question at our quarterly sales conference – not necessarily a physical conference, but at least a video conference. Some things we miss – and we fix them as quickly as possible."

Stephen just confirmed Elton's assessment. His operation was well managed and under control. Once Jaclyn established that, she could move forward.

"I'd say things look pretty good, Stephen. Now here's a challenge for you." Jaclyn paused letting the silence create a positive tension.

"We like the way that you manage the sales/marketing operations. You've managed the People, Process side of things very well. You establish goals, and you meet them. You've identified factors – such as a new CRM system – that will allow you to be more effective, and you've implemented some of these improvements with minimal distraction.

Our Due Diligence team said that you're sales folks have been instrumental in new product development opportunities – from identifying the opportunity straight through to product launch.

And you know your markets – US and on a limited basis, International.

And best yet, you are hungry for challenge."

"Whoa – not crazy mad for challenge. I just hate to be bored."

"No need to clarify, Stephen. We've got you figured out." Her genuine smile disarmed Stephen's half-hearted objection. Stephen was already negotiating – and he didn't know what the deal was yet.

"So here's the proposal. Your shop is clean and you've demonstrated that you can manage a large and successful sales team, selling and marketing a high-tech, complex medical product. One of our goals with this acquisition is to establish a US presence – for all of Hagstrom. We will make Jackson Manufacturing the global device headquarters. We're going to reduce the Berkshire Company to a production and distribution facility, and shift all global device sales and marketing to Jackson – under your control.

The challenge for you? Well, you'll need to understand products from Berkshire and Hagstrom Europe, sift through all the elements – People, Process, Plant, Products, and Market – and develop and implement a comprehensive action plan that gets us under control within 6 months – yes, the first 200+ days."

Stephen, emotionless, sat silently throughout her disclosure. He stood – walked to the window and stared at the pond, hands on hips and without a word. He leaned forward, and breathed a fog on the window, then carefully sculpted a large question mark – never a spoken word.

A short silent pause, and stern-faced, he turned to Jaclyn. "So you want me to run global operations, and get the whole show up and operational within 6 months?"

Only the geese squawking outside the windows broke the silence.

Yes, it was clear to Jaclyn that Stephen was negotiating. He was working with Jaclyn as if she were not aware of his previous discussion with Elton. His goal was to extract more favorable commitments from Jaclyn. Allowing long silent gaps was part of the arbitration process. She nodded.

"When I spoke with Elton, he didn't mention this. He focused only on the US sales force. Does he support what you just mentioned?"

"Yes."

Finally, Stephen broke the deadlocked silence. "That's going to be a big job, Jaclyn. A very big job to integrate and then to manage. I'm not sure that we have the resources to make this happen."

"OK, but remember what Elton and I have said right along. We are now protecting our investment, so let's not think about resource constraints. *Your job, Mr. Phelps, should you decide to accept it…*' alluding to the iconic TV series. "This is not a 'Mission Impossible', Stephen. It's a job that with the proper planning and sufficient resources can be done. That's not to say it will be easy. But heck, that's why we've selected an Ironman competitor to do the job."

Stephen enjoyed the reference to the original 'Mission Impossible' show. It confirmed that Jaclyn had a sense of humor.

"So all I have to do is ask for a resource and I'll get it?"

"Any justified resource requirements that will help us assure a successful integration and help us protect our investment is at your disposal. And, I know you hadn't considered this a requirement." An impish smile crept across her face. "But there will be a handsome bonus when the job is done successfully. And you are the person that can do it."

The flattery and the challenge captured his imagination. Although not yet committed, he was already developing a macro plan that could make this happen.

"Let's get some details of the compensation on paper, but since you've been straight so far, I think that we can work in parallel – I'll start the planning while you document that most incredible financial incentive plan that you'll be offering me."

Jaclyn relished his broad grin as they started to discuss the vision of the global Sales/Marketing operation.

During the next few hours, although unscheduled, Jaclyn and Stephen thrashed through some concepts on the whiteboard. It was obvious that the future state was not just a simple addition of the two organizations.

The Companies had a different sales and marketing mix. Berkshire Ortho relied heavily on an inside sales force which had established prospect call cycles. Sales reps' sole responsibility was to visit customers…typical *hunter style* reps since their products were treated more as commodities than high-tech products. Once a customer ordered a product, the call center maintained the sales relationship.

Jackson Manufacturing invested heavily in building relationships that allowed premium pricing and also provided insight into product improvements and new product development. Personal relationships historically proved to be an excellent barrier to competitive entry.

By adjusting the Berkshire marketing mix, Stephen would establish a blended approach to potential customers.

Sketching a potential organization chart, Jaclyn pressed for personality traits required of each organization level. As the list grew, Stephen was concerned about personnel assessments.

"Something bothering you Stephen?"

"You know, I haven't codified our job requirements in several years – especially since things have been going so well. Now I…" He walked to the windows – a safe place for him to consider major change. Silence embraced the office as Stephen watched the frivolous geese paddling and honking around the pond.

"I'm going to have to make some tough decisions, Jaclyn. I haven't met the Berkshire folks, but it's possible that some of them could be better performers than the Jackson reps – maybe with better growth potential than folks in my group."

Jaclyn had seen this reaction before. "OK – let's go back to the basic premise. The question that you have to answer is, *'How do I best protect the investment?'* Look at some of the steps that we've listed. I'm guessing that when you listed them, you were focused exclusively on evaluating Berkshire's folks. The steps are correct – they make good sense. And yes, I think that you're exactly right that you will be evaluating the entire combined pool, and not just the new folks."

"And to take it a step further, anyone that doesn't fit will be reorganized out of the Company, right? Kick their butts out altogether." His voice trailed off as if he were losing focus. Jaclyn allowed silence to fill the room.

"I'd rather say help them find a challenge that will be a good fit for their skills. But don't think too harshly about the process. As a Company, Hagstrom is committed to a minimal impact on employees. It isn't their fault that the combination happened. And we want to - as much as possible – develop goodwill throughout the industry. So let's evaluate the resources in an unbiased manner, and execute the decision as painlessly as possible."

"I understand – I'm just… well, you know, I've groomed these folks. It just bothers me to move forward."

"Stephen, these will never be easy decisions. But let's look at what the Company is prepared to do. We have generous severance packages. We'll engage outplacement services – and I'm not talking about a two-hour session with a resume writer – but rather in depth career counselors who can challenge the employees to rethink their careers, given the current economy.

Whenever possible, we'll coordinate job-fairs with regional employers, work with nearby companies, provide retraining funds. We'll want the employees to share the responsibility to find new jobs – this isn't a handout, but a helping hand.

When done properly, the personal drama is limited, and often the employee is rejuvenated. But I will not try to minimize the emotional impact.

So let's move past the emotional side of redundancy and focus on how we reorient a combined Company to the competitive marketplace. I like your approach. First you assess, and then you act. You've also considered the kinds of training required – that's both product training and management training. Well done, Stephen."

As she was speaking, she moved to the office fridge, opened and held up a Pepsi. "Interested?"

"Sure –wait, don't toss it. I'll come over."

Jaclyn's experience taught her to sense tension and she knew instinctively when to break the mood. Something as simple as tossing a Pepsi across the room did it.

As Stephen opened the can, he laughed. "I think that we'd both be wearing this sugary soda had you tossed the can."

"For sure. Let's get back on this. Now we've got the preliminary sales target, and I know that you and the sales team have to examine details. Yes, we'll have some new products. And yes, we'll be expanding our reach throughout the globe. We've drafted a potential sales organization, adjusted the distributor organization, and reorganized some of the sales offices. I like it. And then you stepped back from the US operations and said, 'Hey, there are nearly 6.5 billion people out there in the world'. And you've added some international reps.

You've analyzed that entire process for the next 12 months. Not the six months we targeted, but for a first pass at the concepts, this is superb. Well done! Can you spend a bit more time thinking through the timetable? The quicker we move the better off we are in the marketplace, but you are the grand master in Sales/Marketing. And it would be extremely unfair if we held you to the first pass plan before you had any time to interview the folks at Berkshire. So let's put the big DRAFT stamp on this... think about it and can we review an improved version - perhaps tomorrow?"

Stephen agreed... Jaclyn took a picture of the whiteboard for future comparison and to avoid any misunderstandings.

For the next few hours, Stephen used Excel to analyze the notes and consolidate the concepts to a single page reflecting "As Is and To Be" organization, activities and goals.

Jackson Manufacturing
Sales Operations - High Level Transition Plan

AS IS

Each Company now has a separate and distinct sales force. Berkshire uses an extensive inside sales force primarily for initial prospecting and follow-up orders. Jackson relies extensively on professional organization meetings, seminars and professional relationships.

At Berkshire, Inside Sales also do all the sales administration work. The Sales Admin function at Jackson serves as an internal customer advocate that provides the ultimate customer experience, continuously reinforcing the relationship with Jackson.

TO BE

During the next 3 years, the combined sales force will deliver a blend of the ultimate personal customer service for all major accounts, while smaller accounts will get professional order management and follow-up. The shift for Berkshire customers will only be noticeable for those major accounts that get an upgrade to personal service. The upgrade will depend on sales potential, type of account (E.g. teaching hospitals will always get the personalized service. US Distributors will be increased to better serve the rural less populated areas. International operations will expand to Asia an Latin America.

	2017 Current State				2020 Future State		
	JAX	Berk Ortho	Total	Notes	JAX.	Berk Ortho	Total
Revenue *(Millions $)*	35.0	15.0	50.0		50.0	22.0	72.0
Manpower							
Outside Reps	7	3	10	A, B. C			15
Inside Sales	1	6	7	D			5
Sales Administration	3	1	4				4
Managers	2	2	4	E			5
Directors	0	1	1		*n/a*		1
VP's	1	1	2				1
Total	14	14	28				31
Distributors				F			
US	0	3	3				5
International	4	0	4				8
Sales Offices	4	2	6	G			7
New Equipment *(Mil $)*	Amount						
Add Sales Office	0.4			G			
Add Sales Office	0.4			H			
Eliminate Sales Office (W/O)	-0.2			I			

A = Assess sales personnel; rank entire sales force best to worst :
Determine 'why' poor performance   3/ 17
    Training
      Capability
B = Rationalize Sales Force & Inside Sales   6/17
C = Begin Sales Training   6/17
D = Begin Product Cross Training
    Sales Force
    Inside Sales
E = Develop/implement management training; use of CRM   6/17
F = Evaluate current distributors; expand global distribution   12/17
G, H, I = Identify best sales office locations; rationalize geography 12/17

Cynthia clearly understood the challenge of merging so many entities. She was proficient at working through details, planning events and assigning values to the activities.

For Day One, cash management and cut-offs were important to the success of the transaction. As Elton suggested, it was important to establish effective cutoffs – a month end would be ideal.

But there were so many banking relationships – checking accounts, lock-box accounts, sweep accounts, foreign exchange arrangements, letters of credit, term loans and lines of credit. Although some were not used, this could be a real mess.

Thinking through the entire transaction, she considered the US headquarters function, which meant combining the other US subsidiary cash management, general ledger and all the banking relationships. As she listed these topics, she began to hyperventilate; concerned that she would never be able to manage the challenge and diversity of a headquarters operation.

Panic consumed her … she recognized that she was merely shuffling papers around the desk and haphazardly jotting notes on Post-its.

Standing at her desk, she looked for her favorite coffee mug – Pink Ribbon Cancer mug. The mug always rested in a place of reverence, cleaned and with the inscription facing her desk. Whenever she was overtaxed the Pink Ribbon reminded her of those less fortunate. The mug grounded her and dealt a healthy perspective of what is important. And combining 3-4 business entities didn't make the grade.

Mug in hand she purposefully strolled to the kitchen. Slow gliding steps and deep breathing helped to quiet her anxiety. Once there, she selected Vanilla Biscotti Coffee – a wonderful brief reminder of quiet strolls on the Via Veneto in Rome. Yes, that is why vacations are so important - fond memories become enriched with time, and serve to calm anxiety in later years.

Daydreaming about the wares along the Via Veneto, and dining at Café de Paris after an afternoon stroll transported her to a carefree time … a 10-day vacation that lasts a lifetime. Smiling, leaning on the granite counter she carefully sipped the steaming elixir.

"Hey lady, don't hog the mellow. Share some of that daydream so we can all unwind." JB, never shy to intrude on the private moments, meant no harm, but the jolt ruined her visit to Rome.

"Damn! JB you busted the most incredible memories of my Roman holiday. … Suppose I needed to return to reality. What are you up to today?"

"Not much. I decided to spend a few minutes on the integration planning. You?"

"Same way Big Guy. I was a bit panicked a few minutes ago. This is a monster task... not sure how I'm going to tackle it."

"Let's do some quick brainstorming. You never worry about putting too much on the spreadsheet. The trick is to think about the daily-weekly-monthly activity, and list the tasks. Too much detail – shrink it. Not enough – add a few lines. Nothing is permanent and if you put something on the sheet that is just plain stupid – erase it.

This kind of brainstorming is inoffensive and quick. You should give it a try."

"... Hard to believe that this could really be a simple task. But honestly, JB, I'm worried about the integration. Two US Companies... combined with European HQ ... combined with EU device operations... so damn many moving parts."

"Draw a picture, Cynthia." JB selected a few markers and began to sketch on napkins – asking questions as he diagramed their conversation.

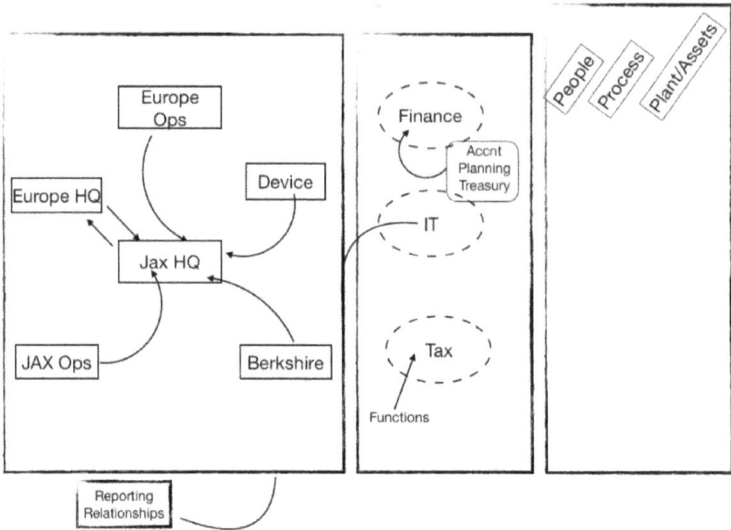

The diagram contains the following labeled elements:

Box 1 (Reporting Relationships):
- Europe Ops
- Europe HQ
- Device
- Jax HQ
- JAX Ops
- Berkshire

Box 2 (Functions):
- Finance
  - Accnt
  - Planning
  - Treasury
- IT
- Tax

Box 3:
- People
- Process
- Plant/Assets

"Jaclyn calls this 'chunking out the thoughts'. She likes to think in groups of *stuff*. I'm not sure of the psychology, but it seems to work. Sort of eliminates the clutter if you can draw a picture to frame the concepts. Once the picture of major issues is identified, then it's just a case of 'who... what... when... and how?' So in this picture, we have reporting relationships that must be enforced... functions that you are responsible for.... And the standard matrix – People, Process, Plant/Assets.

So we have the shape of things. Now just fill in the blanks... freeform – brainstorming. Heck, call it anything you like but just start typing and drawing. Good stuff seems to happen. Not sure if it's a way to kill writer's block, but somehow it works."

"JB, if you had just told me about this, I wouldn't believe that it works, but … well, we've just outlined the framework. I'll just take those napkins, thank you very much. You've saved me a bundle. I owe you a glass of wine."

"Make it a Rigor Mortis Dieu Du Ciel Belgian Quadrupel and you've got a deal."

"Let's do it… whatever the heck that is, Mr. Beer Snob. Find a place that serves that magic and we'll give it a try."

Cynthia's coffee was cold but the solution was at hand.

She quickly moved to her office, fired up the laptop and started typing. Hunched over the desk intensely focused on the screen gradually filling with symbols, words, arrows and numbers, she failed to realize it was now 8 PM.

The first draft of the functional responsibilities seemed comprehensive. As she listed personnel, it seemed to be a good idea to rate the employees, and also consider their long-term potential. As performance gaps were identified, she also determined the training that would enhance the employees' careers.

Personnel				
Accounting	Potential	Curr Rating	Training	Legend
Jackson				**Potential:** A= Outstanding potential; Exec level
J. Shanty	B	B	++	B= Good potential; Director level
B. Cummings	A	B	++	C= At potential; good
J Cummings	A	A	+++	soldier
M Jacoby	B	A	+	
L Schmidt	C	B	+	**Curr Rating** A= Outstanding performance
				B= Performs effectively
Berkshire				C=Needs attention
?				
?				**Training:** +++ = Invest tech &
Europe				
n/a				
IT				
Jackson				
Jason				
William				
Janice				
Mary Ellen				
Berkshire				
?				
?				
Europe				

Within a few hours, she had a matrix of
activities that accomplished the impossible...
activities listed, timing and prioritization
established, all primary reporting and functional
requirements resolved.

While she considered the task to be
impossible, the task was done.

Thinking beyond processes, she concentrated
next on People. She was most familiar with
Jackson and decided to draft an employee
matrix that would be helpful to understand
talent and capabilities. Although the matrix
was incomplete, the template helped her think

through the primary issues of managing Finance (Accounting, Strategy, Planning & Treasury operations) and IT on two continents among 3 Companies and a corporate Headquarters.

Personnel				
	Potential	Curr Rating	Training	Legend
Accounting				**Potentail:** A= Outstanding potential; Exec level
Jackson				B= Good potential; Director level
J. Shanty	B	B	++	C= At potential; good soldier
B. Cummings	A	B	++	
J Cummings	A	A	+++	
M Jacoby	B	A	+	**Curr Rating** A= Outstanding performance
L Schmidt	C	B	+	B= Performs effectively C=Needs attention
Berkshire				
?				
?				**Training:** +++ = Invest tech &
Europe				
n/a				
IT				
Jackson				
Jason				
William				
Janice				
Mary Ellen				
Berkshire				
?				
?				
Europe				

She leaned back in her chair, satisfied that she once again overcame panic and systematically 'chunked out' several solutions. Certainly the analyses were not perfect, but it is much easier to edit than to create. And JB's tip about scratching out the concept was the magic necessary to overcome writer's block.

Thinking out loud, she said, "This merger actually may work…"

Allison's brief discussion with Elton stirred many emotions as he shared his vision of Hagstrom's future in more detail than would be broadcast to the investment community. Profitable, well-managed growth in the *global* device market was Elton's priority. Jackson Manufacturing was the global device platform, and not just the US beachhead.

New product development was critical to the success of the business, but he did not limit new products to those developed in-house. If potential new products met Hagstrom's strict efficacy and financial requirements, Hagstrom would acquire, license or JV with other companies that were culturally compatible. Allison would be responsible for performance and activities she never before experienced. She had not been trained for these new responsibilities.

Historically, Allison worked closely with teaching universities and a few proven engineering firms to identify potential new products. Once potential new products were identified, she would assess the products using a standard template that considered market potential, manufacturing requirements and potential profitability. The review would be a coordinated effort with JB, Stephen and

Cynthia to be sure that the entire team considered the products to be viable.

Quite often, manufacturing capability was an obstacle that could not be overcome internally. Then, JB and the manufacturing team would try to source production quantities at reasonable cost from third parties. This process added more complexity, since implantable devices required exceptional manufacturing control, FDA validated processes, and faultless lot control. Several local manufacturers were often capable of 2 out of 3 requirements. Jackson immediately dropped potential products with more than average risk. Resource constraints at Jackson frequently killed modest risk products early in the process.

Elton expected the Newco to be a global and dynamic New Product Development (NPD) machine. Development would include all continents, and reach far beyond the close contacts now used by Jackson. Language, social norms, legal and regulatory requirements could differ from the basics that Jackson historically enjoyed.

Expectations and job responsibilities would differ dramatically from today's status quo.

Allison was both intrigued and intimidated with such a challenge. The possibilities appealed to her desire to conquer insurmountable challenge, while the wisdom of her many years cautioned that the task would be enormous.

Would the task be too big for her? And was she willing to launch a new phase of her career? The analysis was similar to many she had completed before in her career.

- The first step was to determine all the possible skills required to be 100% successful in the new role of Global VP of R&D and New Product Development. Once she listed broad requirements, what was unique about these skills? For example, could the skills be further segmented by geography – e.g. language proficiency would be far more difficult to achieve in China (with numerous dialects spoken) than in Spain (a common root of romance languages).
- Next *rank the skill from the most important to the least important.* The rigors of biology in a medical device environment would be far less essential than biomedical engineering when considering implantable artificial bones.
- Once the master matrix has been established, fill in the blanks with a personal talent assessment.

Sequence		Rank	Europe						Far East	
			Rank current skills from A (best) to C (needs work)							
		1=Greatest	US	France	Germany	UK	Spain	Italy	China	Japan
1.0	Technical Skills									
1.1	Medical	n/a	n/a	n/a	n/a	n/a	n/a	n/a	n/a	n/a
1.2	Osteo	1	A	C	C	C	C	C	C	C
1.3	Vascular	3	C	C	C	C	C	C	C	C
1.4	Neurological	2	C	C	C	C	C	C	C	C
2.0	Science	n/a	n/a	n/a	n/a	n/a	n/a	n/a	n/a	n/a
2.1	Biomedical	1	A	C	C	B	C	C	C	C
2.2	Chemistry	3	C	C	C	C	C	C	C	C
2.3	Biology	3	C	C	C	C	C	C	C	C
3.0	Business	n/a	n/a	n/a	n/a	n/a	n/a	n/a	n/a	n/a
3.1	Negotiation	2	A	C	C	B	C	C	C	C
3.2	Financial	2	B	C	C	B	C	C	C	C
3.3	Marketing	2	B	C	C	B	C	C	C	C
4.0	Regulatory	1	A	C	C	C	C	C	C	C
5.0	Language	1	A	C	C	A	B	C	C	C
10.0	Soft Skills	n/a	n/a	n/a	n/a	n/a	n/a	n/a	n/a	n/a
11.0	Etiquette	n/a	A	B	C	A	B	B	C	C

As she reviewed her rankings and skills assessment, she discovered that she had no skill for several critical items.

'Now what?' she thought. After a momentary feeling of despair and panic, she circled those ranked a number 1, with a "C" skills assessment and began to develop solutions to these major gaps.

She realized that a language skill across 6 countries and dozens of dialects was impossible for anyone to accomplish.

Regulatory matters became easier to assess, since 5 of the countries were under the European Common (EC) Market control. Despite that, it would be nearly impossible for anyone based in the US to be proficient in

European Regulatory matters. She also understood that the European operation had been working under those regulations for years, and they would have immediate access to the required skills – either in house or through outsourced experts. Besides, she was *expert* in US regulations, and EU regulations often mirrored US FDA regulations.

Her PhD in Bio/pharmacology would serve her well as a basis for understanding specific expertise in medical and scientific areas.

After her initial assessment, she believed that assuming the R&D leadership role in such a global Company was not out of reach. … Challenging yes, but not out of reach. She would begin to identify journals and seminars that would help her upgrade her knowledge in the gap areas.

She would not shy away from this challenge, and she was determined to succeed.

She immediately began to review the Berkshire and European organization, product pipelines, and scientific information provided by Jaclyn. The European information included broad R&D goals, product concentrations, and market characteristics. She would certainly enjoy this challenge, and was thankful that Elton had presented her with the opportunity.

Margaret Brainstorming

Margaret enjoyed brainstorming at her desk using blank pages, #2 pencils, and a large gum eraser. This allowed her to arbitrarily scratch out ideas and if in 2 minutes they didn't make sense, she merely erased the errant ideas or tossed the entire page. This no-fault process allowed her to explore unusual ideas that never seemed to occur to her when thinking linearly.

Today, she had three pages on her desk, labeled respectively People, Process, and Plant – following the themes outlined by Elton.

Concentrating initially on the People page, she drafted an *As Is* organization chart by level, trying to understand how the US beachhead fit an overall Hagstrom organization.

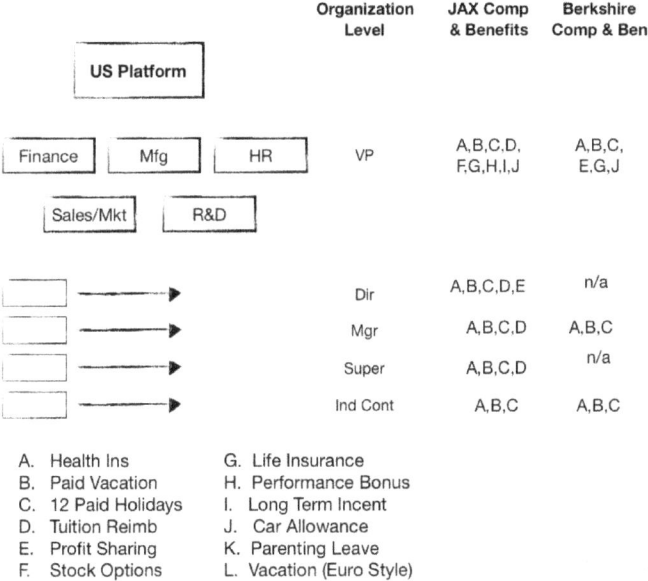

	Organization Level	JAX Comp & Benefits	Berkshire Comp & Ben
US Platform			
Finance Mfg HR	VP	A,B,C,D, F,G,H,I,J	A,B,C, E,G,J
Sales/Mkt R&D			
	Dir	A,B,C,D,E	n/a
	Mgr	A,B,C,D	A,B,C
	Super	A,B,C,D	n/a
	Ind Cont	A,B,C	A,B,C

A. Health Ins
B. Paid Vacation
C. 12 Paid Holidays
D. Tuition Reimb
E. Profit Sharing
F. Stock Options
G. Life Insurance
H. Performance Bonus
I. Long Term Incent
J. Car Allowance
K. Parenting Leave
L. Vacation (Euro Style)

Jaclyn previously sent Berkshire's employee handbook and a summary of Hagstrom's benefits to Margaret, hoping that she would begin comparing the compensation and benefits of the two companies. The rough comparison showed potential increased costs based on additional fringe benefits, and broader coverage for all levels of employees.

For example, Director Benefits at Hagstrom's included Life Insurance, a Performance Bonus and Parenting Leave. All levels at Hagstrom's receive European style vacation benefits – a minimum of 4 weeks vacation.

The preliminary analysis identified several concerns:
- Paternal Parenting Leave was an unusual benefit in the US, and would be excessive.
- Profit Sharing was a great benefit, but never provided to factory *Individual Contributors* at Jackson.
- Minimum vacation benefits of 4 weeks would be excessive at Jackson Manufacturing.

Using broad estimates of these increased costs, she conservatively guessed that the incremental costs would be about a half-million dollars. How had this been considered in the Deal Summary estimated earnings?

Yesterday, Jaclyn mentioned that they were making Jackson the US Human Resources Administration Headquarters. Once the change was made, Margaret would be responsible for all Human Resources policies at Berkshire Ortho and Jackson. This added to the complexity of her job, since all compensation and fringe benefits at Jackson and Berkshire must be rationalized.

Berkshire was a tactically driven commodity business with few creative and motivating benefits. Employees did their job and they received a paycheck. There were few incentives to identify business opportunities to improve performance. Berkshire was virtually the cultural opposite of Jackson.

Berkshire was Hagstrom's first venture into the US market – a relatively small investment to closely manage the risk of international expansion. They'd owned Berkshire for about 2 years, and made few changes. Elton visited the operation semi-annually to review performance and become familiar with the US operating environment. There were no aggressive market goals – just business as usual.

Berkshire had an established product line, but no major new products in the product pipeline – hence a low purchase price for Hagstrom. And now, Elton was upgrading the Hagstrom venture from a *US pilot project* to a full-fledged portfolio investment, by combining operations with Jackson Manufacturing.

Margaret mused, '... has Jaclyn considered the change in benefits that may be required to rationalize Berkshire's operation? ... And the desperately needed lean business training at Berkshire could initially be very expensive.'

More research was necessary to estimate the cost impact to change the Berkshire culture to a more value-add business, if Berkshire were to be included within the Jackson umbrella. Simple continuous improvement processes would be revolutionary to Berkshire.

AS IS

There are 3 Companies & 3 cultures in the mix. Berkshire, Hagstrom, and Jackson. Hagstrom is a well managed global corp. with progressive management philosophy - a creative nourishing environment that rewards performance and encourages stretch goals. Berkshire is a tactically driven, 'daily grind' that established performance goals and expects them to be delivered...top-down management with minimal creativity. Jackson is a progressive US based Company with creative problem solvers ,generous performance benefits but has been somewhat limited by capital availability.

TO BE

Within the next 3 years, Berkshire will become fully integrated with Jackson. Berkshire will perform primarily as a manufacturing operation. Product Development, Sales will integrate with Jackson; Admin functions will be completely shifted to Jackson.

Jackson will simultaneously integrate with Hagstrom, becoming an integral part of their global operations. Jackson will be the Global HQ for implantable devices, and be responsible for European manufacturing, R&D, Sales, Marketing and Admin functions, with the exception of Quality oversight and Regulatory Affairs which responsibility will remain with Hagstrom, UK.

	2017 Current State				2020 Future State		
	JAX Mfg.	Berk Ortho	Total	Notes	JAX Mfg.	Berk Ortho	Total
Revenue *(Millions $)*	35.0	15.0	50.0		50.0	22.0	72.0
Company Headcount	85.0	50.0	135.0				160.0
Manpower							
Administration	2	0.5	2.5				2.5
Managers	2	1	3				3
Directors	0	0	0	A	*n/a*		1
VP's	1	0	1	B			1
Total	5	1.5	6.5				7.5
New Equipment *(Mil $)*	Amount						
Office Renovation	0.3			C			
HR Management Softwa	0.3			D			
Addtl spending - EU trave	0.1			E			
Space holder: Lean Traini	0.4			F			

A = With the assumption of responsibility for the European Device operations, add a Director in US to more closely manage US operations.
B = As the VP HR assumes responsibility for the European operations, he (she) will invest time in Europe. Quarterly trips required to Europe.
C = Jackson offices to be renovated/upgraded
D = HR management software will be required to effectively manage the human assets in the US and abroad.
E = Incremental travel to European subsidiaries will be required. Expected quarterly trips.
F = Lean training never before considered at Berkshire. Estimated required for Lean

After several hours of creative thinking and developing the "To Be" vision of the combined companies, she closed her eyes momentarily, stretched and wondered out loud, "… Will I be able to manage in this new environment?"

Her International experiences were limited to vacations in Montreal, Bermuda and Cancun, and now she would be responsible for the US HQ of an international Company. She reflected upon her 10+ years with Jackson. During the first 7 years at Jackson, her role was limited to US Human Resource compliance - prepare the HR regulatory filings, make sure that the benefit invoices were properly paid, and help manage the workers comp claims. Responsibility for several US operations was intimidating.

A few years ago, after the business consultant arrived, the Company understood that employees truly were Company assets. Payroll and benefits were the largest single cost in the business, and the Company didn't manage them as a critical resource.

During the past few years, Margaret trained and became more valuable to the Company. She learned about how a fully engaged and motivated workforce creates value well beyond the value of a paycheck. As the Company embraced that concept, they rewarded the energized workforce with profit sharing and bonus potential.

Don discovered that treating people as investments in the future was essential to reach peak performance and retain employees.

Upon self-reflection, her challenge was to understand the requirements of being part of an International Company. So many different regulations… different cultures and the travel that may be required. She didn't speak any other languages…

She pondered. 'My dilemma… if not already known, it will be obvious that I don't have the qualifications to do the US HQ job. Should I drag my feet to avoid displaying my lack of knowledge… create some distractions to get a few more paychecks before they reorganize me out of the Company? … Or do I launch into the project like an anxious teenager at a championship football game … all in… nothing left off the table.

All in… that's a lot of work… a major commitment. Do I have the energy and determination to tackle such a task? Do I want the job? …A lot of work – similar to the commitment we went through a few years ago with the consultant. Long days, a few seminars and many hours of self-training. Stressful… and if I jump in and fail, what will that do to me? Am I emotionally ready for failure at this stage of my career?'

Allison just finished a meeting and popped into Margaret's office.

"What's up Margaret?"

"Oh, not much."

"Sounds a bit subdued for your typical bubbly spirit."

"Just a lot to do. I've been scratching around on some pages trying to guess what we need to do in the next 6 months. A 3-way integration won't be easy – this isn't Skyline Chili. And the International ops piece – well, I'm uncomfortable… not sure what to expect."

Allison paused … struggling to find the right words. "OK. Now that we are picking up the European device ops, I'm not sure how I'm going to deal with the increased responsibility. More travel… language, social and legal environments up in the air. And I'm losing the responsibility for Regulatory Affairs… subservient to the folks in the UK. I've always enjoyed working with the Reg Affairs professionals.

But you know me… never say die. So I decided to wrestle with the concept. I know that I'm not ready to take the responsibility now, but I reflected on my skills and career goals. This doesn't quite fit my plan, but it could open up an entirely new career.

So rather than agonize over the future, I decided to say – you'd love this, Margaret – 'It is what it is!' Remember how we used to abuse those who overused that phrase?

So, hold the 'agonize' and lay out a plan. I looked at the overall responsibilities and said, 'What skills and experience am I missing?' I listed the skills necessary for success, and the skills that I have – oh so limited." She laughed and poked Margaret's shoulder.

"I drafted a gap analysis, decided what I could do to fill the gaps, and resolved that some gaps just couldn't be overcome. So for example, in the next 6 months, I can't become fluent in 3 different languages. I decided that conversational Spanish was a good one to select.

As I looked at the technical side of the ledger, I also couldn't become fluent in EU Regulations. Gofigure. Well, execs spend a lifetime studying to maintain proficiency, and I'm not even going to try.

Once I knew the gaps, I outlined a plan that could upgrade my skills when reasonable, and decided that 'outsourcing' technical matters such as language and EU regulations was a simple solution. …The fact-based analysis is done; it's a simple matter of 'Do I want to invest in the skills improvement to reach an acceptable level?' Timing might be important since Hagstrom may not want to wait 1 year for me to become socially and linguistically proficient. At that point, the facts will make the decision – not an emotional 'Gosh, I just can't do it!'

And let the chips fall where they may, but I've given it my best. Whattaya think?"

"I have a similar challenge – and let's face it, all of us will have the same challenge with the European operation. And did you forget the Berkshire impact?"

"Not much for me, since they will be managed as a manufacturing plant, and not a fully burdened business unit."

Yes, that was a worthwhile exchange with Allison.

At her desk, she peeled a clean sheet from the file and sketched 3 column headings labeled: *Today … Future … Gap.* Following Allison's thought process, she filled in the columns. She had to fix the gaps, but was she prepared to dedicate the time?

This new situation was similar to her transition at Jackson during the past two years. When Don hired her as the HR manager about 7 years ago, she was tactically driven and basically the Human Resources compliance technician. Her initial role was to be sure that the Company payroll and fringe benefits were properly paid, and that the Company complied with regulations such as EEOC and Worker's Compensation.

During those early years, Don had full confidence in her ability to fulfill the role defined. Then, as Joseph the consultant introduced the concept of Human Resource – the heart of the Company and probably the largest single cost on the P&L – Margaret grew dramatically, to more of an executive role, thinking beyond the next payroll or compliance challenge. Her proactive analysis of employees – and key outside consultants – as strategic resources helped the executive team to think more strategically. Under her tutelage the Company reprioritized people as a strategic investment rather than a tactical cost to achieve a monthly profit.

She developed Career Path guidelines, succession planning, and a curriculum that included technical skills required for employees to become more valuable – to the Company and personally – and supervisory and management training to allow them to grow their careers.

Overall, she had grown well in the Company. Now she seriously questioned her ability to assume a global role, with multiple facilities and a new 'boss' – a UK headquarters.

Don spotted her mellow mood. "Hey Margaret – what do you think of the transaction so far?"

She and Don always had a close working relationship. Their conversations could be on or off the record, and once the ground rules were established, they would each honor the nature of the conversation.

"It sounds like Elton and Jaclyn have done M&A transactions a thousand times. They know what they are doing. You know, I especially like the way they've handed us the controls. If we don't think we can get the plan together, let's extend the closing date."

"Not my desire, Margaret."

"I understand, Don. This seems to be a great deal for you, and – well, the executive team will do just fine as well. Elton… for such a powerful executive in a global Company – he seems to be spending a lot of time with us. Do you think that he is sincere about the words… sort of giving us the controls?"

"I understand your apprehension, Margaret. I checked out their reputation before I got too far along with this transaction. They have a reputation for integrity – they're tough business negotiators, but when they say they'll do something, history says they deliver.

You comfortable with the transaction? You seem a bit tense. It's a bigger world for you once the deal is done."

"No, I'm not at all comfortable. It seems that there will be a lot of change… a lot of challenge. I'm not sure that I'm ready for this *global* responsibility. I'm just a country gal who's had a great job working for a growing company. I've been stretched quite a bit during the past few years just keeping up with our little Company. And now, Europe and another Company here in the US. This seems overwhelming."

"Margaret, during the past 7 years, you've done a helluva job. You've grown well beyond my initial expectations. But the reason that I hired you initially was your honesty, integrity and willingness to tackle any job we presented to you. My sense is that Elton will give you as much line as you want, but the challenge will be at least as great a challenge as the past few years."

"That's what I'm thinking Don. And I'm not sure that I want to tackle such a monstrous development task. You know at our last round of growth, we worked – what was it 50-60 hours a week – to maintain the day-to-day and then grow into the new responsibility. I'm not sure that I've got the courage to take on that kind of challenge."

"I understand. Have you talked with anyone else about this?"

"Just you, boss…"

"OK – I'm thinking that based on their reputation and the approach they've taken thus far, that they are willing to work with you. My suggestion? Have a one-to-one with Jaclyn exploring the new responsibilities. Nothing definitive, but just a soul searching freewheeling discussion. See where it goes. Maybe change the venue, and take her to the Wine Bar – that keeps it a bit less formal."

A few more minutes of casual discussion, and Don excused himself.

Offsite Meeting: Jaclyn and Margaret

Later that day, Margaret asked Jaclyn to join her for the 5 PM Happy Hour at the Wine Bar.

The Wine Bar was comfortable like well-worn slippers. Hardwood floors were scuffed from years of wear, and a long polished wooden bar included a brass rail footrest. High-backed stools were evenly spaced throughout the 25-foot bar. Well-trained bartenders ensured that customers were properly served, and attended. When a patron wanted discussion – baseball or football teams; local or national politics; the economy - bartenders provided attentive listening with occasional conversation starters.

Margaret passed by those customers who seemed to be regulars, to the stools at the end of the bar. "Chardonnay please." Moments later the attendant served a chilled glass of pale wine accompanied by a small dish of pretzels.

She picked a small napkin as a notepad and wrote a blotchy agenda using a borrowed pen: - Future growth; - Organization expectations; - Managing in global environment.

Moments later, Jaclyn strode through the bar, and waved a 'hello' to Margaret.

"What a great place to meet Margaret. Enough folks so that it's not a funeral pall, yet quiet enough so that we can have a discussion. What do you recommend?"

"Chardonnay works well – wish it weren't such a cliché – but it sure is a nice way to end the day."

Jaclyn nodded to the bartender who was awaiting the order.

"My gosh, times are busy, Margaret. Glad that you thought of getting away from the shop. Sometimes things seem to get far too formal when within the four-walls of the business."

The chilled glass arrived accompanied by a small dish brimming with cashews. "Cheers, Margaret," as Jaclyn savored the first sip.

"I must say that you folks in the states are gracious hosts. We've come in complete strangers, with some big challenges, and you folks have been extremely welcoming. Sometimes it doesn't feel that way when we make an acquisition."

"Part of the reason for our grace is your approach. You and Elton haven't arrived as conquering heroes who have *saved the day*. We appreciate that you respect our history and the work that we've done. Yes, we'd like to thank you for your attitudes."

"I guess we all have the same attitude – respect others as we'd like to be respected."

Margaret casually broke a pretzel into three pieces at the loops – not to eat the pretzel, but more to occupy her mind.

"So what do you think, Margaret?"

"Jaclyn, this sure seems like the big leagues to me… being part of a global half-billion dollar Company while most of us have never experienced such broad exposure. Most of us have spent half of our careers with Jackson. Any guestimates about how successful we will be?"

"Loaded question, Margaret?" Jaclyn paused to let her question mellow.

After a suitable pause, Jaclyn continued. "We fully expect this transaction to be one of our most successful. During the Due Diligence, we noticed the dramatic changes in your operating processes during the past two years. Your team has become much more professional – planning and successful execution have been your hallmark. That kind of culture change is difficult – sometimes fatal to individuals who try to make the transition. Your team has remained intact throughout the change, and that is extraordinary. As a result of that transition and team commitment, we fully expect the team will be successful in the future. That's not to say it will be easy, and there may be some fallout, but we are confident in your team.

That said, two years ago the team might have had a different energy. The payout that you folks will enjoy when the deal closes will be meaningful. That might affect individual commitment."

She swirled the last remnants of the chardonnay, and drained the glass. "Another wine, Margaret?"

"Yes, let's have another. So based on your observations of our earlier transition, you think that we can pull it off?"

"It's definitely within your DNA – if you have the desire."

"Do you and Elton handicap the team members?'

"Good question. We have private thoughts that we don't share. We have one purpose in this transaction – successful integration. Our personal commitment is to ensure that each senior executive gets whatever support they need to be successful.

Look, it's a bit unusual for Elton and me – the CEO and the SVP of Marketing in a global half-billion dollar company– to be so personally committed to your individual success. But we consider this to be a strategic investment in the future of the Company. When you look at our commitment in that frame, it's not so foolish."

"OK – so I understand why you have a personal commitment. But we're a small, family owned Company, and we're becoming a global headquarters for a medical device

Company. We've never experienced either foreign ownership or direct responsibility for offshore operations. Big changes. Risky moves, aren't they?"

Jaclyn tipped her glass and rolled the wine around the bowl, watching the elongated chardonnay fingers glide down the glass.

"You've asked some good questions, Margaret. Jackson Manufacturing executive success is in each executive's hands. A question for you... Are you and the other executives willing and anxious to commit the same energy to this transition as you did several years ago?"

Silence hung in the air as Margaret swirled her wine trying to capture the chardonnay's *nose.*

"So how does this California Chardonnay compare to a continental white, Jaclyn?"

Jaclyn accepted the diversion and shared her assessment of the wine, avoiding any further discussion about the business. She was confident that she outlined expectations, and also properly shared Elton's commitment to the executive team's growth.

With no regard for her personal career concerns, the next day Margaret started the task of *integration planning.* While she was responsible for Human Resources, she took her responsibility much more personally than just a job. She interviewed and hired every person in the Company ... knew their personal strengths and weaknesses... their aspirations and goals ... knew their families. She wanted to be sure that there was no interruption to any HR process that affected the employees – and as she thought about the operations – the longer term independent contractors.

As a guide to her planning, she reviewed her ledger accounts for the past 12 months to identify people or organizations that worked for the Company, certain that this would identify individuals within her responsibility. After several hours, she had a list of every major or repetitive vendor on an excel spreadsheet. In another column, she listed the product or service received from each vendor.

Payments through HR departments		NOTE	Jan	Feb	Mar	Apr	May	Jun	Jul	Aug	Sep	Oct	Nov	Dec
Janson Deli	Food		x	x	x	x	x	x	x	x	x	x		
United Way	Donations	A			x			x			x			
Para-help	Temp Help Agency					x	x	x	x	x				
Ample Insurance	Liability Insurance	B			x									
Ample Insurance	Life Insurance	C			x			x			x			
Cincinnati State	Emp Training	D		x	x			x	x	x		x	x		x
UC	Tuition Reimb	E	x	x	x	x	x	x	x	x	x	x	x	
Griffin Law	Property Lease		x	x	x	x	x	x	x	x	x	x	x	x
Staples	Office Supplies		x	x	x	x	x	x	x	x	x	x	x	x
Gasti Plumbing	Restroom upgrade						x	x						
Toyota Leasing	Truck Lease		x	x	x	x	x	x	x	x	x	x	x	x
Toyota Leasing	Executive Cars	F	x	x	x	x	x	x	x	x	x	x	x	x
State of Ohio	Workers Comp		x	x	x	x	x	x	x	x	x	x	x	x
Hamilton County	Franchise Tax				x			x			x			x

A= Quarterly donations to the United Way, Don's favorite charity. Continue?
B= Will UK-HQ handle liability insurance?
C= Will UK allow key man life insurance?
D= What is the Corporate policy regarding Employee Training?
E= Will UK allow for college reimbursement?
F= Will executives have company cars?

Surprisingly she identified several charitable organizations that relied heavily on Jackson Manufacturing support. She would discuss these charitable organizations with Jaclyn.

Once again, thinking through the exercise, she added several other columns to the worksheet. Columns designating timing – e.g. Day One;………

Pre-Closing: T–3 Days

Jaclyn and Elton arrived at the office the next morning around 8:00 AM, and saw Cynthia, Allison and JB huddled at the coffee machine. Conversations evaporated as Elton and Jaclyn approached. Although smiling, the dark circles under Cynthia's eyes hinted at a sleepless night. Self-consciously, JB punched out a quick, "Heck of a Xavier game last night. Buzzer beater, and they've now got a 4-game winning streak."

Jaclyn nodded agreement to the buzzer-beater assessment. "What's up, folks?"

Eye contact made, Cynthia offered, "Java time for the troops."

"How are things going on the project last?"

 "Overall, well." JB was proud of his accomplishment. "After you and I finished a few days ago, and I polished the worksheet a bit, I stopped over to see Allison and Cynthia – hard at work developing their checklists. I told them about the accelerated Excel worksheet method – showed them the spreadsheet, and explained that in only two hours, we were virtually complete. Sure, I stayed late that night to do a bit more brainstorming – a bit more in-depth analysis – added a few points of contact – but it was so much easier than I expected."

Cynthia held her coffee cup high as if in a toast, "I burned a few hours thinking about the task before JB stopped over – scratching ideas on legal pads – yes, I used a few post-its. It just didn't seem to flow. JB stopped over and showed me his finished product. I'm impressed, Jaclyn. Well, I scrapped my earlier work and began anew. It took a few hours, but we've got a similar worksheet. Wish you would have helped me out before JB… just kidding JB – Jaclyn knew who REALLY needed the help."

"Did it show in Tuesday's meeting? Hey, the least you can do is thank me for stopping over before I left for the night."

"OK- so here's the deal, Jaclyn. When you have those little tricks to make things easier, tell us all – same time & place – so we don't waste our time." Cynthia, mocking the team, shook her finger at each one around the coffee machine.

The Keurig sequentially spurted 5 cups of coffee to the crowd, and they dispersed to their offices.

Planning Meeting

At 10 AM, Don and the team were seated at the conference table in their usual seats, with a laptop and projector prepped for the meeting.

"Good morning, all," as Elton raised his cup acknowledging the team. "Shall we dance?"

Don observed. "The team is a bit psyched. They've done their homework – not sure how this compares to your expectations, but they did their best. I've looked at some of the information. Looks great to me, but you folks are the masters. So let's go."

JB launched the first slide with the expanded matrix he developed. Throughout the morning, each exec presented a similar spreadsheet – some with different headings, but all followed the same concept, starting with their responsibilities.

Throughout the day, Elton smiled at the number of times his name was listed as 'Responsible'. "So who's this Elton gent who's going to do all this work?"

"Hey, boss, you said to make you work. We took you at your word."

"Seems to me that he should have a heavier load … no lackey's on this deal."

The team raised coffee cups in unison – all the while laughing at the exchange.

Throughout the hours of review, the team actively participated in the discussion, frequently challenging the thinking and responsibilities outlined.

Several times during the meeting, the team got sidetracked from Day-One issues. Jaclyn let these distractions proceed for a few minutes since interrupting too soon might stifle their creativity.

Emotions were high as the team reviewed several controversial employee matters. Don's relatives continued to be a sensitive topic, and continued to be unresolved.

As Margaret reviewed pending promotions, Elton reminded the team that the Company should freeze personnel movement for at least 30 days.

Stephen objected. "Excuse me, Elton, but I have aggressive sales goals to meet. Remember the forecast that we discussed a few days ago? Well, I'm going to guess that you will hold us to those goals. I can't achieve those goals without the sales organization that I've defined. I've got a Regional Manager promotion that should happen immediately, and I have an offer out to a new rep. Are we just supposed to cancel those actions… leave those employees hanging"?

"Stephen, once you get me the updated analyses that we discussed, we'll make a final decision. For now, let's consider the freeze in place."

Jaclyn continued, "Now is a good time to refresh some guiding principles of this deal. Our goal is to successfully integrate this Company into the Hagstrom fold. That means that during the next few years, we've established somewhat aggressive goals. One of our goals is to treat all constituencies fairly and professionally. We do not want to disrupt employees' lives unnecessarily. So for example, we wouldn't want to hire someone in the next few weeks and then determine in 2 months that the employee is redundant.

We also would not want to promote someone, and then determine that the organization will change, no longer requiring the higher-level employee and compensation.

In this transaction we don't see much risk in that, since you will be our primary US platform company. But as a guideline for this transaction, we suggest adhering to our overall principles of employee and organization freeze – no organization changes, compensation and benefits. We will review individual exceptions on a one-off basis."

"OK Elton – can we meet today? I've got the analysis ready."

"Will do – how about right after this session?"

Allison's quick note-taking about organizational changes concerned Jaclyn. She made a mental note to follow-up with Allison.

Throughout the meeting, the team was fully engaged, focused, and actively discussed the issues and challenged assumptions. There were no tepid participants in this meeting.

After meeting for hours, Jaclyn stood, looking at each participant. As eyes met, she nodded acknowledgement of a good job. She raised her coffee cup, "Folks, this is absolutely superb. You've taken a rough concept, modified the framework to fit your needs and made it work for you and the entire team. This is perhaps the best that I've seen in any of our acquisitions. …Thorough assessment of the issues – no fluff and fill – no pages with useless *stuff*.

So, as we try to confirm the projected financials, I think we need some placeholders. What I'd like to suggest is that we block $600k-800k expense and $500k capital as placeholders until JB, Allison and Stephen can travel to the other locations to make a better assessment. Any objections to that?"

Stephen cleared his throat, "And when would you suspect that we would have that better estimate defined?"

"Well, Stephen, we're shaping out the 1st 100 days and the 2nd 100 days. I think that we'd like this firmed up within the next 30 days, so that you have time to begin execution."

JB feigned being mortally wounded. "Ouch, that hurts. Are you serious about that timing?"

"Good question, JB. If we've got targets for the first and second hundred days, how much time do you want to spend analyzing, and how much time do you want to devote to *doing?*

And before you answer that question, let's put ourselves in the position of employees, customers, and vendors at those locations. Do you really want them wondering if they'll have jobs – or customers - for more than a few weeks or a month? And do you think our customers want to be in limbo for months before we explain what's happening? I'm sure our competitors would love that confusion. The tough part of that answer is that the best employees can easily find jobs … and if the best employees are the first to leave – maybe poached by our most aggressive competitors - how will we achieve our business goals? And for the customers… do you think that competitors will allow us the luxury of delay, or will they be telling stories about a confused acquisition process, lack of leadership, lack of resources etc.? And it doesn't matter if it's false, if there is a performance vacuum, outsiders will be happy to fill it.

Allison's head bobbed in agreement, and she looked concerned. "Stephen, scary but true. My best research technician got a call last week from a headhunter. Once the rumors about the acquisition started, there was an immediate bounty on our best employees. Fortunately it seems that our best employees like our environment. As long as we don't screw this up, they'll probably stick with us, but it's critical that we move quickly."

"OK, you're right – we can't afford to wait, but my schedule is getting overloaded."

"I understand. Let's recall Don's statement, "if you need resources let me know. Well, now we have Elton in the room. Any thoughts Elton?"

"Folks, we've invested more that $60 million in this transaction. What's it going to take to protect that investment? I know it's a lot of work – schedule compression and perhaps a very tense time for you. Yes, it's true, but we have to remember that the European folks will feel the same time pressure. We're all in this together – that's why we flew the European execs over to work with you. So let's get back to work."

The refocused team started through the agenda, concentrating on each functional area, describing how the functional leader would guide the organization through the analysis and integration process.

Jaclyn kept a 'parking lot' listing of issues that seemed to bog down the discussion, and suggested that, "These open items will be covered in a later meeting. Let's stay on topic today – validate the assumptions in the Deal Valuation model, and finalize the 100 and 200 day implementation plans."

She proposed a plan for the site visits and executive review of the offsite locations. As they reviewed the schedule, several seemed to be concerned about the responsibility.

Seeing the concerned look, Jaclyn asked, "Allison, you ok with the schedule?"

"I've never done anything like this integration. Yes, I'm a bit concerned about the process and how to do it."

"The simple answer is to just understand the objective, and then plan scenarios to get us to the objective. So in your case, you will be responsible for worldwide R&D for Hagstrom's device line. You and I can spend some time together, but for the benefit of those who may not have done integration before, we want to look down the road 2-3 years and describe how we want the business to look and function. So, as we've done here for the Company, we will consider people, process, plant, product and market. Let's take a look at R&D.

You have certain scientific specialties. We've already discussed the nanotechnology, and the fact that we have several PhD's specializing in new product development.

So let's sketch this out on the whiteboard.

Using some of Allison's prework and open conversation, they developed a high-level R&D program.

(Millions $)	2018	2019	2020
Revenue			
New Product A	-	1.5	4.5
New Product B	0.5	2.5	7.0
New Product C			0.9
Total Revenue	0.5	4.0	12.4
Gross Margin			
New Product A	-	1.3	3.8
New Product B	0.4	2.1	6.0
New Product C	-	-	0.8
Total Margin	0.4	3.4	10.5
Development Costs			
NPD A			
Project Headcount			
PhD's	1	2	0
Other Pro's	4	3	1
Techs	4	4	0
Total Headcount	9	9	1
Personnel	1.5	1.5	0.2
Materials	0.5	0.5	0.1
Overhead	2.0	2.0	0.3
Total Cost	4.0	4.0	0.6
NPD B			
Project Headcount			
PhD's	1	0	0
Other Pro's	1	1	0
Techs	2	0	0
Total Headcount	4	1	0
Personnel	0.6	0.2	-
Materials	0.1	0.1	0.1
Overhead	0.8	0.3	0.1
Total Cost	1.5	0.6	0.2

(handwritten note) If PhD's in Europe, how managed?

"OK, Jaclyn, you make this look too easy. What if we're wrong with some of the estimates"?

"Good question, Allison. First of all we're trying to get the major concepts on paper. So if we know that we generally need 2 PhD's to launch Product A, the next question is, 'what support staff is necessary?' Our goal is to size the project in broad terms, knowing that we don't have a detailed project plan. Said another way, let's get the creative part of the task done, and then we can fine-tune the project. If we get too hung up on details early in the planning, we'll miss some of the creative components.

Once the project is reasonably scoped, let's figure out where the talent will come from. So, one of our challenges is PhD location. Since the best people may be in the UK, how would we most effectively manage the project? And if we don't have the right internal resources, where will we find them? Will we need proximity to the regulators? Will we need proximity to the major market – e.g. the US? Many questions, but if we solve these open questions on a white board brainstorming, we aren't really spending any money. Simple, but effective way to solve for the best answer.

As we creatively resolve these questions, the project staffing, location etc. will naturally fall out of the process.

Your next challenge will be costs."

"You read my mind, Jaclyn. I'm enjoying the looseness of the analysis, and can't wait to hear how we estimate costs."

"Gotcha. The question that we're trying to solve is a project with an annual contribution margin of $5 million +-. In this brainstorming phase, what's a few hundred thousand among friends? OK – I'm exaggerating, but the first thing we need to do is identify the actions required. We'll worry about how much the actions cost as we move further down the planning path.

The beauty of this kind of scratchpad planning is that we focus on the issues, not on the specific dollars. So let's say a PhD costs an average of $150,000, and we think it's a 2-year project. That's $300,000. Based on overall ratios, if a clinical requires an average of $.5 million, let's chunk the cost out. In total, I'd say this is a $1 million project, when you include a couple hundred thousand dollars for incidentals. This creative approach will help us get all the right issues on the board.

As we get into more detailed planning, if we truly don't have any idea about the costs or capital required, we'll make a to do list. We may also decide to put in some placeholders – e.g. the nearest half million dollars – so that we don't lose track of the item.

Again, remember, we're only scratching numbers on a page – we're not spending real money yet."

Jaclyn looked around the room and suggested, "We can all use this method in every area – whether we're trying to get a fix on capital or expense spending. Any thoughts, folks?"

Cynthia appeared to be deep in thought. "Jaclyn, I tend to get hung up on the dollars and cents of spending. ... Kind of in my accountant DNA. I'm going to struggle with this 'big-round-nearest-gazillion-dollars' concept. Can you spend some time with me to keep me out of the weeds?"

"Glad to do so – let's schedule some time.

Let's move to the next item on the agenda - develop an implementation schedule. You've all had a chance to develop preliminary plans. Let's take a few minutes for each of you to review the current status. Again, our objective is to be substantially complete in 200 days.

Today, as we listen to each plan, let's think about how the proposed plan may affect the functional area. For example, if Stephen requires a new CRM system in 3 months, that means that Cynthia must dedicate resources to implement the system. Is she prepared to do so?

These cross-functional matters are the items that we're searching for. Also, if during the discussions we identify issues or opportunities never before considered, let's talk about it.

I'd like each person to review his or her plans in about 45 minutes. This will allow us to hit the high spots and also get a picture of the entire Company's integration plans.

In addition to several items identified during preliminary discussions, the team focused on the additional operations that would be under their responsibility – European Device Manufacturing & Distribution, Global R&D for devices, and the Berkshire facility.

To effectively coordinate with the Europeans, the JAX executives would visit the European and Berkshire operations.

"Cheers to you!"

Elton raised his cup in honor of their efforts. "Folks, not only did you think through the Day One issues, but you completed the task in record time. Better yet, some of those sideline discussions focused on issues that must be resolved quickly after Day One. Bravo... and thank you. Don, it seems like we are right on track... just like you said, these folks tackle the difficult tasks – without hesitation."

Elton showed the 'thumbs up' sign to Jaclyn.

"OK - from here we'll summarize all these items, circle back with each of you to go down another layer. Remember, we are all responsible for the success of the integration. If you see something that needs attention –

Day One, First 100 and Second 100 Days - shout it out. Thank you for an excellent start."

JB leaned toward Cynthia, "Wow – it seems like we have a great start. A few days ago, I thought that we were doomed with an incredible amount of work, but Jaclyn knows how to get things done. What do you think?"

"Yes, we have a good start, but oh, there is so much more to do."

As Allison and Stephen were leaving the room, Stephen put his hand on Allison's shoulder. "Thoughts?"

"Well, Elton didn't shy away from his responsibility. As long as we are always equally stressed, we'll get through this – just like every other major challenge that we've survived in this Company."

Elton and Jaclyn cleared the conference table, neatly organizing the pages prepared by the executives. "Elton, they did an excellent job today. I think that this is going to be a good deal. We have a lot to do, but it seems that they are all engaged."

"I think part of the success so far is your contribution, Jaclyn. You made folks feel like we could get through the extra work. You're good at your job."

Jaclyn adjourned to her temporary office – a former storeroom that was cleared to be used by visiting executives. A small desk, phone, 2 yellow legal pads and a picture of Don leaving the air-stair of the Company's King-Air, outfitted the otherwise unadorned office.

She opened the emails containing the worksheets prepared by Margaret and Stephen – planning concentrated on employee and customer matters. These two functional areas were critical elements in every transition.

Stephen was the link to a successful sales process and customer integration, and after today's meeting, was also a challenge in organizational matters such as promotions and new hires.

Once Jaclyn organized all the detail summaries, including the changes made during the group meeting, she had an excellent "Day One" set of activities.

Wednesday, 8:15 AM, the team assembled in the conference room in advance of the scheduled start. The group seemed less tense today. Emotion and concern morphed into a more positive, business-like, *can-do* attitude.

Apparent insurmountable obstacles to the projected results in the Deal Summary now seemed to be achievable. Jaclyn's disarming smile, and meticulous attention to problem solving nurtured the candid discussion necessary to completing the integration task.

Smiles replaced the stern faces and their stressed demeanor encountered during the first integration meeting disappeared. Sidebar conversations now covered vacation plans, sporting events and specialty barbecue recipes. The communications' process – that is no issue too big or small to discuss - was effective – as much from Jaclyn's comforting technique as from the process itself.

Elton's selection of an accomplished, well-qualified senior executive to liaise the integration was criticized as overkill by several Hagstrom board members. Jaclyn was not only one of the most expensive Company resources, but she was now diverted from her primary job – global marketing.

Elton thought, 'Overkill – BS!' Board Members with that opinion failed to realize that the Company has risked $60 million in a single transaction. If the acquisition fails, Hagstrom's reputation will be affected, and it may ruin any opportunity for the Company to enter one of the most important device markets in the world. Elton's response to the cynics, "How much would you spend to save $60 million?"

At exactly 8:30, Elton and Jaclyn appeared.

Elton greeted each team member with a smile and handshake, and a single question, "Everything going OK?" … His sincerity a virtual salve for the executives' anxiety.

He walked to the head of the conference room, gestured to the refreshments and encouraged all to enjoy. "Thanks for joining us today. Jaclyn has updated me about our progress." Elton purposely used the term *our progress* to reassure the team that win or lose, the team was responsible, and he was part of the team.

"She mentioned that you folks have been extraordinarily helpful and have taken her for her word – 'make me work'. Excellent! My role in this acquisition is to make sure that we dedicate all the resources necessary to make this acquisition a success. As we embark on this integration journey, we must remember that Hagstrom invested $60 million to establish a device platform in one of the largest markets on the globe. I encourage you to be tough on Jaclyn." He turned, smiled and nodded almost imperceptibly to Jaclyn.

"Now let's get to it."

With that, Jaclyn raised a carafe of coffee, circled the room asking, "Top off?"

The circuit completed, she punched a remote, and the screen brightened with a PowerPoint slide. "You'll recognize this – the first of several pictures of our brainstorming two days ago."

OPEN ISSUES

-Synergy sales too high***
-Baseline sales - too aggressive?
-Cutting R&D limits NPD
-Mfg cost decrease? How?
-Plant relocation***
-Shifting production to US sister co.
-COGS reduction-too much
-Who's in charge?
-Little Int'l Experience
-Comm with other Hag divisions?
-What happens in 1st few weeks?
-Compliance with US regs?
-FCPA***

-Personnel cuts?
-Comp & bonus plan
-Stock options
-Exec roles & staff cuts
 - Personnel development programs
-What is that earnout $$$?
-Tuition reimbursement prog.
-Maternity benefits
 _ Inventory Turns
 _ -DSO now well-managed...
  improvement can't be done
-Capex $2.5 mil neededShifting
  production to US sister co.

JB smiled, "Never saw this before, Jaclyn."

Jaclyn was pleased that the team was joking. "OK, this is the first page of our brainstorming. We discussed some of the broad principles that Hagstrom's considers sacred... honesty, law abiding, and do the best we can for all of our constituents.

Today we'll go through the high-level response to your questions. We've documented the responses so that we all have the same answers to discuss with employees, customers, vendors etc. Consistency is essential. Miscommunication causes major problems. We're happy to stand with these responses – let's make sure that we understand them, and are comfortable with the information. Again, WE are managing this transition.

First thing, let's look at some groupings." Jaclyn launched the next slide.

OPEN ISSUES
P&L
1-Synergy sales too high***
2-Baseline sales - too aggressive?
3-Cutting R&D limits NPD
7-Mfg cost decrease? How?
20-Plant relocation***
21-Shifting production to US sister co.
11-COGS reduction-too much

General
12-Who's in charge?
8-Little Int'l Experience

9-Comm with other Hag divisions?
13-What happens in 1st few weeks?
24-Compliance with US regs?
25-FCPA***

Personnel
14-Personnel cuts?
16-Comp & bonus plan
18-Stock options
19-Exec roles & staff cuts
 6- Personnel development programs
15-What is that earnout $$$?
15-Tuition reimbursement prog.
23-Maternity benefits

Balance Sheet & Cash Flow
 6- Inventory Turns
5-DSO now well-managed...
   Improvement can't be done
10-Capex $2.5 mil needed Shifting
   Production to US sister co.

"We've identified some of the critical items with
***. Are you comfortable with this
identification? Any priority items that we
missed?"

After a brief pause, she continued, "Ok - you'll
see that we grouped things in common
themes. During the past two days, I've met
with each of you to discuss resolution of each
of these issues and also develop some
preliminary plans. Whenever we can provide
concrete information, we'll do it. There are
some gaps right now, since we haven't
thoroughly analyzed the Jackson and

Hagstrom businesses. We still don't have firm plans about how best to move forward in all areas.

Let's talk about the elephant in the room – money. You've had some questions about the term 'earnout', and you've also mentioned Executive Compensation, Bonus, and Stock Options. We know that you all participated in Don's generous stock option program. Ours is a bit different, since we are a public Company, and our Bonus program is different from Don's.

Our goal is to quickly grow this business, and we are not afraid to compensate the executive team. Elton will be meeting with each of you individually to make offers. In addition to the customary compensation items, we also have a deferred compensation program, and a long-term incentive program that keeps all of our goals consistent with the Company goals.

The earnout is based on your strategic plan, modified for the synergies that we've discussed.

Thus far, our individual meetings with you have, we believe, covered all the other items on this list. Questions or concerns?"

Jaclyn and Elton have spent considerable time with each executive to be sure that integration and strategic objectives were clear. Despite the aggressive goals, the executive team believed that the goals were achievable, especially with Elton's personal support.

"So today, we'll focus on Day-One activities.

We've got a prepackaged template for each of these segments, but the template is a broad checklist. Your insight is critical to success.

Let's look at each business segment:"

People
    <u>Employees</u>
        Compensation
        Fringe benefits
        Offers/promotions
        Job descriptions
        Organization/structure
    <u>Customers</u>
        Key customers
        Other current customers
        Prospects
        Former customers
    <u>Vendors</u>
        Key vendors
        Other current vendors
        Prospective vendors
        Former vendors
    <u>Other constituents</u>
        Agencies/regulators
        Communities
        Etc.

"So when we talk about people, any thoughts about why we include so many categories?"

"Employees, customers and vendors are a no-brainer, Jaclyn."

"Yes, Allison. But why bother including prospects and former vendors? And given that timing is critical, why bother thinking about the organization structure?"

"For 'Day-One' seems like a distraction – a bit of overkill - to think about organization structure. We have too much to do to think about organization structure."

"Fair questions. Let's think about our business. We've gone a bit radical – given our earlier integration experiences – but when we think about integration and Day One, we like to think about People as any person, any organization, any agency that the Company interacts with in the business."

"C'mon Jaclyn. That's absurd. That could be a ridiculous amount of work – and what's the benefit?"

"We thought that initially – in our first acquisition. Here is a story that may help us validate the extreme work. Several years ago we acquired a French Pharma Company. They had a great product pipeline and a very aggressive NPD launch schedule. That fits our culture perfectly. They had a seasonal OTC product virtually ready to go. Package design and approval were the last steps before launch.

As part of our Due Diligence, we looked at the organization chart and talked with each senior exec about their staff. All looked great – we were managing the Org Chart as the basis of 'People' actions and responsibilities. The deal closed, we executed our initial integration plans, and about 3 months later, we noticed that the expected product launch – you know that seasonal product - didn't happen. We did the root-cause analysis and discovered that package design wasn't complete and with the hectic integration activity, no one noticed.

… Turns out that the package design was previously outsourced to a contract designer… someone not on the organization charts since she wasn't an employee. We missed the seasonal introduction, so the product was delayed a year. During that year, a competitor developed and launched an improved product. So we had a double negative – and that's definitely not a positive.

So now our definition of People is any person, organization, agency etc. that anyone in the Company interacts with. And that is why you folks are the keys to success.

When we think of Day One activities, we include changes to what is done. Changes can include approvals required, and at the least, do we want to *communicate* with everyone on Day-One."

"No, but if we have major prospects that we've been cultivating for months or maybe years, I'd hate to lose momentum with them just be cause someone new owns us. Besides, now that we supposedly have a broader product line, we will be a different Company. And not only that, it's a positive reason to reach out to them to present our wares."

"In previous integrations we've asked the transition team to think about every facet of their year – yes, year. Some activities occur routinely – for example, weekly – while others are unpredictable and infrequent – for example, an FDA audit.

When we consider every activity in a normal business year, we have minimized the chance of missing something. When we talk about your activities, we're including everything that you – the functional executive – are responsible for. That means your staff, and their direct reports.

Think about that time commitment.

And since we are integrating, that activity may also affect Hagstrom HQ and other divisions. Let's think about an example. Allison, you're now responsible for Regulatory Affairs. Since our goal is to launch US products in Europe, whom will you work with for the registrations?"

"I think that would be Reginald, according to the contact list."

Yes, that's correct. And do you think that he has routine responsibilities in the UK and Europe?"

"Of course, or he wouldn't have a job."

"So for you to successfully integrate with Europe, you need his time – and probably some of his staff time. Sounds challenging."

"And we'd likely need time from the EU consultants to register and launch products."

"Yes, Allison. Yet another challenge."

Jaclyn continued. "And we'll also be launching EU products here in the US. I'm going to bet that Reginald's goals for this year include successful launches. Whose burden is that? Yours … Reginald's… or both?"

"Both."

"And since we have formed a new corporation here in the US, will that new corporation be required to register to produce and distribute FDA regulated products? …Day One?"

"Yes, for sure some kind of formal registration will be required."

Jaclyn volunteered. "A few years ago, a major freight company acquired a family owned trucking firm. It was a wonderful merger. Everything was well organized, and the day of closing, one of the logistics managers mentioned that the new corporate entity did not have a DOT license. Oops.

It was something that slipped through unnoticed, and unfortunately the acquired Company was unable to legally ship product until the proper license was obtained... about two weeks later. Such a simple thing, and the buyer missed it.

So let me summarize. Everything that you do – daily, weekly, monthly, annual tasks - should be considered in the planning. And that YOU includes any functions that you 'own'. So your entire organization must be considered.

Any contacts within the scope of your operation must be considered."

The next page focused on Processes.

"Any thoughts about this slide," Jaclyn questioned.

Processes
- Cash management
  - Cash/treasury management & FX
  - Deposits/commitments
  - Payroll & other comp
  - Organization/structure/hiring/firing
- Security
  - IT & Other
- Approvals/governance
- Communications
- Customer/contracts
  - Key customers
  - Other current customers/prospects
  - Order processing/approvals/limits
- Vendors
  - Key vendors
  - Other current vendors
  - Order processing/approvals
- Gov't agencies & regulators
- Other constituents
  - Communities
  - Etc.
- Sales
- Purchasing
- Hiring/Firing

"Help me understand 'Approvals/Governance' on Day One. That seems to be a lesser priority overall."

"Excellent question about a Day One priority. Let me pose a question. On Day One, we all come into work and do stuff. Who does it? Who directs the employees? What are their responsibilities?

So, is it OK that on Day One, Cynthia buys a new Company car? Would you like a new Lexus, Cynthia?"

Cynthia smiled and agreed, "…would enjoy a new LS model!"

"Well, without governance, you could do that. And JB, is it true that you'd order that new Laser CNC machine in a Nano-second if you could?"

"You betcha!"

"So governance on Day One sets the ground rules. People will come to work, as always and do stuff – whatever is allowed. The governance allows the new company to establish the ground rules. Most times, the rules are business as usual, with a few exceptions, but wouldn't it be nice to have that defined, rather than have people stand around saying, 'Who's in charge?'

And the next page is plant and other assets. So let's guess why we have that on the list."

Cynthia beat JB on this question. "If ownership of the business changes, we're just looking for control of the assets acquired. And from a financial point of view, some of the assets may not be acquired." Smiling, she turned to Don.

"Will the King-Air be going to the new Company?"

"No, that will be outside of the transaction, but I sure would like to have the new company pay some of the maintenance costs of that beautiful bird."

With that, the team laughed.

Cynthia continued, "Day One... Let's think about how a change of ownership can impact these broad categories."

Plant/Assets
    Cash
        Cash/treasury/FX contracts
        Deposits/commitments
    Intellectual property
    Receivables (notes & accounts)
    Customers/contracts
        Key customers
        Other current customers
        Prospects
        Former customers
        Order processing/approvals/limits
    Vendors/contracts
        Key vendors
        Other current/prospective vendors
    Other constituents
        Etc.

Product
    <u>Current</u>
    <u>Pipeline</u>
Market
    <u>Share</u>
    <u>Growth</u>

"As we think about planning, why bother with Product and Market?"

The team looked puzzled to describe how these should be considered early in the planning process.

Jaclyn continued, "Let's call these catch-all categories in our early and Day One planning. These are more of a macro consideration. Current and pipeline product awareness is important in a competitive business since substitute or near term competitive products may impact our business plans. This is something that we all must be aware of during any planning and strategic thinking.

Market is also a macro awareness… keep our eyes open for things that could disrupt our plans. So, for example, if you hear that a competitor will be showing at a trade show that we historically could not afford…"

Stephen couldn't restrain himself. "We book the show and use the leverage of our half-billion dollar global organization."

Jaclyn cheered, "Bravo Stephen. Now you've got it. Folks we can never have enough information in this market, so let's keep product and market within the planning umbrella."

"So now, we've scanned all five summaries. Anybody want to comment on why we have so many categories for Day One consideration?"

"I think your goal with that list is to make us think about everyone we interact with, so that just in case something needs to be done on Day One, we've considered them."

"Right, Cynthia. But this could take a lot of time to get it right."

JB interrupted, "But I'll bet a lot less time than trying to fix something. I think that your list is for us – the folks that run the business – to use with our local knowledge. Said another way, if we miss someone, we blew it."

"Eloquent as always, JB," observed Allison.

The team laughed and enjoyed the light jabs.

"And next, we'll look at processes:

Allison couldn't resist. "Same shtick, Jaclyn. Just like flying a plane. We always use checklists to avoid problems... and, well, if we're good pilots, we always file a flight plan. Nothing new when we're dealing with major activities."

"And finally, JAX team:

As we've done for the past two days, any problems, concerns or issues, light a flare… send up the rockets. The sooner we hear of problems, the quicker we can resolve them.

Communications – through me - but if you're not satisfied with my response or response time, the boss in the corner is at your disposal – right Elton."

Elton nodded agreement, "Make it happen folks."

"We'll set up a website– password accessible for employees – that will have Q&A and an issues section. We'll review the site for new issues daily, and ideally have a response within 24 hours. Questions?

And while the site is password protected for our employees' exclusive use, we should all assume that anything on the site would be in our competitors' hands within hours… it just happens. So let's be careful about content."

The team was fully engaged and ready to work.

Day One 'Q&A' Summary

She distributed the draft Q&A summary for their review.

Hagstrom's merger with Jackson Manufacturing Inc.; Questions & Answers

Will there be major layoffs after the acquisition?

We don't expect any significant layoffs as a result of the acquisition. However, as we examine the merged organization requirements, it is possible that we will make isolated staff reductions.

Will salaries continue under the same schedules and guidelines that we have today?

We have examined the compensation policies and pay schedules. We will not make any changes to the policies and pay schedules for the rest of the year. Future compensation will be geared to the regional competitive environment, and be consistent with prior years' practice.

We now have a tuition assistance program. Will that continue?

The existing tuition reimbursement benefits and procedures will continue, as it exists today.

Will earned vacation benefits change from current policies?

Earned vacation policies and benefits will continue unchanged. For example, those who have worked in the factory for more than 25 years will continue to receive 5 weeks vacation.

Will sick pay, maternity leave etc. change with the new ownership?

Sick pay, maternity leave etc. will remain unchanged with existing policy.

Health insurance is a critical benefit. Do you foresee any changes in Company contribution levels, coverage, deductibles, or overall costs to the employees?

As far as insurance coverage is concerned, our goal is to provide coverage consistent with the philosophy that Don has implemented during the past years. We expect no changes in coverage or costs this year. Future years' coverage and costs will be negotiated with carriers using the Company's historical philosophy.

If the health insurance will remain basically unchanged, but I have already met my deductible, will the deductible restart with the new Company?

We will make sure that there is no incremental cost to employees as a result of the acquisition of Jackson Manufacturing.

There is a profit sharing program with Jackson Manufacturing. What impact will the acquisition have on the payouts?

We will make sure that the change in corporate entity will have no impact on this year's payout and profit sharing program. In fact, there will be unusual deal costs and integration expenses. These incremental costs will not impact any profit sharing for this year. We will adjust the incremental costs out when evaluating performance.

When the deal is closed, to whom will I report on the first day?

We purchased a well-functioning business based in the US. For the first few weeks, your job will be exactly the same as today. If you report to work at 8 AM today, you'll do the same when ownership changes. You will report to the same organization, and the same people as today. From an operating point of view, only the senior executives will have a new boss – initially Allison, Cynthia, JB, Margaret and Stephen will initially report to Elton.

How will I get paid when Hagstrom's owns the Company?

Payroll will be processed exactly as it is today. For the first few weeks, you'll have the same paycheck – the same direct deposit as before the transaction. Eventually, there may be a different Company name on the check, but everything else should be consistent.

We now use outside service organizations – SAAS, other cloud services, travel agents, freight forwarders etc. How will the acquisition impact these relationships?

We will continue to use exactly the same services as before the transaction. Remember, we purchased a fully functioning, well-managed operation. In the future, there may be changes to suppliers as the scale of the business increases.

Some of us will be retiring within the next year. How will this impact our retirement benefit?

For now, pension benefits for all vested employees will continue as outlined in the benefits booklet. We will be reviewing the Pension Plan benefits and funding during the first few months and keep you informed of our progress.

The 401-k plan Company contribution will continue as is. As part of our management process, we review compensation and benefits annually and try to provide very competitive rates for all our employees.

We've heard that we may be working for a new Corporate entity. Does that mean that we will have to pay additional payroll taxes?

We believe that there will be no additional taxes paid by any employee as a result of this change in corporate entity. The Company will reimburse any incremental payments made by an employee solely as a result of the formation of a new corporation.

Will the facility continue to be located in Cincinnati?

We expect the Cincinnati operation to continue to operate with the existing force.

We now have all functions here in Cincinnati - e.g. Manufacturing, Sales, Finance, and IT etc. Will those functions continue at current staffing levels?

Although we haven't completed all our integration plans yet, we expect that the functions will continue here in Cincinnati.

We've heard that we will be a subsidiary of the Berkshire Company. Does that mean we will be working for them rather than for the UK headquarters?

We've structured the legal entities in a way that Berkshire will own Jackson, but organizationally, Jackson will report directly to the UK.

Your press release says we will be the HQ of North America. What does that mean?

We've made this major investment in Jackson because we have full confidence that this team can successfully lead our US growth. Simply put, we believe that we can rapidly grow the North American business by further investment in Jackson.

Will our fringe benefits change as a result of the acquisition?

Jackson is positioned very well in this competitive environment. We will remain competitive in compensation and benefits.

Will we change the name of the Company here in the US?

One of the reasons we acquired Jackson is the value of the Jackson brand. We don't expect to dilute that investment by changing to a relatively unknown UK brand - Hagstrom. The Company name will be Jackson Mfg. (A Division of Hagstrom LTD)

Will you be adding any of the European products to our line?

As a regulated industry we will apply for approval for any products that may be useful in the US market. Once approvals are obtained, we will begin sale and distribution of the products in the US.

We've heard that Hagstrom has excellent R&D capacity in Nano technology. Will we discontinue our efforts in those areas?

Nanotech is an extraordinary field. As a corporation, we will invest in research where we can achieve the greatest returns for our stockholders. We continue to develop plans that will help us do so.

Please note that many of the questions relate to jobs, compensation, and impact on employees, customers and vendors. A merger is personal for all those involved. A new Company is an unknown environment. Our job in planning the integration is to anticipate constituents' need for information. This list is not exhaustive but could be a conversation starter. We'll build a broader list as we continue planning. Let's develop a master list that is prioritized so that we answer the main questions that concern 'people".

For the next few hours, Jaclyn discussed each item on the pages of initial issues, and frequently referenced the printed documents distributed with the scripts. Answers were thorough, concise and written so that anyone in the organization would understand the statements. There were no acronyms, buzzwords, or complex business jargon.

After Jaclyn reviewed the final point, Cynthia observed, "It's absolutely shameful that you haven't included at least a few acronyms, and a slice of jargon. These responses to questions are so simple and straightforward – well, I think even JB understands them."

JB burst out laughing, while tossing a bag of M&M's to Cynthia. "I only understand them because you've trained me so well, lady."

Jaclyn continued. "Folks, we've been through M&A Integration several times. And truthfully, we've messed things up a few times. Experience has helped us develop a few master checklists to make sure that things go smoothly. If you look at the 'Cue Cards' in the file, you'll see a few of these checklists. Let's all understand that these may not be perfect. As we go through these templates and develop specific plans unique to JAX, we'll no doubt add steps to the masters. If you see things that need fixing, shout it out.

We start out at a high level – People, Process, Plant, Product and Market. In the past we like to address these three areas immediately. Our goal is to make sure that nothing drops through the cracks on Day One."

The team toyed with the deck of laminated checklists. Some bending the cards as if to stress the concepts. Some fanning the deck as if to view a kaleidoscope image of 'integration'. JB's assessment, "Not too shabby, Jaclyn... kind of 'been there, done that."

"For sure, JB. And we have the financial scars to prove it."

"Communicate – could be a monster. Are you talking about one-to-one meetings... phone calls? What are you thinking?"

"Good question, Stephen. First of all, let's think about communications. How should we communicate? What kind of communications? And I've got the marker in hand. So let's list some types of communication."

With that Jaclyn opened the black marker and scribed as people made suggestions.

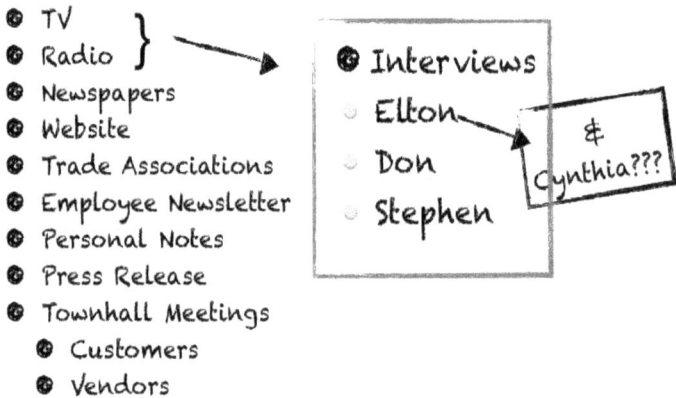

- TV ⎱
- Radio ⎰ → ● Interviews
- Newspapers ○ Elton
- Website ○ Don &
- Trade Associations ○ Stephen Cynthia???
- Employee Newsletter
- Personal Notes
- Press Release
- Townhall Meetings
  - Customers
  - Vendors

"OK – I like the list. There may be more, but let's keep going – we can add more as they pop up. Now with whom should we communicate?"

"Customers!"

"All customers on Day-One Stephen?"

"Yes – wouldn't want any of those scavenger competitors catching us in a weak, confusing moment."

"OK – so are you going to meet with them individually?"

"No time for that."

Cynthia volunteered, "Send an email to the 'C' customers."

"I like the way that you think Cynthia – prioritize based on importance. Stratified customer list. So we want to only touch current customers?"

"Whoa bronco. Hey, I'm just about to close on a major customer. … Been working the contact for nearly a year. I'd hate to lose them during this transition."

"OK – so now we're considering both actual and potential customers."

Jaclyn effectively worked the team. Challenging… writing … directing the quick pace of this brainstorming session, she created an action matrix of how we would deal with 'People" issues on Day One."

	Customers						Employees		Contract	Agencies	Vendors		Retirees
	Actual			Potential									
	A	B	C	A	B	C	Mgmt.	Factory			A	Other	
Telephone													
Personal Visit													
VP/Pres	✔			✔			✔				✔		
Manager								✔	✔				
Reps		✔			✔								
Press Release													
Email													
Video (Web)	✔	✔	✔	✔	✔	✔	✔	✔	✔	✔	✔	✔	✔
TV/Interview													
Letter/Snailmail		✔				✔						✔	

During the next two hours, Jaclyn worked the team into a frenzy of creative brainstorming. Using the white board, she carefully explored Day One activities for People, Processes and Plant for each of the executives.

"OK team, we've just spent a few hours making me work. Yes, I've implored you to do so, but I'm beat. You've done one helluva job – just look at these concepts.

Now, this is just a first pass. Each of you has contributed to this listing. Review the list and personalize it. Yes, I mean think through all of the 'people' in your functional area – that is any person, organization, agency etc. – with whom you interact.

I'd like you to make up a detailed list and think about, 'To whom should we communicate, and what is our message?'

We have some general guidelines – you've seen the frequently asked questions – but what else should we communicate?"

Elton was pleased with the thoroughness of the review and the executive engagement with the process. Their levity confirmed an essential level of teamwork.

Elton congratulated Jaclyn and the team. "Excellent start on this project. But the real work only begins. If you see something you don't like, raise hell about it. Jaclyn, drive on."

"OK team, we've had a heck of a morning. Thank you for your time. Our one-to-one meetings have been very successful. Your preplanning has been thorough and insightful. Thank you for your efforts this morning. Enjoy the evening. Did I hear someone mention a Xavier University Basketball game on ESPN tonight? Enjoy."

Jaclyn established the overall goals to accomplish on Day One. She requested that each executive begin to list Day One activities and concerns. Simple, one-line deliverables on a checklist - e.g. continued health insurance – was really a summary of many steps necessary before Day One could be successful. Such a review required a spreadsheet of all the benefits provided by all Companies involved.

Headquarters

Jaclyn knew that if they were extremely lucky, everything would go well, but that has never happened before.

The executives arrived at 7:30 AM to review the day's schedule, and confirm each person's role. Communications were key today.

There would be problems. Prompt resolution is the best way to minimize long-term disruption and keep the process under control.

Elton and Don were scripted with bullet points for the live webcast to all employees at 8:00 AM. The 10-minute webcast would be recorded for playing to the 2nd and 3rd shifts.

Critical steps, such as physical security and electronic access for all employees, were well rehearsed. There should be no problems.

Timekeeping and payroll access remained unchanged from before the closing.

The functional VP's were the first line of defense for any questions during initial meetings, but in unusual cases, Jaclyn was the decision maker.

Day One instructions included an array of 'what if' scenarios that could ruin a successful Newco launch.

The Newco Corporation had been established, and whenever possible, contracts such as leases and agreements with agencies and vendors were identified and were ready for assignment. The legal work during the first few weeks post close would be time consuming, but based on the review work already completed, there were no major obstacles to the deal.

While much was completed behind the scenes, the activity during the first day was limited largely to communications with employees and key contacts such as customers and vendors.

Preliminary guidelines for approvals – e.g. capital spending and major activities such as financial commitments and employee matters - were established so that routine activity would continue without disruption. The Jackson executives now understood why the earlier role-playing was so important. By thinking through daily activities in each functional area, all major decisions and actions had been considered.

The "Day One" minute-by-minute schedule included every major step considered necessary to ensure a smooth transition. The wire service published the press release at 8:00 AM.

Ref	Resp	Description	Type	Notes	Timing
1	JT	Prepare scripts for personal meetings	Doc	Finalize by 12 PM T-1	T-1: 12:00 PM
1.1	JT	Prepare press release		Finalize by 12 PM T-1	T-1:12:00 PM
1.2	JT	Release Press Release	Doc/Email/ Website		T-0:7:00AM
1.3	EE/DJ	Meeting with local TV channel	Personal	Finalize script by 12 PM T-1	T-0: 2:30 PM
	MM	Kitchen setup	Refreshments		T-0: 9:00AM-5:00PM
2	MM	Security notified that employee badges fully functional	Doc		T-0: 8:00:00 AM
3	CT	Company passwords confirmed & continuing	Doc		T-0: 8:00:00 AM
4		Employee meetings			
4.1		Jackson			
4.1.1		Shift One:			
4.1.1.2	JB	Factory	Personal		T-0: 8:00:00 AM
4.1.1.3	JB	Warehouse	Personal		T-0: 8:30:00 AM
4.1.1.4	CT	Office Employees	Personal		T-0: 8:00:00 AM
4.2.1		Shift Two:			
4.2.1.1	JB	Factory	Personal		T-0: 4:30:00 PM
4.2.1.2	JB	Warehouse	Personal		T-0: 5:000 PM
4.2.1.3	CT	Office Employees	Personal		T-0: 4:30:00 PM
4.2	SK	Sales Force	Video/ Personal		T-0: 8:00:00 AM
4.3	All	Walking around	Personal		T-0: 9:00AM-11:00PM
5		Customers			
5.1	EE/DJ	Critical Customers	Phone		T-0: 9:00AM-12:00PM
5.1.1	EE/DJ	Critical Customers	Personal		T+5
5.2	SK	"A" actual accounts	Phone		
5.3		"A" actual accounts	Personal		T+5-10
		"B & C" actual accounts	Email		
		"A" Potential accounts	Phone		T-0: 3:00PM-5:00PM
6	JB	Vendors			
6.1	JB	Prepare scripts for phone/personal meetings	Doc	Finalize by 12 PM T-1	T-1: 12:00 PM
6.1.1	JB/DJ	Critical Vendors	Phone		T-0: 9:30AM-11:00AM
6.1.2	Engineer	"A" Vendors	Phone		T-0: 9:30AM-12:00PM
6.1.3	Engineer	"B & C" actual accounts	Email		T-0: 9:00AM
7		Banks			
	CT	BB&T	Phone		
	CT	Huntington	Phone		
	CT	JP MorganChase	Phone		

Welcome packets were distributed to all employees including a logo fleece, brief summary of the transaction and printed Q&A summaries. A continental breakfast was served at each meeting site.

Unfortunately at 8:00 AM, a technical failure with the Webcast firm would not allow recording the broadcast. ... Not a major problem. The script could be repeated later this morning for replay on the 2nd and 3rd shift.

Simultaneously, at the entry guard's station, several employees forgot their security badges. While the 'entry' system was properly uploaded for secure entry, the subsystem that allowed 'search and retrieve' employee records was not accessible. The security company mistakenly disengaged employee files at the time of the transaction. Employees were not allowed entry unless their supervisor authorized access, and supervisors were not available, since they were attending the Webcast in the commons area. Employees were delayed, and did not hear the Newco launch webcast.

The webcast was broadcast to both Berkshire and the European R&D device team and Sales Operations.

Executives were stationed strategically throughout the Company to observe employee response to the webcast, and also be available for questions. Upon completion of the webcast, Margaret and Jaclyn encouraged questions. The VP's were stationed throughout the company ready to answer questions at the conclusion of the webcast.

This was the first day on the job for several employees who were visibly upset about the possibility of layoffs – especially since they just left secure positions at a nearby company. The approved Q&A didn't seem to calm their fears. Eventually, Margaret's reassurance in one-to-one discussions reduced their anxiety.

Jaclyn continued the meeting, while responding to questions about, "Who's the new boss? We trust Don... ... why did Don allow a British Company to buy an American Company?"

The phone system was overpowered by dozens of calls to Don's line. As Don was not available, the unanswered calls were immediately transferred in the traditional priority to the functional executive – VP Human Resources... VP Finance etc. The Voicemail system was stressed, but still functional.

Meanwhile, the Berkshire team was upset, since no one was present to explain the impact on his or her business unit. The transition team hadn't considered Berkshire to be a Day One communication's risk, since there was no immediate impact on their business.

Hostile tweets about the Company being acquired by a foreign business quickly turned negative in this era of "Make America Great Again."

Fortunately, the team considered all electronic media in the Day-One scenario. Approved responses to expected Tweets were ready to launch, but Cynthia, who was responsible for media responses, was engulfed in group meetings and personal discussions with key employees.

Unanswered questions from angry vendors, concerned about their ongoing relationship and open account balances, remained unanswered for hours.

During this early critical period, Don and Elton strolled the facility making personal introductions to key employees. Discussions were brief but reassuring. The casual interactions were designed to project calm, and settle the emotions.

After the initial hours of apparent chaos, employees' emotions stabilized. The executive team's calm approach to angry questions, and thorough response to many anticipated questions were reassuring to the employees. Unanticipated questions were noted, and employees were told that further information would be available later that day.

The executive team met at the common area for the scheduled 10 AM status review.

Once the team was assembled, Jaclyn poured the coffee, smiling and reassuring the executives that this was quite a typical Day One.

Jaclyn opened with, "Wow – what a morning! Everyone still on board?" She noticed several nervous smiles.

"I've got to tell you, I felt like I was attending the NCAA championship game, score tied and 15 seconds to go. Lots happening. What did you think?" JB never disappointed with his first remarks.

"This has been a very good start. Yes, there was some breakage, but if you look around, you'll see that folks are heading to their stations, doing their jobs. I think that you folks did an excellent job preparing us for a burst of emotion and flash of activity. Thankfully we were ready for the crush."

"OK – let's hear specific observations – the positive and negative. What did you hear and what did you see?"

Jaclyn facilitated the meeting discussing observations, identifying common threads of information.

People issues dominated the observations. Despite reviewing the approved Q&A that addressed People questions, employees were still unsettled with the acquisition. In rapid fire, the team listed unexpected questions that arose during the discussions:

- Will there be personnel changes at Berkshire?
- There is a headcount freeze. What's next –layoff?
- The Company has been investigating Long Term Care insurance as an option available to all employees. Will the Company continue to investigate? When will we know if such a program is available?
- The Company considered reimbursement for Adoption fees, and was expected to finalize a policy within the next 90 days. What is the status?
- What happens to employees who are out on disability? Will they have jobs after the Newco transition?
- What happens to employees who are on active military duty – activated as reservists?
- Retiree medical insurance cost sharing has been an exceptional benefit for retirees. Will that program continue?
- Jackson has historically supported local charities with funding and special events designed to raise awareness for specific charities. Will our community service orientation continue?
- The Company has an active intern program with the local colleges. Will this continue?

- The Company has participated in a matching gift program for charities. Will that program continue?
- The Company has allowed – and sometimes invited – retirees to work part time once retired. Will this option continue?

During this session, Jaclyn carefully documented all the open questions. She also probed the executives for other observations. For example, were there any groups or departments that were extremely negative or positive about the acquisition? She noted those at the extremes for follow-up.

Negative groups would get special attention – not to encourage them to believe that all things were positive, but rather to listen to their concerns – the true basis of negative opinions. Negative opinions often resulted from misunderstandings or miscommunication. Real issues could be addressed with assessment and Company decisions that would clarify issues.

Positive feedback about the transaction could help the Company emphasize previously unforeseen benefits of the merger. For example, ownership by a global half-billion Company could expand career opportunities for current employees. Also, with a broader base of customers and larger size, the Company may be more secure than a smaller locally owned Company.

Jaclyn shared stories about observations from previous mergers that helped the executives understand perceptions and ways to successfully respond to concerns. She also emphasized that no matter what, some people would not be happy, because change is disruptive and the end result is unknown.

After all the issues had been discussed, Jaclyn encouraged the executives to respond to emails and voice mails, and circulate among the employees to mine information.

The meeting adjourned and the flight teams – Elton & Stephen, and JB & Don - exited for the airport.

Jaclyn took a picture of the open issues listed on the white board for follow-up. The rest of the team filtered out to circulate with their employees.

At noon, Cynthia received a panic call from the freight forwarders, concerned about processing the letters of credit (LC) opened for a recent Jackson shipment to Europe.

"How can I process this if the money is now owed to Hagstrom? That is a different entity than listed on the LC."

"Jackson Manufacturing is still a fully functioning company. Process the payment the same as always."

"And for the LC's now in process? Since the Newco will be selling and shipping the product, I'll have to get a new LC."

"Process the in-process shipments and previously negotiated LC's as if Jackson Manufacturing were selling the product. We'll sort out the details after month end. This is a very friendly merger. Whatever cash we get that belongs to Newco, we'll make the transfer. Any other issues that you envision?"

Cynthia understood the forwarder's concerns since renegotiating LC's could be a cumbersome and time-consuming process.

Later that morning, the billing department called to get a supply of the Newco Company invoicing stationary. Cynthia explained that for the next few days, the Jackson Manufacturing Company stationary would be used. Newco stationary would be available within a week.

Several major customers requested certificates of insurance effective the day of the transaction. Only one hospital required a written indemnification agreement between Jackson and Hagstrom providing identical coverage as was originally provided by Jackson.

Fortunately the team anticipated several of these urgent requirements and the proper documentation was ready to be filed.

While enroute to the airport, Elton received a panicked call from the President of Berkshire. The Berkshire employees were in the midst of an uprising. Employees were upset about the disloyalty of the British parent. The Berkshire team no longer believed that they were a vital part of the merged organization. Several of the mid-level employees left the facility immediately after the announcement.

Jason, the Berkshire President, wasn't prepared for such an event. He believed that there would be some disruption, but the chaos would be short-lived.

Jason questioned, "Elton, is there any way that you can come to the facility today to calm the team?"

"OK, Jason, let's think about this for a moment. We've got an hour-by-hour schedule today – filled until about 10 PM tonight. I'm going to put you on speaker with Stephen, and let's think this through."

They discussed having a live videoconference later today or tomorrow, or a personal visit by Elton within the next two days. As they reviewed the schedule, it was clear that a videoconference wouldn't be the right way to deal with such an inflamed team. The final solution would be to have a Berkshire facility meeting at 3 PM tomorrow afternoon. Elton and Stephen would adjust their schedule and fly in for a one-hour session.

"Jason, do some homework and get a list of the issues as best you can by 5 PM this evening. Send me the list with a copy to the rest of the Jackson team – you've got the roster. I'll get a note to the team so that they expect the list. We'll work through the issues this evening, prepare a draft script of responses that Stephen and I will deliver personally tomorrow afternoon.

We'll have the draft to you by 10 AM tomorrow morning so that you can review and comment on the responses. That will still give us a few hours to finalize the Corporation's position.

In the meantime, walk the floor and calm the nerves as best you can. Also, make sure that we have the cafeteria ready for the meeting. The meeting will be an informal gathering where the folks can ask questions.   It won't be limited to those items that we've scripted.

Get some refreshments – something light so the folks don't fall asleep on us. How's that sound?"

"OK, Elton. That covers the first shift. How will we handle the second shift?"

"Good question. Let's have the meeting recorded, and we'll make it available for second shift viewing. You'll have to handle the logistics of that meeting, but with the first shift done, we will have covered – what would you guess – 75% of the employees? The 25%

night shift will be your baby, Jason. You OK with that?"

"That'll work, Elton. I'm embarrassed that this is blowing up as it is. I sure misread how they would respond. I really blew this one."

"Not a problem, Jason. It's a wrinkle that we'll manage. Let's make it happen. I look forward to your notes this afternoon. This kind of thing keeps us on our toes. Cheers."

After the call, Elton emailed Jaclyn to alert her to the changed plans. He also asked that they arrange for the charter flight adjustment.

Stephen briefly shook his head, "So is this still under control?"

"Yes, Stephen. We can never anticipate every response to a merger, but our principles of engagement – fair treatment and respect – will carry us through. These surprises could be devastating if we hadn't done such thorough planning up front. Instead of 90% chaos, we have 10% chaos and 90% planned activity. That's really a great result."

Customer Visits: Elton & Stephen

Elton and Stephen were visiting a major customer in Chicago when they received Cynthia's email. They ignored the 'email receipt' notification as they discussed the Jackson merger with Children's Hospital.

Stephen was summarizing, "… and overall, we fully expect that this merger will be a positive in our relationship, since we will not only continue to serve you with the same staff, but we will have a broader product line that hopefully will make your purchasing function simpler."

The stoic VP – Supply Chain was expressionless, nodding in agreement. His actions were always difficult to interpret – he'd be a great poker player.

"So what kind of benefits to us – your customer?"

Stephen previously role-played this meeting in his mind, expecting some resistance to the merger.

"Bill, your hospital is one of the largest in the Midwest. Your CEO has made it clear that you wanted a top-ten ranking in the US in some field. During the past years, you've invested in several specialties – one of which is orthopedics.

So let me ask you a question. We at Hagstrom have one of the finest nanotech research operations in the world, headquartered in the UK. Hagstrom's research works with operations throughout Europe – think about having access to this high-tech – that's nanotech and metallurgical resources in Scandinavia, Germany and Switzerland… all coordinated through Allison's R&D shop.

What can you do with access to such resources?"

Stephen was aware of Chicago children's goals. This softball question piqued Bill's interest.

"So exactly what are you offering me?"

"We're not offering anything other than stating some facts. We don't know your business strategy, but we do know our side of a supplier's equation. We're also aware of the keen global focus on joint development of new products.

Let's brainstorm a bit. As a supplier, we can develop new products – new alloys and designs – in a complete vacuum. Produce some of these innovative wonders, send the products to the market, and have a complete bust, because we don't have ready access to our ultimate customers. That would be doctors and patients that will ultimately benefit from innovative products.

Now if we were to have access to these critical knowledge sources, we might be inclined to JV the development and production of these wonderful new products. And they could be quite profitable, don't you think?"

"So are you offering a JV agreement as a result of the merger?"

Stephen leaned back away from the table. "I'm not in a position to make such an offer now. But when you think of the merged Company, you'll continue to get the same great service from a known organization – we're not planning to change anything in our current manufacturing and supply operation – and because we're now an integral part of a global organization, it seems that there is nothing but upside."

Bill smiled. "You're a clever negotiator, Stephen. Elton, hang on to this guy. He's come a long way in the past few years. He's been more creative during the past 3-4 years than I've ever recognized before. Somehow, he's always the source of win-win. Not sure how he does that."

Their meeting concluded, Elton and Stephen arranged the collateral material, and gave the file to Bill.

As they left the hospital, Elton turned to Stephen, brow furrowed, and said, "I don't remember discussing JV's as part of our offering. Do you think it would be worthwhile discussing before we make such commitments?"

"Typically I would, but as Bill started speaking it occurred to me that this could be an ideal synergy that we hadn't considered before. Since I only spoke speculatively, I thought it might be worth exploring.

And let me ask you a question, Elton. If you had the opportunity to partner with a motivated partner in R&D, with access to a qualified group of clinical test subjects, would that be a worthwhile thing?"

"OK, you've got me there, Stephen. You leapfrogged the normal route to a proposal, and your assessment is correct. I guess that you've just demonstrated one of the reasons that you are a keeper. Strategic orientation, thinking outside the lines, and you reasonably considered a probable outcome without committing the organization to a specific course of action. But next time, I'd like to discuss before you present such a proposal. While we don't have any real commitment to do so, just the fact that I was there lends credibility to the proposal. I'd hate to back down now…."

Elton pulled his phone out to review of some messages while reflecting on what just happened. His concern – the type of decisiveness Stephen displayed. Stephen's strategic assessment of value to the Company was impressive – this from an executive that, until now, only worked in a regionally strong FDA regulated business. Once we combine these Companies, the synergy will change all expected horizons. Yes this truly was an exceptional acquisition if we get the integration right.

As they pulled out of the parking lot Elton asked, "So what's next on our agenda?"

"I've organized the charter to get us to Berkshire an hour earlier than planned. I'm a bit concerned that we didn't anticipate the reaction we're getting. I'd like to spend an hour with Jason to better understand what other issues might arise. While they voiced certain concerns yesterday, there may be another layer of discontent that we're not aware of. I'd like to be prepared for the 'what if's' that may arise."

"OK- let's explore the potential downside of Berkshire behind closed doors."

Vendor Visits: Don & JB

On their way to Pittsburgh Metals, just outside of Pittsburgh, Don was flying right-seat today. Since he hired a pilot as PIC (pilot in command), he was able to walk back to talk with JB.

"Well JB – now that you are rich, what do you think?"

"I'm thinking that you made a good deal... found a great match for the Company that you built, and you really took good care of your team. I'm very optimistic about the outcome.

I am a bit concerned about our relationship with Pittsburgh Metals. They've been a bit testy during the past few months. All the 'Make America Great' dialogue could really stir them up with our new British owner. And with this recent talk about a 25% tariff on imported metals – well, they just aren't the happiest campers on the planet."

"Won't that help them out?"

"Yes and no. They don't directly produce anymore. They are more of a distributor of unusual metals. They could take a real hit if prices go up. Their customers – that would be us – won't be happy about price increases, and they have to take the heat."

"Got it. How do we handle the potential ownership issue?"

"I think that we have to stick with the principles that Elton has outlined. What's best for our customers… we deal with folks fairly etc. I think the key will be to emphasize that we will now be a global Company, with a half-billion dollars of sales. That should reduce their risk. We'll also want to focus on broader distribution – global distribution of our products – that could lead to more business for them. We've also got the opportunity to expand our product line with European designed implants.

I think we can make this feel good to them, and it won't be a massage, it will be real."

"I like the idea of less risk, and potentially more demand for their supplies. Do they have any research facilities? Maybe we can tie them into European HQ?"

"That might be a stretch. If the conversation goes that way, I wouldn't discourage it, but I wouldn't volunteer it."

"OK. After Pittsburgh, where are we going?"

"We're off to Atlanta… meeting with a key engineering group. I think they will only see opportunity… upside working with a half-billion dollar Company."

As the flight continued, Don and JB talked about Don's plans for travel after his transition out of the Company.

Executive Team: Jackson Headquarters

Overall, Day One was somewhat chaotic, but a well-versed, confident executive team either responded to all queries immediately, or documented concerns and promised additional information within the week.

The team's long day spanned three shifts. The agenda for the second and third shift was identical – video introduction with Elton and Don, Q&A, walking around to meet with individuals and personally responding to emails and phone calls.

About 2 hours after the beginning of each shift, the executive team gathered to share observations and unanticipated questions.

At 11 PM the local executive team gathered in the common area to summarize the day, while those on the road participated through videoconference. After a one-hour debriefing, Elton summarized the day. "Wow – we've had a great start to this integration. Some of the questions raised have surprised me, but I've learned through several of these integrations that surprises are the norm. I'm pleased and proud of the way you folks have handled the day's events. On the one side, I apologize for the long day, but I'm sure that you can now appreciate that the preplanning completed saved us considerable strife.

As you know, we've had some challenges in the Berkshire operations, so we've adjusted the schedule a bit and Stephen and I will be traveling to Berkshire tomorrow afternoon for Q&A.

We'll gather this team for a meeting tomorrow afternoon at 5 PM - after our session with the Berkshire folks. Let's keep listening to all our constituents and don't be shy about calling Jaclyn or me if something warrants the call.

Thank you for your efforts. And remember, we've got $60 million on the line. Let's keep the focus on how can we best achieve a good integration.

As the call concluded, the team breathed a sigh of relief at the completion of a long day. Offices were somewhat disheveled and cluttered after the flurry of activity throughout the day. Completely exhausted from a challenging but successful day, they quietly migrated to the parking lot to return to their home/hotel.

Day Two

Morning alarm clocks raged in what seemed to be minutes, calling each executive to another day.

After the traditional morning rituals, the Jackson executives seemed to automatically drift to the kitchen for life-giving coffee. Margaret often pranked the team with her unique purchases, and today she brought in a pound of Death Wish coffee.

Quick to recognize the unusual label, Allison queried with a smile, " Do we need to test this for toxicity before we consume?"

"No need to be concerned. While Death Wish, roasted Robusta coffee beans, reportedly has one of the highest concentrations of caffeine on the market, it won't kill us, but I can guarantee that we'll be buzzing around the office like fleas in the dog pound."

After a hearty laugh, they quietly discussed some of the challenges ahead.

Allison mentioned that her lab folks seemed content with the discussion yesterday. There didn't seem to be any undue anxiety, but she would continue to informally meet with the teams. She also had a call in to Jason at Berkshire, just to touch base.

"Allison, have you personally talked to your European team?"

"No – I can't believe I let that slip. While the webcast included both European R&D and Sales, I haven't given it the personal touch. I better ping Stephen as well."

"Here's something that popped up about 4 AM this morning. Antonio DeSteffano, the VP of Regulatory Affairs in the UK dropped me an email. He suggested that we have a conference call around 10 AM. I'll bet that might be his topic – yes, of course the personal touch. At first I was concerned that he was a work fanatic, but then I realized that it wasn't 4 AM, but around 10 AM our time. This 6+- hour time zone difference could be interesting. Any thoughts Margaret?"

"I'm smiling. This could be one of the globalization challenges that we get to enjoy. At least he wanted to schedule the meeting for 10 AM EST – that's, what is it, 4 PM his time. Glad that he recognized the time zone difference. The 6-hour time difference could be new territory for him as well. I've got to run – meeting with the benefits people shortly."

It seems that each executive knew the benefit of communications, and each would be meeting informally with their teams, constantly searching for any concerns about the merger.

Margaret pulled up the internal website with questions and issues. Overnight there were 5 additions to the open question list.

1. How will my tenure with the Company be determined – as a Berkshire employee, will I get credit for my time on the job even though I'm new to the combined organization? Berkshire Mfg.
2. It seems that now that I'm working for Newco my health care deductibles will begin at zero. That will cost me hundreds of dollars. That doesn't seem fair. Berkshire Mfg.
3. Jackson sells high-end products. We sell commodities by comparison. Will the sales force be eliminated? Berkshire Telemarketing.
4. I'm in Berkshire finance. Will the finance function be consolidated to Jackson? Will I have to relocate? Berkshire Sales.
5. I'm in nanotech research-UK. Will I have to relocate to the US? Or will I lose my job?

As Margaret reviewed the questions, she was surprised that Berkshire and the UK were the source of the questions. She had expected more concern from the Jackson folks. She routed all questions to the executive team with a note that requested written responses by 10 AM. This would allow all to understand the responses and comment so that formal responses could be posted to the website by noon.

When JB received her email on his phone at breakfast, he sighed, "…Can't believe the tight timetable… I'll be in meetings with Don and Atlanta until noon. Since the questions are Berkshire and Europe, I don't have to respond by 10 AM, but I'll have to review & comment on the responses by noon. It's truly crunch time."

He looked across the table at Don and said, "We've just gotten a compressed schedule.

So let's shift gears. I really don't expect too much challenge from Atlanta Engineering. They actually may see this as a positive. I've sensitized them a bit to the transaction, without full disclosure so far."

"OK, JB, let's get on the move."

Berkshire Visit: Elton and Stephen

Winds were gusty and variable and the flight in the King Air was very unpleasant, occupants seat-belted throughout the flight. The pilots were not concerned, explaining that the King Air was one of the safest, most proven airframes in the world. Unfortunately that did not make Elton more comfortable.

After their Boston arrival, they rented a car to drive to Berkshire. The bad weather started to pound rain on Boston causing massive traffic jams and delays throughout the area. The expected 1 hour cushion for debriefing Jason was now compressed to about 20 minutes.

Upon their arrival, Jason escorted them to the conference room – set up with refreshments of sodas, coffee and granola bars.

"How was your flight, Elton? Good to see you. And it's a pleasure to finally meet you Stephen. How would you like to proceed?"

Deferring to Elton, Stephen remained silent.

"Jason, we appreciate that you set up the all-employee meeting on such short notice. Can you brief us about the current situation?"

For the next ten minutes, Jason highlighted the main concerns that surfaced yesterday.

"Anything else happening behind the curtain, Jason?" Stephen asked.

"Things have gotten a bit testy during the past few months. Several area businesses have started to poach our best technical workers. They're just making absurd offers that we haven't been able to match. That's causing overtime, missed schedules, and now that we have a new boss – that is Jackson – the folks are concerned about layoffs. I've been aware of their compensation concerns, but yesterday's announcements put them over the edge."

Elton nodded agreement with Jason's assessment. "Ok folks, let's get in front of the team and hear what they have to say."

The cafeteria set-up was ready for the all-employee meeting. Elton would use the slides prepared for yesterday's integration launch to frame the meeting for the first 15 minutes. He planned to listen for the remaining 45 minutes.

As they entered the cafeteria, he turned and asked Stephen, "Can you keep track of the questions so we have a good record? I'm not just interested in the exact question, as much as your interpretation of what they are really looking for – some of your executive insight."

Elton was a master in front of this crowd. His demeanor and British accent resonated well with most of the team. As he completed his final slide, he extended his hands and said, "OK – that's all I've got to say. What's on your mind folks?"

A burly bearded gentleman in camouflage shirt raised his hand. Once acknowledged, he stood and said, "Mr. Elton, I've worked at Berkshire for 18 years. A few years ago, Hagstrom bought us. I didn't like it, but had no choice. Now I hear that we'll be reporting to another Company. I feel like a piece of meat in the market that gets pushed around to the highest bidder. What's my future look like? It's kind of scary for me."

"Sir, thank you for your question. I understand how frightening it can be to suddenly discover that someone else owns the Company. Well, it's still Hagstrom that owns you, but for tax reasons, we've built in another – I'll call it Newco – as the owner. The Hagstrom policies will continue, but our plan is that with the Jackson acquisition, we'll be able to grow the Hagstrom Company faster.

We've got some specialties in the UK – nanotech and metallurgy – that when combined with the Jackson folks will launch us into entirely new product areas. So I understand your concerns and ask you to be patient with us. We believe it is the best move for all the Hagstrom employees."

A young lady – a 20 something – stood and awaited acknowledgment. "Yes ma'am. What's your question?"

"I just graduated with a BS in Mechanical Engineering. This is my first job, and I want a career with a Company that appreciates my accomplishments. As a woman, I'd like to understand what my career would look like while I'm at Berkshire-Jackson-Hagstrom?"

"Thank you young lady. You know, truthfully gender doesn't matter. Although we're a global Company, we're small enough where we cannot afford to have talented people remain unchallenged. We're small enough that when we see intelligent, motivated and dedicated people, we can't afford not to challenge them –

and compensate them accordingly. In a competitive world, these great people will leave us if we don't help them grow in their careers.

So, let me assure you that whether you are a welder, admin assistant, or director of manufacturing operations, regardless of gender, we will provide you, to the best of our ability, with the challenge and opportunity that you deserve. One reason that we acquired Jackson is to make sure that we have the opportunities for our team members to grow."

A bespectacled gentleman in the back row raised his hand.

"Sir, during the past few months, several of our best engineers left for a company around the corner. The other company outbid our compensation schedule. Can you comment?"

"Thank you for your question. Our goal is to provide fair compensation to all our employees. Now, I may be wrong, but I consider compensation to include many things other than just a weekly paycheck. I do not know the specific details of Berkshire's compensation and benefits, but when I think of compensation, I consider performance bonuses, tuition reimbursements, health care coverage and employee contributions, maternity & paternity leave and other things.

Another soft factor is career growth. So let's think about the young lady's question. Our commitment is to ensure that we provide career growth opportunities to those capable and willing to invest in their careers. Without aggressive Company growth, we won't be able to provide that opportunity to everyone when they are ready. At that point, rather than wait for the opportunity, team members leave Hagstrom. I'll apologize, but sometimes we just can't match people's growth capability. But in the meantime, we'll do our best to provide fair compensation to all."

The meeting continued for the remaining 20 minutes, with Jason interpreting and noting the questions.

"And to wrap up this meeting, we'll document your questions and my answers on the integration Q&A website for your reference.

Thank you for your help to grow Hagstrom in a very competitive global environment."

The crowd dispersed and Elton, Stephen and Jason huddled to compare impressions of the meeting. The consensus was that the meeting was a success, effectively covering all the issues raised. It also seemed that the employees appreciated that Elton took the time to meet with them.

"I've found that when there are concerns about a merger it is best to stand in front of the employees, explain the logic, and truthfully explain the expected impact on them and their operations. Sometimes they ask questions that I can't answer, and then it's up to me to get them answers. I'll commit to a time for resolution, and I meet that commitment. I hate the corporate speak where I talk for 5 minutes and don't say anything. Employees can see right through that nonsense."

After a few minutes of discussion, Elton suggested that they all meet for dinner and discussion. He disliked missing an opportunity for casual discussion outside the office.

The seafood restaurant was perfect for a quiet cocktail, dinner and discussion. After ordering a round of drinks from Stephanie, an energetic 20's waitress, Elton took a deep breath, smiled and said, "Glad this day is over. Two tough customers and a work force with some serious questions." The drinks arrived, and Elton was the first to offer a simple toast, "Cheers gents."

After taking a long sip of the scotch, he smiled and said, "So what's up folks. Any thoughts?" Elton enjoyed tossing such an open-ended question to his executives. He hoped that the setting and broad question would encourage their candor.

"So Elton, our flight today was from the dark side of hell. Today's schedule was a gut-buster, and the initial tension at the employee meeting was overpowering. But, I wouldn't change this for the world's gold supply."

"So Stephen, I didn't see masochist in your CV."

They all laughed. Jason raised his glass, "To another successful meeting. And thank you for coming to Berkshire on such short notice."

The meal proceeded with much small talk discussing Stephen's triathlons, Jason's penchant for fly-fishing, and Elton's interest in the history of UK governance. During the next hour+, a delicious meal of fresh-trapped lobster, salad, sautéed vegetables and overstuffed, twice-baked potatoes mellowed each executive.

Jason suggested that they conclude the successful day with a single-malt scotch. "Three Lagavulin's please."

After a sip of the smoky liquid, Elton relaxed in his chair, smiled and said, "Jason, how are things going? Anything that you'd like to discuss?"

Stephen felt a bit uncomfortable discussing Berkshires skeletons – if any. He moved nervously in his seat.

Recognizing Stephen's movement, Elton volunteered, " Gentlemen, we're all in this Company together. We succeed together, or we fail together. I've made a big bet with this acquisition. I've used a lot of political capital to make this happen. So let's talk about stuff – whatever that means."

Jason leaned in, his glass resting on the table while he gently turned the glass.

"The last few weeks have been very difficult. I've lost some key people to the 'highest bidder' in the market. I just haven't been able to grow this Company fast enough to accommodate the team that I've assembled. Sort of what you described earlier, Elton. The folks that I lost are extraordinary. The rest of the team knows they were great, and are wondering, 'why should we stay?'"

"Have we tested our compensation recently? Are we in the game locally?"

"Yes Elton, we completed a compensation survey – the kind that considers everything such as health coverage & contributions etc. We're definitely in the top quartile."

"So maybe it's a good thing that we acquired Jackson. Is there any way we can generate some local enthusiasm because of the acquisition?"

Stephen looked at Elton and said, "I know that I'm not familiar with the Berkshire operation, but one thing that we've tried to do at Jackson is stir up people's careers. So when it looks like someone is getting a bit stale – kind of in a rut – we create a project that forces him or her to develop. So we might ask someone in accounting to help the marketing folks complete a pricing analysis. They still must complete their day job, but we get them out of the rut, let them work with another discipline, and generate some cross-functional awareness."

Elton sipped his scotch, awaiting some kind of response from Jason. A long pause – a dead space – is often filled when people get uncomfortable.

"So do you think that I should have some of the accounting folks do some pricing analysis?" Jason suggested.

Jason and Stephen were now engaged in problem solving. "That's a possible solution, but the real answer is to identify those at risk of leaving and tone up their careers."

They continued to analyze and discuss. After a few minutes, Elton interrupted, "We've just acquired a US operation, and we're a European Company. Why don't we have a management-training program that also considers global projects? Let's have some of the manufacturing folks from Jackson participate in a manufacturing project in the UK? And perhaps we should have the finance folks help us with systems installations in Europe? Or maybe have the marketing folks prepare a competitive analysis in France. We're now truly a global operation, so let's act like it."

Elton enjoyed dropping such drastic solutions into a conversation to demonstrate the Corporation's commitment to career growth.

"When I think of sharing projects like this, I think of the cost of losing a key employee. Do you know how much it costs us to lose an employee? Perhaps 6+- month's of salary costs, when we consider relocation search fees, lost productivity etc. And when we hire someone, there is always a risk that they truly won't fit in the organization. I like the way you folks have challenged the system. So let's think like a global Company and help this Company grow."

Elton continued, "Guys, I'm tired and I've got an early morning call to the UK to give them a progress report on the acquisition. Let's get out of here."

Stephen and Elton left for the hotel, while Jason drove home.

At breakfast the next morning, Elton summarized the acquisition status. "Here's a summary of our progress. Any thoughts?"

1. Day One successful. Initial financial controls established and functional.
2. Data security in place.
3. Employee meetings completed on schedule, despite the failed recording of the first meeting.
4. Meetings with key customers and vendors complete. No major issues.
5. Website for Q&A up and running.
6. Responses to all questions prepared and released.

7. Unscheduled meeting at Berkshire successfully completed.
8. Potential JV with Chicago hospital explored.
9. Executive teams fully functional.

Elton gave Stephen the note and asked, "So what do you think of our Day One? Any thoughts about point #8?"

"I think that you got everything. And of course, I like #8." Stephen was pleased with the compliment that seemed to acknowledge Elton's management style... modest, well considered risk taking without excess delay.

The team met on the afternoon of Day 3, to debrief.

Overall the day went according to plan. While there were problems with some processes – passwords, cash management, employee payroll for new employees etc. – there were no problems to indicate that the transaction would fail.

The team's response to problems, elevating issues to the correct level immediately, conveyed confidence and skill within the entire organization – Jackson, Berkshire and Europe.

The website listing problems allowed anonymous postings so that employees could comfortably raise issues.

For the next 10 business days, the team would meet daily – in person or by video at 2 PM - to raise issues. The 2 PM meeting allowed time for research of issues, and a preliminary response before the end of the day.

One serious problem occurred when payroll for 15 employees, out on disability/illness, were not paid. Given the turmoil of the closing, the Company did not have a plan to ensure that these employees' time sheets were prepared and submitted for payroll. Jennifer, the payroll admin, noticed that those on sick leave/disability didn't have paycheck notifications –the pay-stub informing them of the amount direct deposited in their account. She immediately notified Margaret, who created non-payroll checks for those individuals. She overnighted the checks to their homes, with a note of apology.

Also, the Company credit cards did not work for 3 of the sales reps that were trying to check out of a hotel in Philadelphia. Stephen got the call from the panicked reps. He asked to be transferred to the desk clerk, gave them his Amex credit card number, and let the reps go on their way. He also arranged for an Uber, using his credit card to reduce the reps' out-of-pocket travel costs.

Although these failures were personal crises for those individuals, the Company immediately resolved the problems to minimize the personal impact.

The VP's each assembled their teams to review the Deal Summary and confirm commitments to the Deal strategy and goals. JB's function was the most complex and demanding. JB and Jaclyn developed an agenda and identified the team to plan the integration.

Team Meeting: JB & Operations/Logistics/Engineering/QA

During the first week, JB and Jaclyn reviewed the Deal Summary to brainstorm the best approach to his planning meetings. His team included Berkshire manufacturing operations, the US Jackson team, and associates from the European operations. His headcount responsibility totaled about 90 people.

His delicate challenge was to include those that could accept responsibility and execute plans that achieve the Company goals, regardless of their position in the Company. Jaclyn suggested several European participants that met the criteria.

Within the Jackson group, he would include the Directors – QA, Engineering, Inventory Control, Shipping/Logistics, and the Fab-3 manager. The managers in Buffing, and Fab-1 and Fab-2 would not be invited to the planning meeting. He and Jaclyn made the selection based on historical performance and growth capacity.

Once the selection was made, JB personally met with those excluded. These were difficult discussions, since the stigma of being left out would initially make those excluded very uncomfortable. JB explained the rationale, and encouraged them to continue to excel in their jobs for future growth opportunities, now that Jackson was part of a global Company.

JB and Jaclyn developed a brief agenda that focused on JB's key deliverables – reduced manufacturing costs, lower inventories and European product launches.

"Jaclyn, my impression is that we've scrubbed our inventories clean and I don't see much potential improvement. I'm also concerned about manufacturing cost reduction. Sure, I can get tougher on some of our policies – reordering levels, pushing inventory back on our suppliers for quicker JIT deliveries – but we've already done a lot of that. If we push too hard, we could end up having strained relationships, and in the long run, have delivery problems.

Jaclyn, I think I need some creative help. Do you have any suggestions?"

"I understand your concerns, JB. We don't want to destroy relationships, but we do want those improvements. In addition to the list we've already developed, let's add the logistics VP from Europe. Although you won't be working with him directly very often, he's done a great job in our European business.

He's good at facilitation, so let's get him on the agenda for an hour to generate some solutions."

JB launched his 1-day conference the following week. Jaclyn coached JB behind the scenes to ensure that he could accomplish his goals and that all participants knew he was responsible for the success of the manufacturing and logistics integration.

In addition to Jean-Claude, the European logistics expert, Jaclyn suggested that they engage a 'lean-business' consultant for a 1-hour developmental session during the conference.

The team at the meeting was enthusiastic and focused on problem solving. JB, Jean-Claude, and the outside consultant challenged the team to develop solutions and timetables that would accomplish the objectives. JB was pleasantly surprised that, not only did they develop plans to achieve the merger objectives, they created a parking lot list of potential improvements that would reduce capital requirements, and accelerate US and European product commercialization.

Week 2

While the number of major integration challenges decreased during week two, there were many legal, banking and administrative issues to resolve.

During the week many vendors needed special attention since Jackson Manufacturing had unpaid bills.   Hagstrom bought the assets and, although the vendors knew and trusted Don and the Jackson team, they were concerned about the Jackson account collectability.

Numerous phone calls to Cynthia's accounts payable (A/P) staff cleared most of the concerns. Unfortunately, some calls were harsh and unpleasant for the A/P staff. Cynthia's calendar overflowed with calls from concerned vendors.

In addition to the collection calls, vendors and customers frequently required new applications and valid credentials to become 'approved' vendors and customers. Some of the applications demanded multi-year historical financials, which weren't available from Newco. Interim Hagstrom guarantees were filed, but the delays interrupted the supply chain and timely sales order processing.

Frank and his legal staff were overwhelmed with requests for legal documentation clarifying the purchase transaction and the status of the new company. Simple things like vehicle and office equipment leases were a nuisance, since Jackson leased the equipment, but Newco employees used the equipment. Near term equipment renewals were no longer simple transactions, since historical financials for Newco were not available.

The Company also needed bridging agreements for property and casualty, liability, directors and officers insurance, and other miscellaneous assurances.

Federal and state permits issued to Jackson were technically no longer valid, since all business activity was now completed on behalf of Newco. The attorneys issued legal assurances and agreements to minimize risks.

In-process international sales using letters of credit and other financial instruments, and federal declarations related to pending shipments were reviewed and when necessary revised to reflect the sale.

Unfortunately the Newco banking relationships were not easily implemented. While Newco had an established credit line and sufficient cash on hand, electronic fund transfers (EFT) were disabled since proper 'dual authorization' officer approvals were not on file in the bank's transaction services group. The Company could not process EFT's.

Since the payroll transfer EFT could not be processed, Cynthia received an email notification that there were insufficient funds for the first payroll. After several urgent calls to bank officials, Cynthia resolved the error.

Newco Workshop

Throughout this second week, the team also focused on the upcoming Newco executive workshop. Jaclyn and Elton knew that before the closing, Jackson's executives' responsibility was to Don. Now that the closing was complete, their role was to work for Newco.

Jaclyn prepared the agenda that was designed to update the team on any major issues, and then have a general discussion about the transaction objectives and overall timeline.

Newco
1st Integration Meeting - Agenda

Time	Description	Responsible
8:00-8:15	Introduction & Summary/Welcome	Elton
8:15-8:30	Transaction Overview	Jaclyn
	Functional Updates	
8:30-9:30	Finance/IT	Cynthia
9:30-10:30	Sales/Marketing	Stephen
10:30-10:45	Break	
10:45-11:45	HR	Margaret
11:45-12:45	R&D	Allison
12:45-1:30	Lunch	
1:30-2:30	Manufacturing	JB
2:30-3:30	Legal Matters	Frank
3:30-4:00	Break	
4:00-5:30	General Discussion	Jaclyn
5:30-6:00	Final Remarks	Elton

Elton's welcoming remarks would be upbeat based on the transaction-to-date results. Whenever possible he liked to focus on the positive events.

Jaclyn's transaction overview would summarize the strategic objectives of the transaction, and major issues identified thus far. This would be a positive discussion, although several variances have already been identified.

The Newco executives were allotted 1 hour to summarize their activities during the past 10 days, highlighting deliverables accomplished thus far. They also presented a more detailed implementation schedule of activities during the next 6 months. These summaries included the estimated financial impact when known. The functional plans included deliverables, and would be in enough detail to identify conflicts with other areas.

Once each executive reviewed their detailed integration plan, Jaclyn would facilitate the integration discussion to identify unforeseen conflicts. For example, she already noted that Stephen wanted to fully integrate the global sales force into the CRM system within the first 30 days. This would be nearly impossible, since ERP systems were planned to be integrated within the first 60 days, requiring all the IT resources.

In this first meeting, executives could discuss matters that may not have been appropriate pre-closing. While Elton and Jaclyn expected nuanced, but truthful, answers during due diligence, the executive team now worked for Hagstrom. Their role was now to create value for the new owners.

Key European executives and the Berkshire COO, Jason, were attending this meeting, since the integration could affect their organizations. The Jackson executives were driving the meeting, and the European and Berkshire executives were attending to validate and discuss any coordination issues that may arise.

Elton welcomed the employees to Newco and turned the meeting over to Jaclyn.

"Welcome to our first formal planning session as employees of Newco. It is our honor to work with you to review the detailed plans that will launch Newco to new levels of global performance.

Each of you has a welcome gift."

As the executives opened their package, the scent of fine Italian leather embraced them.

"You'll note the monogrammed leather portfolio that we hope you will use and enjoy for many years. You may have to trade them among yourselves, since we didn't have assigned seating. Hey Cynthia, do you have JB's portfolio?"

After a few minutes of informal communication, Jaclyn began, "Today we'd like to discuss the *To Be* state that we intend to achieve during the next three years. We know that pre-closing, your role was to support the sale of the business. As of 2 weeks ago, you are one of us… and the first thing we'd like to do is reconfirm our goals, with a brief discussion about how we will achieve the growth.

During our previous discussions, we explored broad activities and goals. Yes, we said let's integrate the ERP system in 2 months. Today, we'd like to reconfirm those goals and get your personal commitments about how we will achieve the broad financial targets. We understand that as we discussed some of our objectives during the pre-close meetings, we weren't focused on probabilities – for example, a likely deliverable versus a certain deliverable.

Today, we'd like to confirm probabilities. In fact, we'd like to get to the 90% certainty level. So as we review the details, let's think in terms of 90% - and if there is a reason that we can't commit to 90% likelihood, let's understand the constraint and try to eliminate the concern."

Jackson executives reviewed their "As Is & To Be" functional plan. These were high level plans supported by detailed project plans for each department's activities. In some cases, the executive team needed to better understand the linkage of the detailed plans among the functions.

There were conflicts of resource requirements and deliverables. Some were sorted out immediately, while others moved to the 'parking lot' to be resolved later.

With that, Jaclyn reviewed the details of the *To Be* state of the Company. In addition to the brief Deal Summary, she included many of the enhancements that the executive team discussed during the past few weeks.

During the next few hours, she challenged the team to fully explore any items that may be difficult to achieve, or raise any items that may require additional resources to reach the *To Be* state.

The first month after closing was stable and overall on plan, although several times chaos erupted. When a problem arose, the executive team managed using the integration principles as a guide:

- Every issue gets resolved ASAP.
- Every issue is logged and managed on the integration database so that the entire team is aware of issues and their resolution.
- The executive team is responsible for walking around their respective areas of responsibility to maintain close and open communications with their constituents.

After the first two weeks, mandatory weekly Executive Team integration meetings were scheduled for Tuesday morning, 7:30 AM.

The weekly executive team meetings often raised sensitive topics that, historically, may have been avoided to maintain good team working relationships. Now, under the Hagstrom ownership, it was clear that the team's role was to improve Hagstrom's value – without consideration to customary fiscal constraints. The team frequently raised opportunities that would have been avoided for financial reasons by Jackson, but were acceptable by Hagstrom. Although only about one-third of the opportunities identified were initially accepted, the remainder were logged into a database for future execution.

Most issues discussed at the weekly integration meetings were limited to exceptions to the schedule.

Elton believed that a well-constructed plan should be monitored for significant variances, but otherwise should generally be left alone. The executive team was responsible for execution, and Elton ensured that they felt the full responsibility of implementation.

At the end of each meeting he asked the same question. "Is there anything else that we should discuss to ensure the successful integration of the Jackson Manufacturing operation?"

Two weeks after the close, Jaclyn and the executive team validated the initial Deal Summary including major deliverables and financial projections used to justify the transaction.

Jaclyn prepared an integration summary report to the Hagstrom Board, 2 days after month end. The report included progress compared to the original integration plan, a summary of major variances from plan (activity and financial) including reason/resolution for variance.

During the two weeks post closing, the executive team concentrated on communications – listening and providing quick, well-thought-out responses to questions raised by constituents.

Deal Summary Validation

The transaction was based on several critical items:

TRANSACTION SUMARY / NOTES: / **SUMMARY CASH FLOW:**   YEAR

Purchase Price:	Millions US $
Cash	45.0
Stock Val	
Debt Assumed	5.0
Subtotal	**50.0**
Earnout	10.0
Total Cost	**60.0**

This Acquisition Will:
1. Increase Jackson Sales through expanded US Dist of   **A**
2. Focus JAX R&D on critical products; rationalize company prod line; expand Titanium   **B**
3. Sales synergies-broaden global distribution.   **C**
4. Establish Hagstrom US base.   **D**
5. Reduce Mfg costs.   **E**
6. Improve inventory turns by 2.
7. Reduce DSO by 2 days.

Year One Objectives:
1. JAX sales force to include all Hagstrom products.
2. Eliminate distributors in Central America.
3. Rationalize Corp. product portfolio.
4. Accelerate R&D Titanium & launch new products
5. Add 3rd shift to JAX manufacturing
6. Add JAX products to global distribution.

SUMMARY CASH FLOW:

Description	Resp	1	2	3
			(Millions US $)	
Baseline		12.0	14.0	15.0
Reduce DSO	Cynthia	2.0		
Inventory Turns	JB	0.5	1.0	
Sales Synergy	Stephen	6.0	7.0	7.0
COGS Reduction	JB	1.0	2.0	2.0
R&D Rationalization	Allison	1.0	1.5	1.5
Total		**22.5**	**25.5**	**25.5**

Hagstrom US Operations *(Year 1)*

	Baseline	Baseline	Synergy	Total
Sales	45.0	6.0	7.0	58.0
Gross Profit	30.0	4.0	5.0	39.0
SG&A				
Marketing			2.0	2.0
R&D				
Duplicate			1.0	1.0
Incremental			1.5	1.5
IT Reduction			0.5	0.5
Total SG&A			5.0	5.0
Pretax Profit Impact	30.0	4.0	10.0	44.0

NOTES:
A= Sales will increase due to broader distribution nationwide rather than
B= Rationalizing R&D will eliminate Corp duplicate projects and focus on
C = Sales synergies due to selling US products in EU, and EU products in US.
D = Hagstrom will now have a major presence in the US.
E = Upgrading manufacturing equipment and introducing new metals technology will reduce manufacturing costs.

The team concentrated on 'Year One Objectives:"

1. Jackson will integrate all FDA approved Hagstrom products into the product line. The integration team assessed each item, considering the first year timeline. Detailed plans were developed for approved product launches in the US

and throughout Europe. While this was a daunting task to be completed during the first year, the team believed that the approved product launches could be completed as scheduled by using outside consultants. The original integration plan did not consider using consultants, resulting with a $150,000 variance to the plan. The contingency pool was adjusted to reflect this variance. Estimated sales would reach the commitment.

2. Newco will eliminate all distributors in South America. Eliminating the Latin American distributors was more of a challenge than initially believed. The Panamanian Distributor decided to appeal to the local government to assess financial penalties against Hagstrom, a global half-billion company. They believed that Hagstrom would be willing to pay a bounty to discontinue the contract. Rather than pay an exorbitant penalty, Hagstrom decided to let the Panama contract expire, without financial penalty. Although the Company 1st year goal was not achieved, there would be little financial impact. The Panama Distributor would be an administrative nuisance for the next 12 months, until contract expiration. The contract would not be renewed.

3. Newco will rationalize the US product portfolio. Product rationalization would

extend through 18 months rather than the planned 12 months to minimize the financial impact. Since no adverse financial impact was included in the deal summary, this was only a timing issue.

4. R&D will accelerate development and launch new Titanium products. R&D assessed the progress against the original, conservative launch plan. By adding additional analysts, R&D now expected to launch within 4 months of the acquisition – an improvement of about 6 months. The additional analysis would cost $200,000, but the early launch would add gross profit of $800,000 during the first year. Analyst spending was approved and the net affect of $600,000 was included in the contingency summary.

5. Newco will add a 3rd shift to production. Based on the timely global launch of European/US products, the Company expected to be able to staff the third shift. Although the schedule required a 3rd shift to be added within 3 months, the third shift would not be added until the fifth month. The lost gross margin of $100,000 was reflected in the contingency summary.

6. Hagstrom US will add Euro approved products to their European sales lines. The original plan to launch European product in the US remained at the

original goal until Stephen and Allison could travel to Europe to develop a preliminary detailed plan.

The team also identified the need for an additional multi-axis machine tool that was not considered in the integration plan. As they completed the detailed integration planning, it was best to upgrade to a multi-axis machine. The initial negative cash flow impact totaled $400,000, with a payback of 18 months.

Cynthia and Jaclyn prepared the summary report. The team was concerned about Elton's response, since all tasks were not to be completed within the initial integration timetable.

At the conclusion of the report, Elton's broad smile confirmed his satisfaction. "Congratulations to all. While we have missed a couple of our estimates, you've done one hell-of-a-job. My gosh, this is superb."

The team, relieved at his response, settled comfortably in their seats.

Elton continued, "Folks, we at Hagstrom HQ recognized you as a team of pros, and in the first few weeks, you've proven that 100%. So far, this has been an excellent start. Jaclyn, is it next week we're scheduled to update the entire 6-month timeline for the integration?"

"Elton, we've run into a few glitches, so we'll postpone the review for 10 days. We'll miss the original schedule by a few days, but I think it's the smart thing to do."

"That's a deal, Jaclyn. Thank you folks for your dedicated efforts on this acquisition and integration. As always, if you need me, don't hesitate to call. Shall we say meeting adjourned?"

During the next 2 weeks, the executive team reviewed, assessed and tested their assumptions for every step of the detailed 6-month integration plan.

At Jaclyn's insistence, their Tuesday meetings continued on schedule, although some required video attendance by those traveling. It was even more challenging for Allison and Stephen, since they traveled to Europe to meet with the R&D and Sales/Marketing teams.

Allison Fly-over

Allison scheduled a 5-day trip to meet the European HQ and the R&D team. Her trip was compact with two days of travel, and only 3 days on site. Her first stop was at the Company headquarters to meet the team responsible for regulatory affairs, since she would coordinate all US activities through the Hagstrom central organization.

Hugo Fitzworthy, a barrister by trade, was a slight man with bookish appearance. He startled her with his strong baritone speech, but was very pleasant, focused and intense.

Her impression was that he was extremely conscientious, and a very practical executive. Although a barrister, his initial university training included an advanced chemistry degree, followed by legal training.

She particularly enjoyed meeting him because of his dry sense of humor. Yes, he understood his corporate responsibility, but he also understood that there is more to life than 60-hour workweeks. In his spare time, he worked with an amateur theater group.

This would be his first transatlantic responsibility, since previously Berkshire engaged consultants for any US regulatory support, and the Berkshire product line was low risk with little product development.

After an hour, she understood that he was equally apprehensive about his global responsibility. Yes, she could easily team with Hugo and they formed an informal pact to succeed through routine communications and coordinated business goals. It was also useful to have such a comrade in the headquarters that shared her approach to business.

Next, she met with Jeremy Fitzworthy, the CFO, who was a traditional green-eye-shade stereotype – numbers were his life – always shuffling papers filled with spreadsheets. His office was cluttered and in disarray, with stacks of financial statements allowing little workspace. Allison didn't understand how such a narrowly focused person could work successfully with Elton and Jaclyn, who had many outside interests, were more personable and creative. During their discussion, she realized that he was somewhat of a technical wizard who knew every number in the Company's history. His role was that of historian and quantitative genius – neither creative nor business beyond the numbers. Thinking back to discussions with Elton and Jaclyn, it became clear that they were the creative side of the executive team, and they needed someone with Hugo's talent. Unfortunately Allison had never worked with such a finance person. This working relationship would require effort to be successful. She promised herself that she would share her observations with Cynthia.

Her next stop was the R&D facility. These folks anxiously awaited their new boss. Upon arrival, the team had a "Welcome Allison" sign in the lobby. The receptionist was excited to meet the new R&D leader, and with a strong accent, welcomed Allison.

"Please be seated until I can get Reginald, our local chief scientist. Would you like a tea?"

Allison declined the tea, and mentioned that she would catch up on some emails while she waited.

A few minutes later, a toothy Reginald appeared, and with his long strides across the lobby, he made a quick entrance. "Welcome

Allison. So good to meet you after the phone calls. Please join me in the conference room."

It was difficult for Allison to keep up with Reginald's quick pace. After the *sprint* to the conference room, she was somewhat out of breath.

Reginald apologized for his speedy pace. "I'm sorry for the jog. I often forget that I'm nearly 2 meters tall, and, well, I consider walking sort of non-value transit time.

I've taken this opportunity for us to summarize our portfolio of R&D device projects. I've included the original approval documents, and the last 2 quarters' status reports. The Executive Summary is prioritized using two methods: first, prioritized based on 7-year payback of the projects, and secondly based on expected launch date. Of course, each of these criteria can change based on the development process.

Later this morning, we'll have lunch brought in so that you can meet the entire R&D team, and then you can have a select session with your device group. Since the R&D team is fairly compact, I wanted the entire team to meet with our US partner. The select session will allow you to become acquainted with your team.

I understand that you have asked for personal meetings with each of your direct reports. We'll get that scheduled later today, so that you have some time to get adjusted to the jet lag. Are you comfortable with these schedules?"

"That sounds great Reginald. I would like to return to the hotel early this afternoon … having arrived early this morning has been tough on me."

Reginald ordered some coffee and they began the review. Reginald volunteered, "Your team has never reported to an International boss. While I don't expect any major problems, they're a bit nervous."

"They're not the only one a bit apprehensive. We'll move cautiously and concentrate on the business tasks and see how things go."

Overall, Allison was impressed with their analysis and documentation for the in-process projects. Reginald's discussion about the personalities in the device group was very helpful. Surprisingly, they were all women.

Reginald summarized, "This international responsibility is new for us, and we have some financial hurdles in our model. Dealing with the unknown means we should have a contingency fund – let's call it a placeholder until we get more information about our global operations. Elton and I can give you an overview of the operations, but that won't be enough to lock down performance objectives.

For now, I'll let you meet with your staff."

Allison enjoyed their first meeting. Later that day, she met with the device R&D leadership team.

Stephen just returned from Germany – pale, with dark circles under his eyes, the result of jet lag and a brutal trip.

"How are you holding up, Stephen?" Margaret was perpetually observing the health of the executive team.

"Always doing well, Margaret. This trip was a tough one. I had to let two reps go. It was tough for a few reasons. One is the emotional side of terminating employees. The other is the extraordinary financial impact on our financials.

I'm not overly concerned about the emotional impact, since we've given these employees several written warnings, provided weekly coaching and they just refused to get with the program. I was initially concerned that I wasn't communicating effectively with the German sales force, but 90% of the folks got the message and really delivered performance.

I'm guessing that the two *graduates* just didn't want to work for a US boss. It's a shame, but I tried.

Can you believe what it takes to terminate someone in Germany? More documentation required than to end the Korean War, and the cost – well let's say it was cheaper to land someone on the moon than to sever a German employee.

And yes, I'm exaggerating, but we've now got a two-fold P&L hit. The first is the year's severance pay – with full benefits – but the second, which is much more expensive - is the lost time in the market. I've had virtually no performance in those two territories for nearly 3 months. The other sales team members had to up their game to cover the shortfall from the two laggards.

I guess that is the value of teamwork. Interestingly, I was thinking there might be some blowback from the other team members about the termination. Not a word.

In fact, several of the team members cornered me and said, 'It's about time you figured out Josh and William were not doing their job.' I guess that what I've read in all those Human Resource articles is true. In a high performance Company, the workers know who the non-performers are, and they resent the fact that they have to carry the non-performers' shortfall as the Company strives to achieve its goals."

Margaret nodded agreement, and added, "And if you don't catch the problems early, non-performers will poison the entire organization. Others in the Company will ask themselves, 'Why bother busting my butt if non-performers are allowed to get paychecks?' I know that separations are no fun, Stephen, but you did the right thing."

"Well, I'm beat. I hope that today's meeting goes quickly."

Jaclyn entered the room and greeted Stephen. "How did the trip go for you?"

"Not a fun trip. Too short for a transatlantic crossing, but it had to be done."

"Yes, I heard that it went well, considering your objective. Feedback from the rest of the organization was that you handled the separation professionally, and the two individuals almost expected it. Now they are enjoying their one-year's severance package. … Sure not like here in the states. The 'at-will employment' is more of a performance mantra – get with it or get out. Welcome home, Stephen.

Folks let's get through this meeting so that we can get Stephen off to slumber land.

OK – here we are at week 12… we had 3 primary goals for the week.
1. Finalize integration of the European operation into the Hagstrom/Jackson CRM system;
2. Migrate the Berkshire accounting system to Jackson/Hagstrom;

3. Establish the performance management system of goals setting and review for all employees.

And believe me, Elton and I know that you have been working late hours to reach these goals, but when you look at why the timing was critical – well, we appreciate the efforts that you've put in.

So how'd we do?"

Cynthia spoke initially. "Just to give Stephen a bit of breathing room, I'll talk about the accounting system migration. Overall, we made great progress, but we didn't complete the task. As we dug into the historical details of the Berkshire system, we noticed that they upgraded the IT system 18 months ago, but didn't map history. As a result, we don't have a clear apples-to-apples performance trail for the past three years. We properly sized the equipment, trained all the personnel, ran parallel for about 4 weeks, and reconciled accounts. The mapping went well for all the current information – that is during the last 18 months – but before that, there were fewer accounts and financial information was a mess before they made the change.

I guess the disappointment is that we don't have the 3-year performance history that we'd like, but the system now works well – with a few minor exceptions that we are still resolving.

I'd put us at 90% complete, and we are fully functional."

"Ok Cynthia. That sounds good. Would you change anything about the process?"

"The only thing that would have been helpful is to have learned before the migration that account detail was lacking. We might have shortened the transition time had we known about that."

"Margaret, how's the performance management system working out?"

"My turn in the box? Ok. As you know, we have 5 employee levels … executive, directors, managers, supervisors, and individual contributors. We haven't been able to roll out the Performance Management (PM) system as we originally planned. The director level and we –the Executive team – are well on-board and fully functional. All managers and supervisors here at Hagstrom-Jackson have also been fully indoctrinated, and we are managing using the process.

But it took a lot more time than we expected to get the training and goals/objectives established. That pushed back the implementation schedule for the Berkshire team.

Once Margaret concluded her report, the other executives shared their progress against objectives. Overall, the integration was on track. The US and European teams worked well together by focusing on universally accepted goals.

2nd Hundred Days

After the first 100 days, the integration workload decreased significantly. Major governance controls had been implemented and become well established. Throughout the first 100 days, the continued to meet weekly, resolving any issues that arose.

Once the deal reached 100 days, integration meetings occurred bi-weekly since the number of concerns dwindled.

Allison and Stephen made monthly scheduled trips to Europe to manage their new organizations. JB made trips as required for technology transfer, related to the exchange of US and European products. Elton was particularly impressed with JB's grasp of managing in the International environment. JB quickly realized that he must delegate authority to subordinates and manage his environment differently.

He conducted weekly operations phone calls, monthly performance meetings, and task force meetings focused on technology transfers and new product launches.

When Margaret cashed out her options, the extra half-million dollars combined with her 401-K rollover distracted her from accomplishing her integration goals. Jaclyn met with Margaret at the Wine Bar to discuss her performance. They concluded that the international responsibility and travel were more an unpleasant responsibility than an enjoyable challenge.

In the end, Margaret decided to leave Jackson Manufacturing and seek a position with a local manufacturing company.

Integration Checklist

DAY ONE

1 The Executive Workshop - Framework

Overall, the integration/transition process includes three segments:

- o <u>Day One:</u> Activities that require immediate attention, such as compensation, benefits, cash management, insurance, contracts, communications, systems.
- o <u>First 100 days:</u> Confirm preliminary analysis and strategy developed before full access to the target company business and personnel. Early integration activities should concentrate on critical areas identified in the acquisition strategy.
- o <u>Second 100 days</u>: Continued plan execution, progress assessment versus the workshop goals defined, and reassessment of the overall strategy.

Conduct an Executive Workshop as soon as possible once the Due Diligence review is completed. Ideally, executives from both the acquirer and the target company should attend the workshop, although it is unlikely that the target company would allow its executives to begin thorough planning with the acquirer's executives until the deal is executed. Assemble key executives in the executive workshop to:

- o Confirm the acquisition objective, focus executive attention on the issues and broad plans for integration/transition, including reporting metrics;
- o Define a governance process to manage the integration/transition;
- o Identify and resolve conflicts in schedule and priorities among the functions;
- o During the workshop, executives will review planned activities and define priorities, define communications and

governance processes, and establish accountability for the transition team to deliver a completed project.

Workshop participants should include executives who represent the functional areas in the value chain for the companies involved in the transaction. Based on the team leader's judgment, the team should be composed of the best people, *not just the acquiring company executives*. The workshop leader will coordinate the meeting by first reviewing each participant's work prior to the workshop to better understand the issues, prioritize the agenda items based on importance, and facilitate the process.

The workshop agenda will require one-to-two days, depending on the deal size and complexity. During the first hour of the meeting, the facilitator will review the integration process rules, integration team organization structure, and the companies' current and "To Be" state. The "To Be" state will be time scaled to reflect major events, such as year-one Company goals.

Throughout the executive workshop, executives will review functional assessments and integration plans, share plans about how the activities will be coordinated among functions, and establish their vision for the *"To Be"* business. Executives will develop the integration master plan, measurable business goals including forecast P&Ls, Balance Sheets and Cash Flow, Capital spending, and other metrics unique to each transaction - i.e. headcount, sales per headcount, and production targets.

The executive workshop is not a process for the executives to develop their plans, but rather a process to review their assessments and functional plans - - *"As Is"* today, the projected *"To Be"* state, and high-level transition plans - - and coordinate major events among all the functions in all the companies. Before the workshop, each executive will develop and review the completed plans with their functional teams.

The facilitator will review the executives' plans before the workshop to understand each function's plans. After completing the one/two-day workshop, execution plans will be refined to reflect the group conclusions during the week following the workshop. The team will develop financial summaries and other metrics in the subsequent week. Executives will define reporting and future communications during the workshop. The workshop and outcomes should proceed as follows:

- o Facilitator to learn the deal 2-3 days in advance
- o Workshop activity: 1-2 days
- o Refine integration plans:1 week
- o Refine financial and metrics: 1 week
- o Execution: less than 1 year

The facilitator should become familiar with the deal elements, and all available background related to Due Diligence, business forecasts, issues and opportunities. This background will allow the facilitator to focus on the most important issues.

Deal complexity will determine the length of the workshop, but ideally, the workshop will never be longer than two days. If the integration is too complex to finish in a two-day workshop, have mini workshops in advance - e.g. with the source of complexity such as Manufacturing Operations - to narrow the issues.

Once the actual workshop is finished, functional executives often refine their plans as they have learned more about the transition priorities, as well as the costs and benefits of the overall transaction. The executives should review the adjustments with their functional teams to develop consensus about the revisions. This should be completed in the first week after the workshop.

The workshop facilitator should assemble the modified plans and update the deal summaries to reflect the current planning status. Ideally, changes made to early plans will be consistent with guidelines developed at the workshop, and another executive workshop will not be required. If extensive changes are made, the facilitator should schedule a brief meeting to gain consensus on new objectives.

During the workshop, each element of analysis and deliverable will be prepared based on information known pre-deal, since it is *unlikely* that a seller will allow full and complete access to all personnel, processes, customers and vendors. Once the deal is closed, first actions include validating all assumptions and plans after the buyer has full access to people and processes.

1.1 Facilitator review

The facilitator will review the overall transaction as a framework for the functional presentations. The high-level introduction will summarize key elements of the deal, costs, significant transition activity, and contingency plans. Later in the workshop, other executives will share their detailed functional plans to ensure a well-coordinated process.

1.1.1 Review/modify/confirm a high-level business model and financial goals

The facilitator will present the high-level business model that describes the current state and the proposed or "To Be" *state of the companies.* The introduction will establish a common understanding of the *"To Be"* state, identify reporting metrics that are significant to the business, such as gross margins, SG&A ratios, cash flows, and asset intensity. It will also help to identify obstacles in reaching the *"To Be"* state. Obstacles to completion should either be resolved, or managed using an open items summary. The high-level business model consists of two elements:

- **Structure:** The structure describes the companies' physical attributes at each location. For example, a company location will include functions such as sales operations, Customer Service, Human Resources and so forth, and a description of the facilities themselves.
- **Responsibilities:** Define the organization role at each location, separated between strategic leadership and tactical performance. Briefly outline the strategic and tactical requirements.

Once requirements for the high-level business model are defined, identify key personnel, organization structure, and business processes. The business model presents the acquisition's strategic goal. *Prepare the model using input from key executives. The overall model will be the framework that other executives use to demonstrate fit within the new strategy.* The business model will include the company description - - physical sites, number of employees, and key financial metrics, such as return on sales, ROI, growth expectations. The model will also include a broad description of how The business will operate, using a high-level organization chart and description of authority and responsibilities.

1.1.2   Confirm the keys to valuation

The facilitator will prepare the acquisition summary including the strategic goal, proforma financial statements and highlights, incremental integration costs, and critical success factors that will guide the integration/transition process.

Review and Present the Complete value chain

Workshop attendees will review the entire value chain to share their vision of the future Company. They will develop and approve the transition plans, and through the business plan review and coordination process, develop creative contingency plans to achieve acquisition goals. It is possible that one executive's plans will not be easily implemented. For example, the Vice President - Sales may require a fully implemented Customer Resource Management (CRM) package by the first quarter, but this may not be a feasible goal to the IT department. Problem solving capabilities of the best executives attending the workshop will develop innovative solutions to conflicts and create a consensus plan, including contingency plans that ensure the success of the merger.

1.1.3   Financial cost estimates

Costs and investment decisions should be evaluated based on the impact to reach the planned "To Be" state.

WARNING - Executives responsible for routine activities may consider each cost in relation to their annual budget, rather than in relation to the investment in the merger. Executives may be reluctant to invest $500,000 in new systems in the normal course of business, but when the investment is considered as protecting a $50 million acquisition, the decision would be made. Summarize financial results, including cost estimates for the following:

o   Hidden costs total as much as 50 percent inefficiency for each organization. Costs reflecting lost customers, sales and profitability may also be significant. Evaluate expense investments using this as a basis of comparison. For example, if hiring a $25,000 consultant will accelerate the integration by two months, saving $50,000 of duplicate resources, the investment is justified.

o   Incurred costs to execute the integration process can include both capital and expense items, which should be identified during the Due Diligence, integration planning, and execution.

o   Baseline costs exist if nothing is changed. For example, a merged company with two identical IT departments would include all costs in the baseline costs.

The financial statements include baseline spending (financial results before the combination), and the estimated combined entity. The sum of the two are not necessarily equal to the *"To Be"* state. *Identify major changes from current state and hold executives accountable for delivering the expected results.*

Establish accountability over both the P&L and balance sheet in the planning to ensure that the company achieves the acquisition goals.

1.1.4 Summarize/assess key personnel/ constituents

The integration team will Identify key personnel and organization, and discuss plans to retain them, recognizing that certain matters should remain confidential. Summarize expected key personnel losses or major gaps in the organizations to be resolved during the workshop. Key personnel/constituents include any person or organization that interacts with either company.

1.1.5 Summarize the high level plans

Outline the high-level activities that will be required to reach the future state. Examples of the high-level issues may include replacing data systems, implementing *Lean Manufacturing* concepts, eliminating factories or replacing functional areas with outside resources. This segment of the workshop will educate the participants about the major points of change, and allow them to view their functions as they relate to the total company. For example, if the company were replacing all data systems in the next 12-18 months, it would be foolish to upgrade existing systems to a more current version of the old software.

1.1.6 Develop a communications strategy/plan

Outline a preliminary communication's strategy and communications plan. The communications plan should include constituents served, major events planned, mode and frequency of communication. The plan will sensitize executives to the communication approach and strategy so that the workshop can build on the plan as issues develop.

1.1.7 Develop contingency plans

Regardless of how thorough the pre-planning, actual results are seldom achieved as planned. *At the conclusion of the workshop, the executive team will develop contingency plans that include activities, names, dates and milestones to activate the contingency plans to assure delivery of the acquisition goals.*

1.2 Participants/Attendees

Select workshop participants who can effectively assess, plan, and execute the integration process. The executive leaders who will implement the transition/integration plan may be from either the buyer or the target organization, but should include only the best executives regardless of prior company affiliation, as determined by the executive responsible for the integration project. Consider executives from all organizations as participants. The workshop team should be limited to 15 or fewer senior executives who wield enough organizational power to make decisions and allocate resources to the project as required. If executives do not have all the skills required to effectively plan and execute the assessment and planning, supplement their knowledge with specialists, as required, to achieve the goal.

1.2.1 Leaders – both sides of the transaction

The CEO or Chairman of the Board will select executive attendees, based on skills required, experience and anticipated business priorities. Teams should include executives from both organizations, if possible, to avoid the appearance of a dominant organization. There must be a single agenda, and a common purpose to achieve integration success.

1.2.2 Integration teams: only the best people

Select the best personnel on the broader integration teams to assess the goals, develop the creative plans to achieve the goals, and share their information with other executives at the workshop. The workshop will then empower these executives in their transitional role and in the future organization.

1.3   Executive Advocates

Assign Executive Advocates (EA) to be responsible for segments of the transition, including people, processes and plant/assets to ensure there are no gaps in performance in any functional areas. Executive advocates are those executives who are personally accountable for the success of specific elements of the transition. The EA will coordinate the assessment, planning and execution of any transition activities. The EA will also be responsible for communications - - listening -- as well as outbound communications for all constituents within the defined area. Publish the list of EA's, using a newsletter, organization charts, and/or websites so that constituent questions or problems are resolved on a timely basis. For example, if the VP of Human Resources is the Executive Advocate, for Human Resources, the EA is responsible for the physical assets, such as adequate computer equipment, office space, and software accessibility, the processes within that responsibility, as well as all the people issues involved in the Human Resources function. The following items are the EA responsibility:

- o   People/constituents: Any group or organization touched by either organization, including employees (current/retired), consultants, outsourcing organizations, vendors, governmental or regulatory agencies Etc.
- o   Processes/activities: Any process or activity completed by either organization, anywhere in the business, including processes and activities performed by outside organizations.
- o   Plant/assets: Any physical plant or asset (tangible or intangible) whether directly

controlled or owned by either organization, or rented/leased or used by the organization.

1.3.1 Identify constituents

Define people/constituents, which include any individuals, groups or organizations touched by the acquiring or target company. This includes employees (current/retired), consultants, outsourcing organizations, vendors, governmental or regulatory agencies Etc.

Executives responsible for the support functions, such as Finance or Human Resources, serve a dual role since their functional responsibilities may span the entire company. A finance executive is therefore responsible for financial controls, reporting and planning in all functional areas not just within the finance function.

1.3.2 Related processes

Identify all related processes/activities, which include those completed by either organization, anywhere in the course of business. This includes processes and activities performed by outside organizations.

1.4 Establish rules of governance

Establish the rules of governance. This should include the overall management process, reporting, accountabilities, decision processes, approval levels, hiring/firing personnel, contract negotiations, purchasing authority, project approvals, and communications. The facilitator will establish the rules with the CEO/Chairman in advance, and review the rules with the leadership team to ensure that executives understand the process and expectations.

1.4.1 Define integration leadership

Determine the integration team leadership based on the acquisition's strategic objectives and the best-qualified personnel to complete the job. Team selection should be purpose driven, and not politically driven. Leadership during the transition and integration process may differ from the day-to-day business management due to the acquisition strategic priorities. If, for example, R&D intellectual property transfer is critical, a technical expert may have a leading role in the integration. Assign the best people to roles to ensure the merger success. If necessary, hire an outside consultant to manage the successful transition. During the integration period, this individual may have significant authority within the organization, since the individual may manage the entire integration.

1.4.2 Structure/organization

Develop guidelines before the meeting, to manage the interim structure and organization throughout the integration project. The structure and organization will define the operating principles used throughout the integration process, such as authority to spend expense or capital, hiring/firing, compensation and bonus, operational approvals authority. All functional areas, regardless of their importance before the combination, will participate to avoid missed opportunities.

Activities are separated between Strategic and Tactical. Focus on both long and short term objectives when developing the organization, since the longer-term perspective will help you make better strategic decisions. One executive may prepare the summary for multiple functions - e.g. logistics, and operations. While the number of entries in either the strategic or the tactical responsibilities may vary, focus on key items to avoid diluting resources. Prepare one summary for each functional area. Executives may prepare similar, additional lower level summaries for locations around the globe if they are significant to the integrated "To Be" company.

Freeze all headcount changes, all salary changes, promotions, new hires or reorganizations until both organizations have been reviewed to identify if any major changes will occur with the transition. You do not want to promote individuals and then terminate as redundant two months later.

1.4.2.1   Decision processes

Identify the processes that will be affected by the integration effort, and establish rules to be followed during the integration process. The best way to identify such processes is to work with the employees that actually perform the activity, who also understand the "To Be" state. Develop procedures for significant processes required during the integration such as hiring/firing, compensation, bonuses, stock options, purchases of expense/capital, and customer trade terms. Prepare a matrix of all affected procedures to be sure that there are no control gaps.

1.4.2.2   Reporting frequency, content, and audience

Determine the frequency, content and audience for reporting. Develop reporting requirements based on the integration objectives, and the "To Be" state of the companies as well as reporting requirements to manage the day-to-day business.

- Formally monitor critical short and long cycle metrics. Monitor short-cycle metrics daily or weekly as required. This may include sales; order flow, cash reporting and borrowing, headcount, hiring/firing, capital spending, project spending and progress. Formally monitor longer cycle activities such as new product development, plant closures, and product sourcing changes at the executive level monthly.
- Define integration/transition goals in sufficient detail to establish metrics and accountabilities throughout the organization. Report content should reflect the goals and the responsibility levels within the organization. For example, daily cash reporting should

display total cash received at the executive level. However, cash receipts may also be summarized by region in lower level reports, so that the regional executives can be measured against goals. Sales orders may be total or by product line at the executive level, while accountabilities may also be established at the product level for mid-level executives. Mid-level executives may receive daily order reports, while senior executives may receive weekly or monthly activity reports.

o   Audience: Restrict report distribution to those that need the information to manage effectively. Avoid the temptation to expand the report distribution to create a status symbol for those receiving the reports.

Use three types of reporting *to manage the integration:*

o   Develop financial reports that include:

- Integration project reporting for incremental capital and expense spending. During the planning process, executives will identify incremental spending for outside assistance, registration fees, and licensing. Include these estimates in forecasted financial results, and establish executive accountability.

- Essential financial information that relates to the total company project such as P&Ls, Balance Sheet, and financial performance metrics including DSO, and Inventory Turns. P&L and Balance Sheet performance metrics can be helpful to manage synergy, incremental sales, and improvements in balance sheet metrics for the entire company.

- Develop project reporting within the functional teams, and summary reporting to the Integration/Transition teams. At each progress review, the leaders should confirm that, "The project will be completed on schedule." When leaders do not expect to achieve plan performance, they should outline the actions required to reach the plan schedule, and then fully integrate any major schedule changes into the overall project schedule.

1.4.2.3   Communications: Formal & Informal

Plan a total communications strategy to both report on progress and maintain an open and free flow of information to those requiring it. Good communications are essential to the integration process, and formal reporting will assist in that process. Communications are both outbound and inbound - listening.

Develop a master communications matrix during the planning process to communicate goals and accomplishments to your constituents. As you develop and execute the plan, inform your constituents, and monitor feedback throughout the integration process. Integration leadership and their teams must observe and listen to the constituents. The communications planning matrix can use one axis to define the information requirements, and the other to define frequency and audience. As you plan the communications matrix, identify noteworthy events and activities and manage the flow of information in a fair and responsible manner to keep your constituents informed.

1.4.3   Review the Deal

The workshop leader will present, to all workshop participants, a high-level deal transaction summary including all-important information such as investment summary, assumptions, expectations, timing, and key measures. Key measures can include such items as sales, earnings, gross margins, headcount, and capital spending. Throughout the workshop, executives will present their function's plans, to ensure consistency with the overall company investment goal. Each deal summary will include different information, because each deal will have unique critical items. Distribute the transaction summary to the executive teams to establish executive alignment, which is essential for success.

Deal summaries should include:

o Acquisition Proposal - - High-level summary that describes the heart of the transaction, such as key elements of valuation, financial projections, key employees, and approximate timeline.
o Key deliverables and assigned accountabilities.
o Integration planning cost details.

1.4.3.1 Transaction Summary

Prepare a transaction summary that briefly describes the deal's strategic objective, the "To Be" state, and any important elements of the "To Be" state. For example, the "To Be" state may be described in one year and then again in three years if significant change will be made during that period. Be brief, but with sufficient detail so that the company goals are understood by workshop attendees.

1.4.3.2 Purpose

Describe the deal's strategic objective and summarize the "To Be" state and its important elements. For example, the "To Be" state may be described in one year, two years and three years.

1.4.3.3 People

Identify critical people/constituents and activities at both companies. "People" includes critical vendors, key customers, and regulatory agencies such as the Food and Drug Administration (FDA) or the Department of Transportation (DOT). Also, identify potential constituents, such as new customers, new customer classes, or new vendors who may become critical due to the combination of the companies. For example, if the combined company will become a global service provider, additional legal counsel or tax expertise may be required.

1.4.3.4 Processes

Summarize all critical processes, whether internal or outsourced. Critical processes are those that are essential to make the acquisition successful. For example, perfecting the patent on a unique new product could be an essential process that would cause the deal to falter if not properly managed.

1.4.3.5 Plant/Assets

Identify all significant plant and assets including all physical and intangible assets, whether owned, leased or used, if the assets are used in the business. For example, if an airport or shipping facility in close proximity to a production facility were essential to timely delivery of product, the facility would be an essential element of the transaction summary.

1.4.3.6 Key elements of valuation

Summarize the key valuation elements. Aim for fewer than 10 elements at the highest level that will make the transaction successful.

1.4.3.7 Known upsides/downsides

Develop contingency plans that describe alternate ways to achieve the acquisition goals. These plans will initially be developed during the Due Diligence process, and will be expanded during the executive workshop as each executive reviews their transition plans and risk assessments.

1.4.4 Review the Operations/Functions – Functional Executive

After the high-level review by the workshop facilitator, each executive will review the operations under their direct control. Since the only source of information about the acquired company is that obtained during the pre-deal process and Due Diligence review, plans presented are still preliminary, pending further review starting on Day One. Assign responsibility for every person (constituent), process (activity), and plant (asset) to an executive to manage to the "To Be" state. Executives should summarize:

- o The "As Is" business,
- o The "To Be" state,
- o The plans to achieve that goal.

Assign each executive's review time based on importance to achieving the acquisition goal. For example, accounting may have a minor impact on the success of the transaction, while the sales force will be essential. The Integration executive may allocate the sales function two hours for review, while the finance function will receive 30 minutes since there may be less business risk in the finance function. The individual executive review will ensure organizational alignment. If executives disagree about the goals and structure, differences will be resolved at this time.

This segment of the workshop will be similar to the high-level summary, and will include information *from each executive such as:*

- o Confirmed valuation assumptions
- o High-level business model
- o Process review and changes required
- o Organization structure and key constituents
- o Keys to valuation as applicable to the functions
- o Gap analysis
- o Financial summaries

1.4.4.1 Entire value chain by function

Functional executives will review their portion of the critical value chain elements to ensure agreement among the workshop executives. During the workshop, executives will review up to 10 summaries. They will review one summary for each element of the value chain.

1.4.4.1.1 Confirm valuation assumptions

Each executive will review the critical valuation assumptions as they relate to their function to ensure that all executives have a thorough and common understanding of the deal. For example, if a key to valuation is increasing manufacturing throughput by 25 % without any increase in manufacturing overhead, the executive should state that the saving is achievable. Functions that are not essential elements of the valuation will support the overall value statement.

1.4.4.1.2 "To Be" state

Prepare a summary of the "To Be" state of the combined operations at specific and significant time intervals. Important time intervals may be at 100 days, six months, and one year. These intervals will vary with each transaction. Identify factors that are measurable and consistent with the overall acquisition strategy. For example, if a key to valuation is increasing manufacturing throughput by 25 % without any increase in manufacturing overhead, the executive should state that the savings are achievable.

1.4.4.1.3 High Level Business Model

While considering confidential matters, each executive will review the personnel/organization, and constituency. Factors such as critical personnel, or other constituents, organization size and structure, changes in compensation, benefits, and expanded and reduced staff levels should be discussed, if critical. Each executive will summarize the "As Is", and the "To Be" organization, and review transition plans to reach the goal. During this process, executives will identify and discuss organizational or constituency gaps and plans to resolve the gap through hiring, improving processes, or investing in plant/assets to eliminate the gap. For example, if the manufacturing organization in the acquired company does not use Computer Assisted Design/Manufacturing (CAD/CAM) equipment, add CAD/CAM trained engineers to the organization to raise the performance standards at the target company.

1.4.4.1.4   Processes (... facilities, assets etc.)

The executives will discuss each process in both the "As Is" and the "To Be" state and identify integration issues and performance gaps. They will discuss factors that are significant to the integration, or items that are essential for other executives to understand. Prepare gap analyses that identify the issues and the proposed solutions to the gap such as capital, work force, and training.

A matrix identifying significant processes used in the organizations will highlight opportunities for change. The matrix can include descriptions of the processes, assessment of the quality or robust capabilities, and compatibility.

1.4.4.1.5   Capital/incremental spending

The executive will identify the preliminary incremental capital/expense, carefully considering confidential matters that should not be disclosed - e.g. individual performance incentives. Each executive will review his/her capital/incremental spending including significant elements required to achieve the "To Be" state. These elements could include spending amount, timing, type of spending such as lease, capital spending, and program commitments, and justification.

1.4.4.1.6   High-level deliverables

Identify deliverables at both the corporate level and functional level to demonstrate alignment. The review will demonstrate alignment with company goals for financial results, organization structure and processes. So, for example, the Sales VP cannot unilaterally decide to establish an international distributor network organization. While corporate deliverables may define a total sales value, functional deliverables that contribute to the corporate goal will be more specific, such as regional sales targets, or perhaps product line sales targets.

1.4.4.1.7   Contingency and communications plans

Executives will review their high-level plans with the workshop team. These plans are summaries of those developed by the executive with the functional experts who manage the business day-to-day.

1.4.4.1.8   Unresolved issues

Not all issues or opportunities identified will be resolved, during the executive workshop. List items that are not satisfactorily resolved, and include a priority, timetable for resolution, the individual responsible to complete, and the expected goal. The goal may include investment, increased sales, and change in headcount. This summary should be part of the meeting minutes.

1.4.5   Identify Integration Issues – Group

Throughout the workshop, executives will present integration plans that explain how they will complete the integration process. Plans will include organization and personnel changes, investments in people, processes and plant, as well as potential write-offs. During the workshop, feedback from other executives may require changes to their proposed plans.

    o   Designate an executive to document decisions made, changes to the goals and plans to achieve them, and open items. Document changes for any significant changes to the plans, such as task name, deliverable description, timeline, costs, resources required, and task dependencies. For example, the Sales VP cannot obtain sales reports until the sales systems are implemented. Conflicts due to prioritization and resource constraints will arise during the integration/transition planning, and should be resolved immediately or listed for follow-up later.

o   The facilitator will review all significant changes to the original plans, and coordinate final updates to the original workshop documents. This includes the deal summary, the financial summaries, and gap analysis. Revise the transition plan immediately after the meeting - e.g. during the week following the workshop. After updating the operational plans, the facilitator will review the plans to ensure that the most recent financial summaries are reasonable in relation to the operational plans. Finish the update process, including the detailed operational plans, and the updated financials as quickly as possible - e.g. within two weeks of the workshop.

o   If the facilitator believes that the changes made require a formal review, convene a brief workshop to validate the final working plans with the executive team,

These plans are tentative working plans until the executive team can actually validate all the assumptions and activities once the deal is complete and the team has access to the acquired company personnel and facilities. During the first 100 days, validate the plans through discussion with the target company personnel, observation of actual activities and facilities, and review of documentation to support the assumptions.

1.4.6 Create Detail Plan & Timeline - - Group

Detailed plans and timelines may be created using project planning software such as Microsoft Project or other software developed specifically for M&A transactions. These programs are available either as web-based applications, or for those doing numerous transactions per year, by purchasing the software.

2   Day One

Successful Day One activities establish a framework for the entire transaction. If constituents arrive at the company and cannot get into the building, or do not have proper computer passwords to function, it will be obvious that there is poor planning. Functional executives must develop a master matrix of critical activities, in all functions and locations, including all constituents. Once the matrix is developed, assign the Day One activities. Include all companies in Day One planning, even if some companies will have no changes, since the master matrix will minimize omission errors. One caution - do not change something on Day One unless it is essential. Too much change can quickly become chaos.

2.1.1 Brainstorm critical operating issues

Develop a checklist of all possible activities, which consider all constituents, to identify the activities to complete on Day One. The brainstorming team represents the functional executives and any employees, customers, vendors or other constituents necessary to identify the critical items. During the brainstorming session, identify high impact activities that are critical on the first day.

- o   Identify critical constituents to contact on Day One. The President may want to personally visit or call key customers, vendors or employees with the integration message and plan. The company may also use web-conferences, teleconferences, email, and websites to open a consistent dialogue with the constituents.
- o   Items that need Day One attention include: (Note: These items need not be fully resolved, but the company should communicate with the involved constituents to manage expectations.)
    - Press releases and media packets to explain key elements of the transaction to the constituents.

- Employee compensation, such as salary, bonus, commissions, health and life insurance, and benefits.
- Outstanding employment offers, current-hiring processes, pay raises, promotions, and transfers.
- Security clearances, access to company processes, cash, travel requirements, credit cards, and computer processes.
- Cash management and control activity, loans, advances, and company credit cards.
- Customer pricing, payment terms, contracts, and open purchase orders.
- Vendor pricing, current and negotiated contracts, delivery schedules.
- Government registrations and filings such as Department of Transportation and the Food & Drug Administration.
- Insurance, performance bonds, and licenses.
- Freeze all in-process contracts, employee hiring, expanded outsourcing, and capital spending until the merged company can evaluate how these actions fit within the strategy.

2.1.2 Review negotiated company purchase, supply and performance contract terms to identify any Day One requirements.

For example, certain executives may be terminated upon deal closure, so it is important to notify the constituents that those individuals are not able to represent the company effective Day One.

2.1.3 Establish real-time communications processes

- Establish a clearing-house -e.g. web-accessible for all issues that may affect the success of the transactions. Develop communications processes so that any constituent (inside or outside the company) can raise issues with a designated responsible person, if necessary.

o   Establish feedback loops so that constituents who identify issues receive prompt feedback.

Ensure that executives and other management personnel know contact information - e.g. by function and location. Executives and managers should actively listen and observe for Day One integration issues. Tactics can include:

o   Management-by-Walking-Around;
o   Phones, teleconferences, Webinars;
o   E-Mail;
o   Blogs, which may require close supervision depending on the tone of the transaction.

2.1.4 Conduct integration team meetings to discuss/resolve issues.

Coordinate Day One activities well in advance of the event. If possible, include the Target Company employees and executives in the planning process prior to Day One. Despite thorough transition planning, errors and oversights will occur. If you have a process to record, manage and resolve issues, the integration will succeed.

In the value chain, support functions perform services for the primary functions. Include representatives from these functions on all other functional teams, since they will respond to Day One issues. For example, the Information Technology group should implement a plan to establish passwords, security control, and access to critical systems such as fringe benefits.

o   Implement a real-time communication process so that errors and oversights are immediately communicated to the correct level for fast resolution. Resolve all issues as quickly as possible, even if it is a temporary solution.

○   List all functions on the vertical axis, and identify constituents across horizontal axis. The matrix should represent all functions, activities, and constituents affected in any company involved in the transaction. While it seems to be a daunting task, a 1-2 hour meeting with the constituents/representatives will identify all the major items requiring attention. Not everything need be resolved immediately, but any actions that require immediate attention will be addressed.

2.1.5 Day-One Execution

The ideal Day One has little major change, but rather is one of open communications discussing the transaction, and the philosophy of the combined company. Do not change anything on Day One that is not essential. However essential items, such as updating a license to operate a fleet of trucks, must be completed on time, or the Company may not be able to serve its constituents. Execution will be the key to Day One success. Organize the integration teams to anticipate problems immediately at the opening of business. Establish clear communications lines so that constituents understand how to raise questions - e.g. personally, by phone, E-mail, blog etc. Implement a tracking system to identify trends as transition issues arise. In addition to providing an immediate response to questions from constituents, schedule a brief daily transition team meeting for the first week to identify and resolve issues. Team members should be proactive and prepare summaries of issues and trends to manage the environment, and not just react to individual issues.

3 First 100 Days

There are three major operational elements of the transaction:

  o   Day One activities and deliverables
  o   The First 100 days of activities and deliverables
  o   The Second 100 days of activities and deliverables

The First 100 Days will include the integration team's validation of all the assumptions, plans and expected results developed in the executive workshop. It will also include a rapid execution of those near-term plans, which will be the foundation of a successful integration. Executives will now have open access to the constituents who may have been unavailable prior to the closing and can now review all the assumptions and plans developed previously without their insight. Identify broad strategies and deliverables in the workshop to establish the magnitude and pace for the integration process. Once the high-level strategy is acceptable to the M&A leadership team, finalize more detailed planning using the functional resources that will actually complete the work.   For example, it would be a waste of time to plan an engineering Bill of Materials process on a new SAP data system, if the company changes strategy to use an Oracle system.

  o   During the First 100 days, constituents should meet frequently to validate, assess, plan and begin execution of plans to merge the entities. Meetings should take place on a scheduled basis. Short cycle tasks such as cash management controls may take place daily, while a function's overall review meeting may take place weekly. Executive management attention is critical during the first days after the merger to assure the constituents of the merger's importance, and to listen and respond to issues that surface. Decisiveness is essential.

o   Throughout the First 100 days, the Executive Transition Team should meet at least weekly to monitor performance versus objectives, and to modify goals based on real world information. The transition executives will prepare formal and informal communications for all constituents, including vendors, customers, employees, and agencies. Constituents recognize that the First 100 days will be disruptive and require more work than usual. Extra staff, overtime, frequently changing short-term priorities are the norm. Know that your competitors are anxious to take your best employees and customers during this period, and adjust your actions to avoid such losses.

3.1   Analyze & Develop Strategies

Thus far in the transition, the "To Be" state has been defined, the executives have assessed the "As Is" status of the companies affected by the transition, and high-level plans have been developed and approved by the executive team. Once the deal is closed, implement the following actions immediately:

o   Execute the "Day One" activities identified in earlier meetings to avoid business disruption in any function, in any location affected by the transition. Validate "Day One" activities with the target company constituents before the close to avoid business disruption.

o   Within the first ten days after closing, the transition team leadership will coordinate high priority activities to validate the key valuation assumptions, high level plans and strategies, organization structure, policies and costs developed and approved in the Executive Workshop. The leadership will have direct access to the target company personnel, vendors, and customers, possibly for the first time. Conduct a mini-workshop with key personnel so that they can begin the detail planning.

o   Within the first ten days after close, company employees will develop detail transition plans, including people, processes and plant, to achieve the defined acquisition goals. Detail planning should include accountabilities, costs and required resources, timing and coordination among all the companies and functions involved in the deal. Prioritize the plans based on company benefit, cost and resources available, for the overall master plan approved at the Executive Workshop. In an ideal M&A transaction, complete the planning before the closing to accelerate the integration process.

> o   Execute the detail plans and communicate - outbound and inbound. Carefully manage the environment, which includes employees, customers, vendors, other constituents, since the environment may now differ significantly from pre-deal. At each major transition plan milestone, notify the transition team of any significant variance from plan to be sure that other areas that may be affected can modify their plans.

> o   After the First 100 days, reassess the transition strategy and status versus the acquisition plans.

3.1.1   Understand Keys to Valuation

Coordinate a mini-workshop meeting with the integration team members to review the transaction summary and the keys to valuation, so they can align their activities to achieve the goals. Validate the assumptions related to the high-level summary so that all team members have a common understanding of the goals and interim objectives. Review any significant variances with the integration team leaders immediately to determine whether the strategy should be adjusted.

3.1.2   Assess Hi-level Business Model

Review the approved high-level business model (as confidentiality permits) with all the team members, and validate the assumptions developed at the Executive Workshop so that the teams can align their activities to the approved strategy.

3.1.3   Review Organization Structure

Based on the high-level business model approved at the Executive Workshop, develop detailed organization charts, identify actions and develop job descriptions, and complete training within the first few weeks of deal closing. Include constituents, from any organization involved in the transaction. For example, new systems and operating procedures may require training for vendors and customers to use a new website effectively. Assess the span of control, the number of layers in the organizations, use of contractors and temporary employees and confirm the ""To Be" organization.

3.1.4   Assess Personnel

Evaluate the constituents to understand current and future capabilities, and their fit within the "To Be" organization. Identify and develop retention plans for key employees and constituents, including those both inside and outside the company who are essential to the successful merger. Develop transition plans to align the organization with the approved organization. Evaluate personnel performance and the required performance in the "To Be" state, and identify any gap to reach the "To Be" status. Determine if the gap is due to inexperience, poor training, or capability, and develop a plan to train, reassign or terminate employees not expected to meet future requirements. Identify the specific actions required for every employee throughout the organization(s) within the first 30 days.

Develop a plan to transition redundant employees and other constituents. Treat employees with dignity and respect, pay fair termination settlements and retraining costs, and provide job search support. As you complete these transitions, know that your competitors, customers, vendors and local communities will evaluate your actions as a guide to your normal business methods.

3.1.5   Review compensation and bonus; fringe benefits

Evaluate the elements of constituent's compensation (inside and outside the company). Develop the expected "To Be" state and timeline, and a transition plan to achieve the goal. There are three steps in the compensation review:

- o   Document and evaluate the "As Is" structure at the companies, and include every form of compensation and benefits to any constituent (include vendors, government agencies, active and retired employees, temporary and contract employees). Compensation and benefits include salary/wages, bonus, stock options and grants, perquisites (auto allowance, tuition reimbursement etc.), life, health and dental insurance, 401K etc. *Follow the money* to avoid missing a compensation element. For example, outside contractors may not be included on organization charts.
- o   *Evaluate compensation such as union representation and contract status, expected negotiation timeframe, employee contracts, vendor contracts, and terms and conditions for all other payments.*
- o   *Finalize the "To Be" state details* based on the assessments, and compare to those approved at the Executive Workshop. Document major variances and review the variances with the transition team leaders.
- o   *Once a final "To Be" state has been accepted, define action plans to reach*

the "To Be" state, which includes expense and capital, as well as other critical information, such as headcount, and organization structure changes.

3.1.6   Review Processes/Systems

Evaluate all systems and processes, including outsourced systems such as FedEx, logistics, in all companies involved in the transaction to determine if transition plans are required. Validate the systems and processes identified in the Executive Workshop, as well as all other systems and processes that were not considered in the Workshop. List and assess the quality of the processes used in each location, and their potential use in the "To Be" combined company. The "To Be" performance should meet an established standard. The summary will identify duplicate or questionable processes that may be eliminated, or optimized if moved to other locations. As multiple locations are identified in the master matrix, assess the process quality and scalability.

Reviewers should always seek a better method to complete the task, and not just assume that one of the existing methods is the best. Since the companies are involved in major process and systems changes, consider upgrading all the systems instead of just patching existing systems together. For example, each company may have outdated CRM processes, and the best solution is to upgrade to a new system. This type of summary should be prepared - on a priority basis - for every significant location, and for every significant activity performed in the merged company.

3.1.7   Validate Hi-Level Gap Analysis

Validate the Executive Workshop process gap analysis. Also, identify any processes that require improvement, based on a more thorough review, and summarize the key elements of change required.   Summarize essential information that describes the issue, expected resolution and timing, the potential benefit, and costs, and identify whether the costs are capital or expense. These summary pages should be logged and monitored at periodic meetings. Comparing the "As Is" status with the "To Be" state will identify the gaps.

Prepare a gap analysis (the difference between the "To Be" organization, technology, plant) and the "As Is" operations. The gap analysis will describe the issue and the proposed solution. The gap analysis also will describe the costs and expected benefits to evaluate in the context of the overall integration process.

3.1.8   Prioritize Activities

Prioritize activities based on the acquisition objectives and resources available. An integration project will have major priorities managed at the senior level, and lesser priorities within the functional areas. For example, the president may personally meet with every major customer in the First 100 days, while the sales manager may update the customer data base files within the First 100 days. Quite often, the plans will require constituents to complete activities during the first few weeks of the integration. Since plans are seldom executed exactly as expected, changes in priorities may be required. Based on the governance rules established for approved activity changes, revise the priorities to achieve the integration goals using current information rather than an outdated plan. Review these gap summaries with the Executive Transition team at periodic meetings.

3.2   Analysis & strategy – Deliverables

Review the detailed strategy. A thorough review may not take place until after the closing, since the acquirer may not have access to the target company's records, staff, and plans. During the Due Diligence and negotiation phase of any transaction, high-level analysis and strategy will be developed to estimate the amount of investment, including expense and capital, resources, and approximate timelines for implementation, as a basis for negotiation and valuation. Since the plans are at a high level and somewhat imprecise, these broad plans are often not executable at a department level.
Expand the plans to reflect specific resource allocation, deliverables, priorities and timelines to meet the strategic

goals, and manage these plans in a traditional project management process. For example, it may be clear at a high level that the company needs a new $1 million engineering design data system, and the system implementation will require 5 months of effort. However, a detailed implementation plan including work force project loading, specific activities, and specific capital and expense spending will be required to execute the plan.

Major changes from plans identified during the Executive Workshop should be reviewed at the Executive level to ensure alignment within the organization. If significant changes are made to spending levels, the transaction may not meet established objectives.

3.2.1 Organization structure

Design the detail organization structure that best fits the expected "To Be" state outlined in the valuation process, without regard to the existing organizations or personnel, such as unions, and existing locations. Detail design includes specific job titles and responsibilities, and reporting structure. When the overall design is completed and approved by the integration team leadership, assess the existing structure, personnel, and process to develop a detail plan to move from present to future. The structure should reflect the "To Be" state span of control, number of layers, management philosophy (centralized, or decentralized), and culture.

3.2.2 Organization Culture

Validate the organization's culture in all locations, with the understanding that cultures may vary by location or function. Identify inconsistent cultures in high priority areas as an unusual culture may disrupt integration plans. Identify the "To Be" culture, and develop plans to migrate to the "To Be" state. For example, some cultures are very formal, rigid, and well organized. If such a company acquired an informally managed entrepreneurial company, by design, the culture of the acquired company may never change, since their value is based on their entrepreneurial spirit and creativity.

Culture is a major variable in a successful merger, and culture change is one of the most difficult activities to complete. If there are major culture differences, detailed plans to explain the culture goals as well as the path to achieve the goals are essential. Validate the initial observations from Due Diligence once you have access to all personnel and all locations.

3.2.3 Compensation, Bonus and Fringe Benefits

3.2.3.1 Compensation and Bonus Plan

Assess compensation and bonus plans for all companies involved; develop the "To Be" state, and create a bridge plan to achieve the "To Be" state. Thoroughly analyze all elements of the compensation at the companies. Ideally, complete the analysis before the merger is finalized so that announcements discussing the compensation plan can be made upon deal closure. Compensation includes salary, wages, bonus, stock options, stock grants, 401-k, pension, deferred compensation plans. Realign performance driven programs as soon as practical to avoid conflicting priorities. Also, since the integration will require exceptional work and effort, develop a program to compensate the team properly for delivering a successful merger. Compensation programs are extremely personal and should be immediately addressed. If compensation and benefits are not properly assessed and changed to motivate, the constituents will not effectively support the transition.

3.2.3.2 Fringe Benefits

Fringe benefits include all non-cash benefits to any constituents, including both formal and informal programs. Benefits can include, but are not limited to, vacations, sick time, personal days, tuition reimbursement, birthday recognition, and special performance awards. Discuss the programs with the acquired company executives to determine the best course of action.

3.2.4 Personnel alignment

Prepare organization charts, job descriptions, approval's authorities (capital and expense spending, hiring and firing, and contract approvals levels), and span of control. Personnel alignment will directly affect the organization's performance. As strategic and near-term goals are developed, align the organization to the company goals. Document and distribute the goals to affected employees. Prepare a master summary that describes the overall organization, and key elements of the alignment. Integrate compensation, such as incentives, bonuses, and recognition programs, with organizational goals throughout the structure to reinforce alignment.

3.2.5   Processes & systems

Develop a matrix of all processes and systems for any acquired organization and the base organization. Identify every activity in any organization to determine actions required:

- List and document all activities for every function.
- *Assess the quality* of the activity to determine if the activity meets the requirements. Determine if remediation is required for those not meeting standard, and estimate the resources, such as personnel, expense, and/or capital, required, estimate time to complete, and benefit to the organization. If similar activities are performed in all locations, always select the best activity for future use, or plan to upgrade the activity to the "To Be" state required.
- *Prioritize the activities based on costs and benefits*, and coordinate with other functional areas and locations to get the best results more quickly.
- *Plan resources to meet the priorities established.* Use external resources if adequate resources are not available in-house. It is often far more expensive to miss priorities than to invest initially.

3.2.6   Implementation timetable

Establish detailed implementation schedules, but also ensure that the senior executive team reviews suitable macro-project timelines periodically. Establish critical milestones and report progress against these objectives on predetermined schedules such as at the weekly executive meeting. Each time the high-level implementation timetable is reviewed by the integration team leader, confirm with the executive team that activity objectives are on track, or review remedial actions to bring the project back on schedule.

3.2.7   Financial assessment

Assess the established acquisition objectives and reconfirm that all significant issues have been identified and resolved. Each executive should confirm that the financial aspects of the project are on schedule or explain remedial action to achieve the goals. Complete this step after the entire organization has reviewed people/constituents, processes, and plant/assets to understand the "As Is" and the "To Be" state, the gaps between the two states, and the organization has created detailed plans to move to the "To Be" state. Include a financial summary of any significant changes from plan. This should include timing, since inefficiencies during integration are potentially significant, and the impact on constituents, such as customers, vendors, and employees, may be significant.

3.2.8   Contingency Plans

Develop contingency plans that allow the combined organization to meet the established merger goals. Discuss contingency plans at each formal review. Determine if the plans need modification at each meeting, and/or begin contingency plan execution if the integration project is not meeting objectives. Each element of the contingency plan should have an executive sponsor who owns the responsibility for execution.

3.2.9 Communications strategy

Review the communication's strategy, and reconfirm the key elements of the strategy with the new company executives. Consider all the constituents, both inside and outside all the companies, timing and frequency of communications, media that can be used and the probable audience response. Media may include newsletters, e-mail, web posting to the company website, personal town hall meetings, and small group meetings with the constituents. For example, if a company discontinues operations at an acquired business location, the employees at that location will be affected. However, all company employees could be concerned about their continued employment, since employee seniority or specialized skills may affect employees throughout the company. Anticipate the constituent reaction and plan accordingly.

3.3 Detail Design/Build/ implement – Activities

Earlier in the M&A process, high-level plans were created to integrate the companies. The design/build/implement segment of the First 100 days will focus on execution. Management will design processes, train personnel, and develop systems as described in detail plans developed by the integration teams. Execution describes specific activities, timelines, assigned personnel, costs and so forth, for the entire integration project, including all departments, functions, locations, and personnel. This may affect both companies, as each functional executive who attended the Executive Workshop and their staffs will implement the plan to achieve the "To Be" state. Complete these activities throughout the organization, and involve all constituents - employees, vendors, customers, agents, and agencies.

In addition to completing the tasks, the team will prepare and review with management periodic project status reports. The integration teams will conduct formal project review meetings throughout the organization, as you would do with any major project, to ensure that the detail activities are being completed as required.

Meeting frequency and content will depend on the task priority and complexity. Conduct department or function meetings. Daily or weekly - - depending on the nature of the tasks. For example, cash management procedures should be resolved immediately so daily meetings may be appropriate. However, changing paper stock, logos, and selected printed material may be managed weekly. The definition of assets includes any asset used by the company, whether they are tangible or intangible; owned, leased, or borrowed.

3.3.1 Design Process Flows

The merger goal is to combine companies or selected functions into an organization that provides more profit to the overall organization. Each company often has a complete value chain, resulting in duplicate functions or processes within the functions. Process flows must be modified or eliminated to reach the merger goals. As process flows are modified, people and systems need change or replacement, retraining/programming. Each element of change requires time and investment. It also entails risk. The integration team is responsible for understanding the "To Be" state, the "As Is" state. They must define the change required, and then manage the risk so that the change is properly implemented. Design process flows for all processes requiring modification, and prioritize the flows based on greatest value to the organization. The process flows will describe the business processes that will be in effect when the "To Be" state is achieved. Identify all the steps necessary to move from the status to the "To Be" status.

3.3.2 Technical systems and facilities identified

Inventory and document all technical systems and facilities in both organizations, and include in process items on order/under contract. This summary should provide a level of detail that allows the executive to assess the required changes to reach the "To Be" state. For example, systems documentation should include summaries of hardware and software used in the day-to-day function, as well as those systems in development. The summaries will describe the status of technical assets and facilities, and include items such as unlicensed software, or facilities not in usable condition and might require extensive repair or replacement. The summary will identify additional investments required to have a fully functional technical structure and facilities when the "To Be" state is finally achieved.

At the conclusion of the review, the integration executives will formally confirm that the expected "To Be" state can be achieved, with a summary of resources, expenses/capital, and timeline necessary to reach that level.

3.3.3   Develop Procedures

The integration team and all participants throughout the organization will review every function, every activity, and every procedure and identify and change procedures necessary to achieve the "To Be" state. Procedures should be thoroughly documented and complete whereby the standard of performance, defined within the scope of the "To Be" business model, can be achieved.

3.3.4   ID/Train Personnel

As procedures and facilities/assets have been modified, select and staff the redesigned processes with appropriate personnel, and train them to meet the required "To Be" state of performance.

3.3.5   Execution

Execute the implementation plans. Develop and achieve aggressive execution plans since delays in execution will disrupt the constituency. The best employees, customers and vendors etc. may leave the merged company and go to the competition. During integration periods, good competitors understand the confusion and inefficiency and lure the best from the merged companies.

The hidden cost of Inefficiency during the integration process can be as much as 50 percent, and only the after-affects will be observed in lower profits, lost customers, employees and vendors. Effective project management during the initial 100 days is critical and will include formal and informal reporting and performance measurement.

3.4 Detail Design/Build/Execute – Deliverables

The First 100 days establish the performance expectations for the entire integration process. Develop and maintain open candid communication channels throughout the entire constituency. Sub-groups within the merging companies may have their own agendas, their own cultures, and business drivers. During the First 100 days, team members should continually assess the environment, modify plans as necessary, and flawlessly execute. Prioritize deliverables to provide the most benefit to the merged companies, and identify dependencies that can affect the entire project. For example, if a company does not properly develop new system specifications, systems cannot be designed and implemented. If deliverables are delayed, understand the impact on the integration project and assign resources accordingly.

3.4.1 Detail project plan

Prepare a master detailed project integration plan, which includes all significant steps, costs, and resource requirements that are based on a thorough understanding of the project interdependencies. Manage the plan using progress reports in progressively more detail as you proceed down through the organization. Schedule progress report meetings based on level within the organization, the critical nature of the tasks, and the impact on the company as a whole.

3.4.2 Develop Procedures

Modify activities and related procedures as organization responsibilities change. Prepare and document detailed procedures to reflect the changed activities. Procedures should include a statement of purpose, required resources, contacts and activities to be performed, estimated time to complete, skill levels and advance training required, and a description of the ultimate deliverable. Develop procedures consistent with the integration priorities and accelerate those that add the most value first.

3.4.3 Train Personnel

Train all personnel as to the purpose, all the required steps to complete a task, and the basic skills to perform the task (both hard and soft skills). Consider training in groups so that personnel are cross-trained on essential processes, and train in advance of going live to ensure that there are fewer missteps. Maintain up-to-date training processes to reflect the current procedures.

3.4.4 Active project management & reporting

Aggressively manage the First 100 days based on the established priorities. During the first week of the transition, conduct daily update meetings to resolve new issues, and resolve open issues from earlier tasks. After the initial weeks of activity, executive meetings can be weekly. Use judgment to determine the meeting content and frequency, but concentrating on exceptions to the schedule will yield the best results in the least time. Discuss only significant activities that are off schedule, or significant new issues. The meetings should be action oriented, decisive, and brief. Prepare minutes and schedule follow-up sessions. At the conclusion of each meeting, each executive participant should be able to state that either the project is on schedule, or the listed actions are in place to bring the project back to the required timeline.

3.4.5 Processes implemented

Implement the integration processes as scheduled in the prioritization. Monitor the process changes to ensure that the desired result occurs; progress toward the "To Be" state. Modify processes if they do not achieve the desired goal, and modify the written procedures and training to reflect any changes. The business world, competition, and constituencies change frequently and may often require changes to the plan. Maintain open communications throughout the organization, and be flexible to a changing the schedule.

3.4.6 Communications strategy execution

Review the communication strategy that outlines long-term objectives and the short-term tactics outlined at the Executive workshop. It is essential that both outward and inward communication processes be established. Establish "help" lines for reporting problems, and issues, establish and publish e-mail addresses to receive feedback from inside and outside the company.
Consider establishing blogs that provide an uncensored communication process, since feedback is essential to a successful integration process.
Plan these communications so the participants can achieve their goals on schedule and enjoy the feeling of success. Provide routine updates to the constituents to inform them of accomplishments, and subsequent merger steps. Updates may be provided through the following:

- Weekly newsletter (e-mail or web posting) with overall integration/transition progress.
- Periodic town hall meetings
- Periodic live or recorded web casts, which may also be available on an integration website for later viewing.

3.4.7 Contingency planning

At the Executive workshop, executives prepared contingency plans that may offset major unfavorable events. Unfavorable events, such as product introduction delays, increased competition during the transition period, or lost key employees or customers can affect sales, profits, cash flow, plant/assets, systems and processes. Contingency planning identifies those potential unfavorable events, and creates alternative plans that will offset the unfavorable impact. During the First 100 days, validate the contingency plans, and begin to execute those that are required.

4   Second 100 Days

During the Second 100 days, longer-term projects will continue to be implemented. Project management skills will focus on the routine changes in those items that are less visible, but still essential to the successful transition. Constituents who are working on these projects will require positive reinforcement since the initial impact of the merger is gone. Invite constituents who are meeting their objectives to periodic executive meetings to present their results, gain exposure, and feel a sense of accomplishment. Congratulate them on their performance.

During the Second hundred days, begin to harvest the improvements planned. Document the value created, and broadcast the success. The Second 100 Days is a chance to reassess and realign expectations and tasks to be completed. The meeting format should be similar to the first Executive Workshop, but with considerably more insight into the processes, risks and opportunities.

4.1   Second 100 days – Activities

At the beginning of the Second 100 days, coordinate a one-day Executive Workshop to reassess the progress of the First 100 days. Transition executives will report their progress against the established objectives and discuss the next 100 days goals and activities.

4.2   Sustain & Harvest Benefits

Compare benefits and major accomplishments achieved to plan, and explain major variances. Include financial results for items originally planned during the First 100 days, such as reduction of Days Sales Outstanding (DSO) in accounts receivable by 5 percent or $2 million.

4.2.1   100 Day Status Check

Coordinate the Executive workshop to understand the existing "As Is" situation, the planned "To Be" goal, and the status of scheduled major projects. All the value chain elements and the constituents will be included in the status check. Effectively, update the presentations used in the first Executive Workshop to reflect the knowledge gained, and revised goals and objectives.

Once again, executives will discuss their assessments of the integration, and the "To Be" state. The "To Be" state and the activities that will be used to achieve the objectives may be somewhat modified from the initial workshop. Review of all the activities will ensure a coordinated effort, and common goals among the executives.

4.2.2   Reassess Priorities

Reassess priorities with the newly gained knowledge from the First 100 days of observation and activities completed. Expect changes to established priorities, since the earlier workshop did not include complete insight into the target organization. Unfortunately, change may be required since not all the initial objectives established during the First 100 days may have been completed.

4.2.3　Align Activities to priorities

As necessary, adjust the priorities to reflect the knowledge gained from the First 100 day's results. Priorities may shift during the meeting, as other executives goals may require adjustment for the company benefit, such as delayed installation of data systems, or spending beyond budget. Adapt priorities to new facts arising during the integration.

4.3　Second 100 days – Deliverables

Once the priorities are established, align the activities to the priorities, and develop/reconfirm specific deliverables for the next 100 days. The project plan will include names, dates and specific deliverables so that the activities are coordinated within the company. The project plans will have enough detail so that daily, weekly and monthly meetings can measure performance against the objectives.

4.3.1　Updated project plan

Once the transition executives have updated the detailed plans, the workshop will again familiarize the entire team with the expected activities and deliverables, and will allow overall coordination among the functions.

5 Synergy

At the conclusion of the second hundred days, reflect on the progress achieved and identify the benefits realized thus far. Synergies planned are often not realized, and the end of the second hundred days is an ideal time to reassess the acquisition in total. In addition to planning an abbreviated workshop to understand the integration status when compared to the plan, this is an ideal time to reevaluate the acquisition strategy and synergies realized.

Other Books by Michael P. Gendron

Cashing Out @ Full Value: A Novel/Guide for Boomers Selling the Family Business

Doing the M&A Deal: A Quick Access Field Manual & Guide (2nd Edition)

Doing the M&A Deal: A Quick Access Field Manual & Guide (1st Edition)

Creating the New E-Business Company: Innovative Strategies for Real-World Applications

Integrating Newly Merged Organizations

A Practical Approach to International Operations

About the Author

Mike Gendron (CPA-inactive) is the founding partner of CFO Insight LLC. He has extensive experience throughout Europe, Asia and Latin America in companies ranging in size from Business Week's 'Hottest Growth Companies in America' to Billion-dollar companies. Industry experience includes high-tech electronics, telecom equipment, FDA regulated operations, and industrial instruments.

During his career, he has been the CFO of global corporations – both public & private – and he has extensive experience in Fortune 500 corporations. He has participated in M&A transactions in France, Germany, China, Mexico, Canada and the US in industries such as high-tech electronics, telecom equipment, FDA regulated and industrial instruments.

He frequently speaks and writes about mergers & acquisitions, strategy, and high-growth companies, and he maintains a website (http;//www.cfoinsight.net) dedicated to financial management and M&A.

In addition to flying high-performance airplanes as an instrument rated pilot, Mike enjoys backpacking, skiing and golf. Mike is Vice-Chairman of the Management & Entrepreneurship Advisory Board at Xavier University, and a member of numerous private company advisory boards.

www.ingramcontent.com/pod-product-compliance
Lightning Source LLC
Chambersburg PA
CBHW060316200326
41519CB00011BA/1750